BRAVE NEW CHILD

Liberating the Children of Liberia—and the World

Lessons in Peace Education
From a War Torn Country

Marvin Garbeh Davis
Common Ground Society, Liberia

With an Introduction by
Dr. Terrence & Jean Webster-Doyle

Based on Dr. Terrence Webster-Doyle's Book and Curricula
Why Is Everybody Always Picking on Us?
Understanding the Roots of Prejudice

A Youth Peace Literacy Project
A Cooperative Effort Between
The Atrium Society USA and The Common Ground Society Liberia

Robin Alys Roberts was happy to have the peace-inspiring job as editor of *Brave New Child's* second and third editions. Sharing her editing suggestions from her office in Canada with Marvin Davis in Liberia and the Webster-Doyles in the USA was an uplifting experience in positive, forward-moving, international communication.

Adryan Russ was editor of *Brave New Child's* first edition.

Order this book online at www.trafford.com/07-0354
or email orders@trafford.com
Most Trafford titles are also available at major online book retailers.

Note for Librarians: A cataloguing record for this book is available from Library and Archives Canada at www.collectionscanada.ca/amicus/index-e.html

Printed in Victoria, BC, Canada.

ISBN: 978-1-4251-1947-8

We at Trafford believe that it is the responsibility of us all, as both individuals and corporations, to make choices that are environmentally and socially sound. You, in turn, are supporting this responsible conduct each time you purchase a Trafford book, or make use of our publishing services. To find out how you are helping, please visit www.trafford.com/responsiblepublishing.html

Our mission is to efficiently provide the world's finest, most comprehensive book publishing service, enabling every author to experience success. To find out how to publish your book, your way, and have it available worldwide, visit us online at www.trafford.com/10510

www.trafford.com

North America & international
toll-free: 1 888 232 4444 (USA & Canada)
phone: 250 383 6864 ♦ fax: 250 383 6804
email: info@trafford.com

The United Kingdom & Europe
phone: +44 (0)1865 487 395 ♦ local rate: 0845 230 9601
facsimile: +44 (0)1865 481 507 ♦ email: info.uk@trafford.com

You've Got to Be Carefully Taught*

You've got to be taught to hate and fear,
You've got to be taught from year to year,
It's got to be drummed in your dear little ear,
You've got to be carefully taught.

You've got to be taught to be afraid
Of people whose eyes are oddly made
And people whose skin is a different shade,
You've got to be carefully taught.

You've got to be taught before it's too late
Before you are six or seven or eight
To hate all the people your relatives hate
You've got to be carefully taught…
You've got to be carefully taught.

*From South Pacific © 1949 Lyrics by Oscar Hammerstein II
Music by Richard Rogers

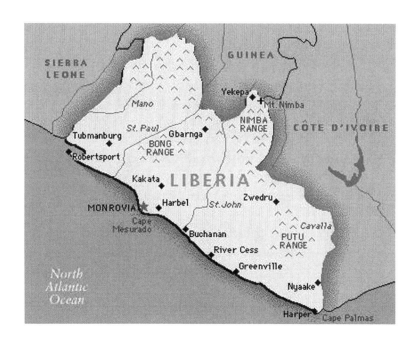

Liberia

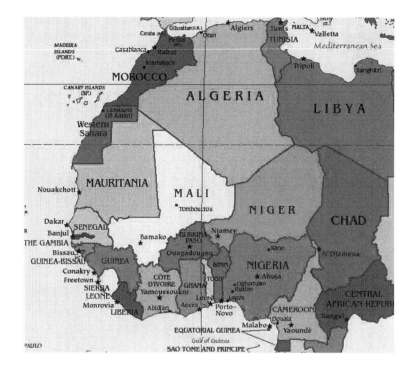

West Africa

Table of Contents

Illustrations

Introduction

"TILL AT LAST the child's mind is these suggestions, and the sum of the suggestions is the child's mind. And not the child's mind only. The adult's mind too—all his life long. The mind that judges and desires and decides—made up of these suggestions. But all these suggestions are our suggestions… Suggestions from the State."

Aldous Huxley – From Brave New World

Aldous Huxley's famous novel highlights how a state controls it citizens through conditioning. No matter the name ~ brain washing, programming, inculcation or socialization ~ the devastation is the same. Twenty brave children and their courageous teacher, Marvin Davis, in Buchanan, Liberia worked together to understand the underlying causes of the 14-year civil war they had grown up in. The compilation of Marvin's letters is an amazing story about how these children are liberating themselves from the confines that have time and again driven the human race into war. They are brave new children because they are questioning the conditioned mindset that has caused such terrible violence in perhaps the worst civil war in recent history.

Political upheavals began in the 1980s, extended into brutal civil war and thrust the country's living standards into a steep decline, ravaging its education, social and economic infrastructure. The civil war in Liberia was one of Africa's bloodiest, claiming more than 200,000 lives, displacing another one million internally and shoving more than 150,000 into refugee camps in neighboring countries.

Over the next fourteen years, life for most Liberians was hell. The entire country lacked electricity and safe drinking water. All major roads in Liberia fell into disuse and many parts of the country became inaccessible, making it impossible for relief organizations to provide assistance to people living in rural communities. The breakdown of central authority because of the war meant people had to find individual ways and means to stay alive. Fighters roaming the countryside constantly disrupted farming cycles. Even after the war, unemployment stood at 80%, and rice, Liberia's staple food, cost US$30 per bag: more than a civil servant's monthly salary. Nearly all Liberia's three million people lived in desperation or close to it, yet Liberians were not daunted by the hopelessness that engulfed them.

Against all these odds Marvin Davis, having fled Liberia under the threat of death, came back to his country to help these children of war. He hoped that if he could teach them to understand the roots of prejudice which creates war, they would not carry over the tribal vengeance that remains a seriously dangerous and inflammatory concern.

Searching the Internet for peace educating organizations that would help him, he found the Atrium Society in the U.S.A., the Youth Peace Literacy Program which we created. Internationally acclaimed, the training and materials in this award-winning peace education program enabled him to do what he wanted in Liberia. Working together as a team, the three of us helped establish the Common Ground Society Peace School of Liberia.

The lessons that follow come out of the Atrium Society's peace educating program entitled *Why Is Everybody Always Picking On Us? – Understanding the Roots of Prejudice*,. Transporting this program to the 20 war-indoctrinated children, Marvin has begun to change their conditioned, prejudicial attitudes. These 20 lessons demonstrate that no matter how heavy the conditioning for violent behaviour, no matter how habitual the resulting war mindset, liberation is possible. And if these Liberian war children can be liberated, so can all children who face daily conflict ~ whether they're bullied on the playground or bullied on the battlefield.

The most fundamentally significant thing they have learned in these lessons is that the world they have been conditioned to see is the outside picture of an inward condition. They now understand that projection creates perception. Through these lessons, these 20 young people have learned to change their mind about the world, and therefore change the world.

As anthropologist Margaret Meade said, "Never doubt that a small group of thoughtful, committed citizens can change the world; indeed, it's the only thing that ever has." And this could never be truer than with these Brave New Children freeing themselves from their divisive tribalism. To emerge free of its influence, they are creating a new world, a world that is peaceful because they now understand what prevents peace, and thus what causes war.

Terrence & Jean Webster-Doyle

The Beginning

WHERE DID MARVIN *Davis come from? What led up to his commitment to peace education, especially to the establishment of the Common Ground Peace School in Buchanan, Liberia? What did he have to do to get that process started in a country ravaged by war? We truly wanted to know more about Marvin.*

— Terrence and Jean Webster-Doyle

In 1989, the National Patriotic Front of Liberia, led by Charles Taylor and backed by northern ethnic tribes, began its disruption of my home country. Despite an onslaught of massacres, tortures, kidnappings and political assassinations, the Samuel Doe dictatorship, backed by inland ethnic tribes, lasted another eight years before Taylor managed to proclaim himself president. Ethnic identification has produced a see-saw of corruption and wars. Thus, our life as a family has had its share of turmoil over the past decade—but at least, contrary to many thousands of others, we managed ultimately to reunite.

In October of 1992, at the moment the National Patriotic Front rebels launched their Octopus attack to take our capital, I was spending the weekend a few miles south with my uncle in Sinkor. My wife, Emily, and our eldest daughter, Rochelle, were caught on the other side of Monrovia's People's Bridge. Once again, we were separated. Weeks later, at the end of November, the forces of the Economic Community Monitoring Group managed to expel Mr. Taylor's rebels.

I worked as an editor for a biweekly newspaper published at the Center for Law and Human Rights Education in Monrovia. Journalists' lives were constantly threatened, especially for the kinds of articles we published. As a human rights paper editor, I was certain that I would not be spared if any rebel fighter caught me. The possibility of my death preoccupied me.

So on April 6, 1996, we fled to Ghana, living for a year as refugees. At the end of the year, I left my family at the Buduburam Refugee Camp and went to Nigeria to study computer software. In 1997, I returned to Liberia to search for a safer job than journalism, so that I could bring my family home. In 1998, they finally arrived, but with the conflict escalating, we soon and often had to move. The newly installed Taylor administration was well known for its human rights abuses.

Sometimes we just moved out, packing our household goods without knowing where we were heading or how we would get there. We left good friends, took our daughter out of school often mid-semester, felt briefly exhilarated by an exciting period of travel, and then plunged her into the disturbing confusion of strange new classrooms, teachers and classmates. While my family has a strong sense of responsibility toward each other, I was constantly aware of the pressures of the capricious uncertainties of our movement from place to place.

In October of 1998, I left Emily and the children in Tarr's Town, Monrovia, and fled north to Gambia, to a friend who wanted me to join him writing for the Daily Observer in Banjul. Within two weeks, I realized the life of a journalist under President Jammeh's military government was also too dangerous. A few years previously, the editor of the Daily

Observer was detained, flogged and deported to Liberia. I told my friend that I just wanted to lie low for a while, until things shaped up in Liberia.

But political conditions moved from bad to worse in my homeland. By early 1999, I had run out of every cent I had. Not wanting to continue living as a beggar in my friend's house, I used my Liberian teaching skills and my Nigerian computer software certificate to land a job teaching English as a Second Language. Although the salary was not fabulous, it beat sitting at home and gave me an entry into the system.

During my first six months of ESL teaching, I started to worm my way into the social fabric of Gambian society—and I also started pondering my future. If I did not return to Liberia, what would I do with my life? Get a better job? Acquire additional skills? Try a graduate program? I had been obsessed about starting a career in peace education since the end of Liberia's first civil war, and dreamt of a graduate degree in Peace and Conflict Studies.

At the end of 1999, I resigned my teaching position and began work as a public relations officer at the Peace Society of Gambia. My duties were similar to those of my old job as editor in chief of Liberia's Human Rights Review. Here, I provided documentation, cultivated media contacts, wrote press releases, arranged press conferences and developed a public relations plan for communication objectives. I also supported all rights-based advocacy campaigns and helped in HIV/AIDS campaigns for refugees from Sierra Leone and Liberia. The job was challenging, but I enjoyed my relationships with my colleagues and executive director. The salary was better than teaching and the work environment and service conditions in this non-profit organization were satisfactory—for a foreigner.

In addition to saving money for my home and growing family, I began saving up for a graduate degree. I had hoped to go to a school in the USA, but realized I could sooner afford a university in Europe. When a more lucrative, contract-teaching job at a local computer school opened up, I resigned from the peace society and taught for six months. Just before we were to be paid, the Nigerian proprietor ran off with the contract money to the Netherlands and left me in the cold.

Towards the end of 2000, I began working for a British man who accepted my proposal to help him open a computer school in Gambia. He paid six months' rent, bought a new generator, installed telephone lines, furnished the office, sent over the first set of ten computers and issued ads. Within weeks, we opened the doors to twenty students, and soon the school acquired more teachers. Once again, I started saving for my graduate program, increased my monthly allowance to my family in Monrovia, and began helping my wife with her own fees at the University of Liberia. About four months later, just as suddenly as the Nigerian proprietor, this owner, jilted in a love affair, decided to return to the U.K. He told me to run the school on my own, but neglected to take financial responsibility for the rent or the bills.

When other teachers and the night watchman left, I slept in the building to protect it, and taught all the courses myself. I tried to save the school by advertising for an investor, but as a foreigner in Gambia, I was unsuccessful. By November, up to my neck in debt, I sought my wife's advice. "Sell everything," she said. "Pay your debts and if anything is salvaged after that, raise your own money to start your own, small, computer school." In the end, I managed to pay all the debts, including the staff's salary arrears, and was left with my own computer, two desks and one table, which I moved to my house where I started a home study program. Emily and the girls were able to join me in March of 2001.

Once again in possession of some income, I applied to the European University in Austria, including a refugee scholarship and even appeals to friends who supportively chipped in. In July of 2001, the European University accepted me, so I sold my computers, a satellite dish and even my mattresses so that I could pay the initial deposit while beginning my visa application. In the end, I was unable to raise the required money, and the school fortunately refunded my fees.

Never one to give up, I enrolled in an online Human Rights Advocacy program in New York and went back to work at the Peace Society of Gambia, this time as a volunteer. I also began a serious online search to find institutions involved in peace education. Thus I found the Atrium Society of the United States. I emailed them for information. President Jean Webster-Doyle responded, wanting to learn more about the Gambia Peace Society. Her letter was a major turning point in my life.

In 2001, I started implementing Atrium Society's *Education for Peace* curriculum, targeting mainly Liberian and Sierra Leonean refugee children. Located in the Gambian community of Ebo Town, we called this after-school program the New Generation Peace Club. This doubled as my practicum in Peace Education with Atrium, and developed so well that I was joined by a Sierra Leonean psycho-social worker. By 2002, classes had increased from 10 to 20 children. As this work was part of my volunteer work with the Peace Society, I was still trying to find a job to increase my earnings.

In March, 2002, SOS Kinderdorf International hired me to be a high school computer teacher. By the beginning of 2003, I was promoted to Kinderdorf's Northwest Africa Regional Office as a computer technician. The environment was far superior, and the pay my highest since arriving in Gambia. To my joy, this job took me to eight countries in Northwestern Africa, where I set up computer labs, employed and trained teachers, updated software and distributed computer parts and accessories. Out of Gambia for two weeks every month, my weekly per diem sometimes added up to more than my monthly salary.

During this time, I continued to work with the New Generation Peace Club, and Jean continued to assist me in both the teaching process and the curriculum. By mid-year, enrolment had jumped to 40, including five Gambian children. The Ebot Town Primary School authorities agreed to give us two classrooms at the school. Our peace club developed football and kickball teams with the voluntary services of one of the Gambia Football Association coaches. In 2003, Gambia provided sporting gear for our team to participate in the Federation Internationale de Football Association's Global Peace gathering in the Gambia SOS Children's Village.

The Atrium Society offered me a scholarship in 2003-4, to study education for peace online and to further my training to teach their peace curricula. In September, I was invited to present a paper at a program marking the celebration of world peace. In October, a British tourist funded our Peace Club to erect Peace Poles in three Gambian middle schools. By April, 2004, 180 children had graduated from our peace school.

When I was certified as a Peace Educator from the Atrium Society, I made a trip to Liberia to register the New Generation peace program under the name "Common Ground Society." In July, 2004, Liberia notarized, incorporated and accredited our society to operate as a Non Governmental Organization (NGO). Jean and Terrence Webster-Doyle made it clear that I could continue to count on their assistance, offering funding for Common Ground Society's start-up costs. Meanwhile, my boss at Kinderdorf had been encouraging me to continue my computer technology and engineering training, saying that they would like me to grow to the top and become one of their international staff members. But my heart was not there.

I was engulfed in thoughts of a non-profit peace education organization in Liberia. By the end of 2004, I began preparations for heading home to Liberia. On February 24, 2005, I resigned from SOS Kinderdorf. Although my good friends, colleagues and I all assured each other that we'd stay in touch through phone calls, emails and periodic visits, I was certain we were bound to become estranged by widely divergent lives.

Leaving SOS without any real evidence of the concrete realities in Liberia really challenged me, but that afternoon, I felt strong and confident. A challenge has always been a tonic to my spirit, and for no reason, I had the feeling that my resignation from SOS might have some fascinating compensation. Whenever I talked about the Atrium Society, USA, I had to mention Jean. To my family, the name 'Jean' was a household expression. Even though no one in our family had met Jean or her husband, Dr. Terrence, my daughter used to tell her school friends, "I have three grandmothers. Two of them are black, and one is white and lives in the USA. I'm going to visit the one in the USA when I finish school." To her teacher she one day said, "My white grandmother is teaching my father peace education."

That evening, our talk at home over dinner maintained a cheerful level of excitement about the prospects of starting the new peace school in Liberia. Although we would soon be separated again, our eldest daughter Rochelle was happily anticipating her examinations for the West African Senior High School. Younger daughter Mardell Joy would stay in school also, awaiting Rochelle's completion. As a way of assuaging the pain of the recent loss of our newborn son in hospital, where he had died a few minutes after birth, my wife had enrolled in the gender and development program at the Management Development Institute. Immersing in academia could be healing.

We talked about the challenging adjustments my family would soon have to make. They would have to leave our three bedroom apartment for a two-bedroom one. They'd need to shop at the credit facility at the STOP'N'SHOP supermarket. They'd have to reduce electricity consumption and keep family expenses at very minimal levels. They understood the need for these new, more stringent realities because they backed me in Common Ground's goal: to help Liberian children understand the roots of conflict and to resolve their differences without resorting to violence. Their white grandmother had agreed that the Atrium Society would provide funding for our new organization until it was strong enough to seek outside resources.

On the 5th of March, Emily and I bought my ticket for two days hence, and took the girls to Sam's Fast Food on Kololi Highway. Over glasses of ginger ale, we watched the girls savour their favourite: chicken sandwich delight. I called Jean to assure her that everything was finalized, and called Liberia to arrange for my cousin Felix to pick me up at Roberts International Airport. I would be staying with him and his wife until I could find my own home and set up office.

On the eve of my departure, my office threw a farewell party attended by all the staff of the Northwest Africa Regional office and friends of the Association of Liberians in Gambia, for which I had served as secretary-general. They honoured me with letters, gifts and speeches about the innovative information technology development I had brought to the SOS schools in the sub-region.

In bed that night, I reviewed my six and a half years in Gambia. As a foreigner, I had been constantly suspected of having a criminal record, and at the very least, doubted for some imagined, potential, shady activity. As a result of the war, many Liberians—especially young people—were distrusted. Many were involved in money doubling, scams and fraud. Lots of Liberians were serving time in Gambian jails for a variety of crimes. I had survived by pushing through these constant judgments, working hard to build an honest reputation, making good friends and going back home with my reputation intact. Many considered it quite unusual that I, as a Liberian, would be welcomed back to visit any time. More remarkably, I was leaving my family in a foreign country based on this accumulated trust.

As another day of departure dawned, the kind of day that we thought our family had become accustomed to, we learned yet again that no matter how extensively I traveled, we never got used to the separation. Somehow departures never lose their pain. The Banjul International Airport was packed with passengers heading south along with me on the early morning flight to Freetown, Monrovia and Accra. The girls stood stoic and seemingly indifferent, for which I had empathy. Emily looked frightened and her face was drawn with lines of sadness. As we looked frequently into each other's eyes, her many smiles could not erase her fears or the turmoil in her heart.

As I hugged my girls, I told them to take care of their mother, not give her hard times, and do well in school. Departing words, hugs and kisses with my wife both hurt and soothed. I trudged through the gate to the departure lounge, heard the boarding calls and before I knew it, was on the last ramp of the 737 Slok flight called Jammeh—named after the President of Gambia. I thanked the cordial, pert stewardess who showed me a lonely seat, sat next to a window and fastened my seatbelt.

The plane whirred and whined, reached its takeoff point, gathered momentum and launched itself with a roar toward the morning skies. Banjul, Emily and the girls were obliterated by veils of gray vapor rushing past my tiny windows as we hurtled along an invisible airway towards Sierra Leone. Gambia, which had been so long a part of our lives, was fading beneath me in the early morning dew. I felt that lately I had been doing nothing but flying away from everything I knew and everyone I loved.

I thought I had prepared myself well when I decided to come home, but Liberia is full of surprises and living here is a battle full of uncertainties. My basic concern was security: the greatest preoccupation for many like me, who have lived out of the country for many years, is the threat of death.

I spent my first two weeks with Felix and his wife, Minnie, in a suburb of Monrovia called Gardnersville. Even though I was establishing Common Ground Peace School further south, in Liberia's second-largest city, Buchanan, I needed to open an account in Monrovia, as it was the only city with banking facilities. Due to Liberia's fragility after fourteen years of warfare, inter-bank transfers were neither instantaneous nor direct, and we finally had to settle for a Western Union money transfer for Atrium Society's first funding deposit.

In line with our budget, I bought a second-hand utility vehicle and subjected it and my-self to the pot-holed journey to Buchanan in search of office space and temporary housing. After fourteen years of continual neglect, Liberia's asphalt highways have been steadily disappearing with every rainy season so that now they are a mockery of the original. Giant ruts and frequent wash-outs demanded my constant agility as a driver. Once we made it to Buchanan, it took me several days to get over the pain in my back. When I finally re-covered, I took an evening stroll along Tubman Street, Buchanan's major thoroughfare, searching for a house or an old friend who might have an idea for a rental location. The rainy season was fast approaching, and Buchanan was stifling.

Like all other cities in Liberia including the capital, Buchanan had no electricity for lights, let alone luxuries like air-conditioning. To get our computers up and running, we have to find a working generator, which usually takes hours to kick to life. There has been no running water in Liberia for the past fourteen years, and the few hand pumps scattered around Buchanan are miles apart. A seemingly simple flush of a toilet entails the big prob-lem of first finding a bucket of water. Poverty is our burden—all over Liberia. Every day we breathe it, walk through it and work in it. Rice is our staple food, but many Buchanan families cannot afford it. Some survive on bulgur wheat, and even that is difficult to find.

As the sun was setting, Buchanan drew me into its soporific, heat-soaked darkness. Mosquitoes were as fat as flies and bit like snakes. Malaria is on the increase here. Some attribute the condition of the city to the war, others to negligence, inefficiency and govern-mental corruption. One faction blames all the country's woes on former president Taylor, who, they say, exploited the country and left it in ruins. But this is a country that is full of hope and possibilities. Liberians manage to smile despite the stringent adversities of their lives. These are the smiles of hope for their children, their families and the return of their great nation. Hope keeps them alive.

However, every house we saw was in deplorable condition. Their roofs had been punched with holes, their walls busted by bullets or rockets, their door-frames hung empty, their windows smashed or missing, their floors stained with dirt. Despite this, the owner asked for one year's rent upfront, and we'd have to use our own money to make the place habitable. Renovation costs would be adjusted in next year's rent. If we had to use a generator, we had to do our own wiring. The landlord would demand payment in U.S. dollars, as if to say our country did not have its own currency.

"What have I done to myself?" I pondered. "I've just thrown away a good job, left my family on a belt-tightening budget, and here I am in a shell of a war-torn country. What do I think I'm doing even contemplating setting up a non-profit school in this second-largest of our Liberian cities, where all the good houses have been looted, vandalized and almost totally wrecked? Where homeowners are craning their necks to find someone to salvage their lives by charging exorbitant rents for a headache of a shack?" Some whole days I would sit there, devastation filling me, feeling embarrassed and ashamed.

Finally, we found a house along the road leading to the old LAMCO camp. Or at least, we thought we had. I paid for six months rent, and then, needing to contact Jean, I jolted and jerked back over the road to Monrovia, the only email centre. No sooner had I arrived than I received a message from my Buchanan friend saying that the extended family who owned the house I'd rented had started bickering and was demanding not only the agreed-upon U.S.$17 per month but an additional $50. My brother advised me to return right away, get a refund and look elsewhere. However, when we immediately went all the way back and met the landlord, we had to cajole, coax and beg him to remit the refund in three instalments. My friend advised me that this was the current way of business in Buchanan.

If I'd taken the man to the police station, as we did in the old days, I'd have had to pay the fare for the police, or forced the man to ride in my own car. After a preliminary investigation, the policeman would say, "Give me something to eat," which means "Wet my palms." However, if the police realized that I, the complainant, was better off financially, then he would delay the case as long as possible in order to gain a few more dollars while I lingered in uncertainty. Besides wasting more time, I'd also have to pay the court costs. I found it hard to take in that this was the Liberia I thought I knew, but my friend stressed that Liberia was indeed not the country that we had known as boys, or even before the war.

One evening, my brother was speaking to one of his students and discovered that the boy's grandmother had an apartment right on the main street. We drove over, paid for a year's rent, and began restoration. Within seven days, we'd finished renovating the interior. Within two more days, we'd cut the grass, painted the exterior and readied the signboard. By the eleventh day, we officially opened our office. Would the sun shine on our program?

My first job was to start recruiting staff and students. On Radio Buchanan's "Radio Gbehzon" talk show, I explained the purpose of our program and called on parents to enrol their children. Before the end of my first week of work, we had ten children registered, and by the following week, we had the total of twenty that had been our goal for the pilot program.

I gathered the parents and guardians for a meeting at our office to orient them to the Peace School and describe the activities they could expect the children to participate in. I asked them to encourage their children to attend class regularly and to be on time. Many parents were extremely happy that there were no fees. Some said they were grateful to know exactly where their children would be on Peace School days, while others expressed appreciation that their children would be spending after-school hours in a valuable way. The gathering concluded with a photo and light refreshments. Regardless of the number of points on an agenda, Liberians fondly refer to this as "Item 13." As food is so sparse, it is a big drawing card to attract community members to meetings. After the snacks, we shook hands and I assisted some of the parents to get a taxi home.

Saturday, May 28th, 2005, burst upon our opening ceremony bright and sunny, dispelling fears that our guests would be drenched by the month's recurrent rains. The newly registered students turned up at our office before 8:00 a.m., neatly dressed in their Peace School T-shirts. Supporting me on this momentous day, my oldest daughter, Rochelle, and our youngest daughter, Mardell Joy, had flown in from Gambia, while son Marvin Jr., had arrived from Ghana, where he'd been living with my sister during the school year. Unfortunately, Emily could not come, as she was facing final exams in Gambia.

The county band—four men playing two big drums and a couple of saxophones—serenaded the 20 students, 10 of their parents, several of Common Ground's office staff, my family and five special guests, including the Mayor of Buchanan. After marching the length and breadth of Tubman Street within forty-five minutes, we returned to the office where we had assembled chairs inside the building. All of us rose, as one of the town's dignitaries gave the invocation. Mardell Joy welcomed the guests. Cindy Reeves, the first girl to register at the Peace School, introduced the guest speaker, Dr. Abba Karngar, Buchanan's most senior citizen. Dr. Karngar stressed the importance of peace education in postwar Liberia. "It is especially essential to give the younger generation tools to help them resolve their differences," he said, "so that Liberia will not have a war again."

All the time I listened, I thought about Jean and Dr. Terrence Webster-Doyle. How I wished and wished they could have been here! For seven years, we had planned and worked towards this special moment together. It was right for them to be here. But Liberia was currently on the list of banned countries for American travelers.

I held in my hand a letter from Sr. Carletta Bondi that helped fill their gap. A wonderful friend and social worker, she had helped me get a scholarship to go to high school. As my father did not have money, I had agreed to take a plantation job for a few years to save up for my education, so when Sr. Carletta said I was qualified to enlist in the Liberian Agricultural Company academic scholarship program, this was a major turning point in my life. After graduation from high school, I saw Sr. Carletta only once before the 1989 start of the civil war. Returning to Liberia this time, I had tried to find her missionary station, but learned that she had been suffering from cancer for years, had gone to Italy periodically for treatment, and was currently in Kenya serving as principal at the only all-girls' high school. I wrote to tell her that I was back in Liberia and about to start Common Ground.

I received her response on the morning of our opening ceremony. "I am so proud of you and your achievements in Liberia, and nothing comes to me as a surprise. I am happy that you are back in Liberia not running for political office, but helping young people to learn about peace. I wish I were in Liberia to share in your success and I am so happy that out of the hundreds of tappers' children from the Liberian Agricultural Company plantations, you were able to get an education and return to work with underprivileged youths. You have my best wishes every step of the way in your work."

Sr. Carletta was more than a social worker. She was one of those people who reach out and touch other people's lives so as to forever alter them for the better. This was my own challenge now. I wanted to touch the lives of these kids. I was going to work to the point that they would be able to look back and remember everything with joy and happiness.

Looking back a few days to when I could not find an office space, I now found it unbelievable that I was sitting in a building with these people, opening the Common Ground

Society Peace School. I was moved, not only because I was accomplishing something I had looked forward to for years, but also because I just could not believe I had reached this point today.

The children sang two songs Rochelle had taught them, and a couple of parents made remarks. Then I stepped up to the podium to explain the importance of Common Ground Society, and its work with young people. I explained the history of the organization and all our plans. Then, out of a file, I pulled two photographs I'd received while in Gambia in 2003.

"The pictures you see in my hand here," I say, "are of two people I've never met in my life. They are Jean and Terrence. They have never seen Liberia. But because of these people, we are here today. Dr. Terrence and Jean provided the training I needed to start Common Ground and have been working with me for seven years. They provided every cent needed to start this project in Liberia.

"We don't need to know people before we share our resources with them. I want you young people here to understand that if a cause is important enough to believe in, no matter where it is, you should give your life to it. These two people believe in global peace, and they know that to achieve this peace, we must understand what prevents it. At Common Ground Society Peace School, you will be learning about these roadblocks to peace. Jean and Terrence are ready to provide every ounce of their energy to ensure that the world becomes peaceful.

"Only with peace will you be able to achieve your dreams. Many of you know what happened in this country over the past fourteen years. To achieve our dreams for the future, we need to start pooling our resources now. The first step is to make sure that this generation learns the causes of violence in human relationships. We must work to gain an understanding of why we have been in such turmoil. Only then will we be able to build a new and peaceful Liberia."

Great applause greets the end of my speech. Then of course, we roll in Item 13. As the children start to eat, the music begins and soon they are dancing. Other children from the community pour in, while I see my special guests off. Finally, the children have eaten their fill, we turn off the music, and I am ready to take Rochelle, Marvin, Jr. and Mardell Joy home.

So at last, Common Ground is officially open. But is it ready to implement its goals and aspirations? As this question rumbles around in my brain, I kick my car to life and drive away, past the people standing on the roadside watching my departure, all with their own expectations for Common Ground.

I call Emily before going to bed, to tell her about the opening ceremony. "I'm so happy," she says with a voice full of longing to be here. As I lie in bed, I think about our separate lives and how I want us to be rejoined soon. Then I think about the success of the evening. I had anticipated trials and inevitable deficiencies just getting to this stage. But for now, I want to do my work one day at a time—solve future problems as they come, instead of creating them with no basis in my imagination. Right now, the Common Ground Society Peace School is open and I expect to start work on Monday.

I hear a couple of dogs barking. My dog responds. I want to get up and find out what they're barking at, but I am too tired. I feel a touch of headache, take two pain tablets, pull my bedding over me and switch off my bedside lamp. Before long, I am deep in sleep.

Lesson 1

Where Does Prejudice Begin?

"Many theories have been put forward as causes of the Liberian civil war, including unemployment, abuse of human rights, political patronage, illiteracy, lack of development and tribalism. While it is true that all of these factors may have contributed, the heart of the Liberian conflict—and the fundamental cause of all human conflict —is psychological conditioning."

— *Marvin Garbeh Davis*

Dear Dr. T and Jean…

For more than 150 years, we have tried to turn Liberia into one of the best places in the universe. The country has been full of resources and potential. We believed that if we worked hard enough, we could make it better. That's what we were doing when the civil war erupted in the 1990s, and everything we had built came tumbling down like the Tower of Babel. We destroyed everything we had cherished as a people, losing some of the finest citizens the country had produced. Our young people turned into beasts, killing each other in our own jungles.

Fifteen years later, we are starting to put our pieces together again. We are rebuilding our schools, hospitals, and bridges. We're rehabilitating our young people by providing them with life skills. In short, our goal is to remake our country. But there is a plague raging across our land. We can't dig a hole and, like ostriches, bury our heads in the sand and pretend it isn't there.

This plague is prejudice. It is eating away at the core of our existence as a nation. Even now as we preach unity among our citizens, the plague of prejudice prowls among our people, devouring the very fabric of our interconnection.

People are obsessed with getting jobs, rebuilding their houses, climbing financial and social ladders, and enhancing careers and lifestyles, while the undercurrent of prejudice spreads across our land without people even recognizing that it's there. Everyone has forgotten what prejudice has cost us, and will continue to cost, unless we wake up, realize its manifestations and begin to do something about it.

I hear our leaders calling us to put our hands and hearts together to rebuild our nation. They say, "Let's forget the past and reconcile our differences." They are failing to talk about the root causes of our problems.

How can we rebuild this country when we are so divided along ethnic, religious, social and political lines? How can we rebuild this country when the Bassa man thinks he is better than the Kpelle man? When the Gio man cannot live side by side with a Krahn man? When some of us think the Congo man is responsible for all our problems, or that Mandingo people are not considered to be Liberians? When certain families can't live together in the same communities? How can we rebuild when people fight and hate because of political differences? When one group thinks that it is superior—that its values, traditions and practices are the best? When another group believes their people can never be defeated by anyone?

All these beliefs are based on prejudice. How can we raise a new generation of children when we continue to raise them under the shadow of hate, bigotry, and tribalism—all these conditioned responses to life? We want to build roads, schools, bridges and skyscrapers. But if we don't get to the root of our problem, the children we are raising now will be the ones to destroy these new structures, just as they did fifteen years ago.

No one talks about prejudice. We don't read about it in the newspaper. No one talks about it on the radio. No one cares. What kind of money will a newspaper or a radio station make for writing about it? Besides, everyone has a personal perspective about this country, and what does it matter if sometimes the perceptions are off base?

Many people say that I sound like the prophet of doom. Many say I exaggerate. It is a democratic country, they say, so everyone is entitled to his views. But I want the skeptics to spend a day with me at my Peace School and I know that if they do, many of them will turn into believers. They may not accept what I myself am saying, but they will believe the children.

How many people will accept my invitation? Many will not have the time. Everyone is hustling now. "Times are hard in Liberia," they say.

Others say, "Why should we give a damn about something that has nothing to do with employment or the economy?"

But the children know what I am talking about. They will recognize the truths in this book. Our children are our jewels; they are the people destined to rebuild our country, a new generation that fills us with hope. They are the ones I want to help most, because when they understand prejudice and learn how to deal with it in an intelligent way, then when I am old, I will truly live in peace. I will be able to sleep and enjoy a hearty retirement.

Every time I talk about prejudice with people I know, I watch their faces twinge. Some are scared when I simply cite an example of prejudice and the dangers it promotes. The mere mention of the word sometimes disrupts the lives of people; they fear its discussion, as if touching a sore. But if rebuilding our nation and living in peace are important to us, we must begin to talk about prejudice.

We have to find out the root causes in our society, to help our young people maximize their intelligence and guide them to recognize prejudice in their own lives. We need them to see how they are conditioned to think and act in ways that are destructive, and how—with insight and new thinking—they can eradicate everything that *prevents* peace in their lives.

This is what the Common Ground Society is about. This is our inspiration for the Peace School. This is why I left my job and came back home. This is why the Atrium Society is asking people for funding and other help to enable us to carry out this task in Liberia and around the world. When our children understand the causes of violence in their lives and have the skills to deal with these causes intelligently, we can truly remake Liberia.

Located 125 miles outside Monrovia, Buchanan is our capital and second largest city, as well as the administrative headquarters of Grand Bassa County. It is in this town that we established the Common Ground Society. Buchanan, with its population of 30,000, is home to the second largest international seaport in Liberia. Here, iron is exported by the Liberian American Swedish Mining Company and the Oriental Trading Company, who exploit it from the Nimba Mountains of northeast Liberia. The Liberian Agricultural Company is 25 miles outside the city, and the Liberian Flour Milling Company is situated at the outskirts of Buchanan. These companies have provided employment to many inhabitants of Grand Bassa County, especially Buchanan, and the booming iron ore business has made the city a thriving town. The possibility for employment attracted a lot of people — from across the length and breadth of Liberia, neighboring African countries, Europe and the U.S.A. Their arrival added a rich diversity to the city, and despite their differences, harmony and peace remained a hallmark of its inhabitants. But that was fourteen years ago.

The region has a history of unrest. The economic factors associated with Buchanan made it a central theater in the fourteen-year civil war, leading to the deaths of thousands. Intensive battles between rival factions (especially to capture the port of Buchanan and the Liberian Agricultural Company) left most of its population massively dislocated. Different warring groups recruited its young people. Companies operating in the country were looted and vandalized and, at the height of the war, closed down operations. Companies working on a number of so-called development projects during the Taylor regime harmed the complex ecosystem of the region, through deforestation and depletion of wildlife habitats. These problems have caused pain, suffering and losses to large communities of citizens, young and old.

The economic reality for single mothers and their children is even more ominous. The population is severely affected by a high level of unemployment and lack of access to basic services such as food, water, health care and education. The social safety net provided by family and neighborhoods has broken down. With the ceasefire of August 2004, many people outside Buchanan started pouring into town from different parts of the country, including many who had been displaced and sent to refugee camps. Left with nothing to do, many have returned to fishing, petty trades and backyard gardening.

Children have no meaningful after-school activities. Many have joined gangs playing war games and mimicking war scenes, some even naming themselves after the most feared generals of the civil war. The arrival of ex-combatants from disarmament and demobilization camps—many of whom are young people with no marketable skills—puts many communities at risk.

Buchanan is a town of great cultural heritage. The native Bassa chiefs are greatly admired for working to provide land to settlers and helping to peacefully resolve many disputes between natives and freed slaves from the United States of America.

Nonetheless, the town was in a constant state of conflict during the civil war, and was always prisoner to some new rebel group. But in all that time, the people never surrendered their streets without a fight. In fact, no individual rebel group was able to take over the town and use it as a base. The inhabitants risked their lives to ensure that no gunmen treated their compatriots like animals, as soldiers had done in many other parts of the country. When the National Patriotic Front of Liberia (NPFL) rebels started killing innocent people in Buchanan, the residents chased them out.

Now the fields are burned and left barren, the factories bombed and bare, their port destroyed. Where there was once hope, hunger now resides. Where once great dreams filled the hearts of people, nothing more than the somber acceptance of a humiliating life unfolds.

Buchanan has the potential to become a source of initiatives where everyone has a hand in building peace and harmony, and where doing so provides a good example for other peacekeeping initiatives around Liberia. The significant progress made, particularly in disarmament and demobilization, should serve as incentive and opportunity for engaging young children of the country in peace building. Many of these children are forced to bear the burden of adulthood, surviving on the barest essentials, living like cornered animals in need of shelter. They are scattered all across towns and cities in Liberia.

Common Ground Society's office is located on Tubman Street, less than 400 meters from the "Welcome to Buchanan" sign. The house used to be occupied by another local nonprofit, but the landlady asked them to move out. I am happy that we have this office space that is conspicuous, sitting right in the heart of Buchanan. I love the office and I am particularly happy about the space both inside and out, since we moved to our new, bigger building. The children can run around during breaks, and we have lots of room for dramatizing and role-playing, activities that teach our children how to recognize prejudice and other conditioned thinking.

Today the sky is a faultless blue, without a single cloud, and radiant with unexpected sunshine. This is going to be our first day at the Peace School. I have always looked forward to it and finally it is here. Now is the time to bring the dream to life. My mantra for success has always been to aim for a single-mindedness of purpose through grueling work and dogged determination. I still have a great deal of vitality surging through me. I want to apply it to achieving my goals.

My first set of 20 young people—12 boys and 8 girls—has arrived at the Peace School for a new after-school program, right before class time at 4:30 pm. The children look excited. In Liberia people generally don't respect time. When a meeting is expected to start at 2:00 pm, for instance, they start to leave home at 2:30, and even then may be the first ones to arrive. When people disrespect time, they just say "It's Liberian time," as if Liberia were a world of its own. So it bodes well that these children have arrived on time.

The average age of the children is 14, and most are fifth and sixth graders. The war left a great impact on the young children in this country. The ages of many young people are not commensurate with the classes they are in. The last time I went to visit the literacy school program at St. Peter Claver, which my 7-year-old daughter attends, I saw a 14-year-old learning the alphabet.

All the children are dressed in their new T-Shirts provided by Common Ground. We are starting with your curriculum, Dr. T, called: *Why Is Everybody Always Picking On Us? – Understanding the Roots of Prejudice.* I start with a small welcoming remark, as I usually do. I want the children to have an idea of why they have come to the Peace School.

"I am sure many of you heard about the importance of the Peace School and that is why you registered. Here we are going to learn about conflict—how people create it—and how small conflicts can turn into big conflicts such as war. We want to learn about conflict so that it does not continue in the future and lead us to kill each other, as our predecessors have done. We don't want to destroy our country; we want to live with each other in peace, no matter what tribe or family we come from. This is what the Peace School is about. So you are welcome, and I am sure that by the time we finish our training, all of us will be ambassadors of peace in our homes and communities.

"We are going to start by learning about prejudice and how it affects us. Do you believe you have no prejudices?" Taking a look around, I notice some nodding, and some shaking their heads.

"Would you be surprised to learn that you do? If you discovered that you do, would you want to hang on to your prejudice? Change it? Talk about it? I will ask you questions such as these when we begin.

"In the Peace School, everyone is free to speak his or her mind. We must respect the rights of others to speak. All questions in the Peace School are intelligent, and no answer is wrong. We must learn to respect all perspectives in any situation."

Each child stands and recites his or her name. Some of them say their parents' names, the school they attend and the community they come from. Then I open our conversation with a rhetorical question.

"What is prejudice?" Knowing a dictionary definition would be easy for me but boring for them, I jump in with a real-life example.

"A new boy comes to your school or church or community. You don't know him, but you are against him, or don't want to be his friend, or you don't like him because you heard he has just returned from Monrovia with his parents to live in Buchanan. You don't even know the boy's name or any member of his family, but you don't like the boy because you assume that because he's from Monrovia, he might behave in a superior way—perhaps he'll think that he is better than you. Now I want to ask you: Do you believe you have no prejudices? If you hate someone for no reason or because he comes from a different community, town or school—aren't you prejudiced?"

"Yes", says Mai Tarr.

"I have hated someone in that way before," Cindy Reeves says.

"Can you tell me how, Cindy?" I ask her.

"I used to be friendly with a girl called Lucy in our community. We were close until another girl moved into our community who also got very close to Lucy. Then things started to happen differently. Lucy barely came to visit me again. She spent all her time with this new girl. Even though Lucy told me the girl was nice and friendly, I never cared to know her. Instead I started hating her, including my own friend Lucy."

"Did this new girl do anything to you?"

"I think she took Lucy away from me."

Wanting to open their minds to the possibilities for change, I ask them, "If you learn from today's lessons that you do, in fact, have prejudices, do you think it will be helpful to keep talking about them? Do you think it could be helpful to change them?"

"Yes," they answer in one voice.

"Have you ever questioned some things you learned at home, at school, or at church—things you learned from friends or your parents?"

"No, I never question what I hear from adults," says Magnus.

"A good child should not question big people," Cindy interjects.

I continue to probe. "Do you accept as true the things people tell you, or do you listen to other people's opinions and then make a decision based on your own thinking?"

"I believe many things people tell me, especially when they are older than me," says Pius.

"Sometimes, I don't believe what I hear, but I don't want to disrespect the person, so I just say 'yes'. But in my heart, I don't believe the person," Wodokueh reveals.

"Sometimes when I hear something, I compare it with what I know. If I think I am right, then I don't accept what the person said. But I never try to make the other person feel bad," declares Janet.

"Sometimes I don't want to believe what people tell me, but I have no way of finding out if it is true or not," Mardell Joy interjects.

"To not believe older people is disrespectful. And you know that, Mr. Davis," Cindy challenges, a seriousness coming over her face.

The discussion flows and the interchanges grow more interesting.

I ask them, "If you have prejudices, what do you think would be their roots? How would they start?" But they look a little blank, so I elaborate. "Put it this way: If you hold a grudge against someone for no apparent reason, what do you think is the cause? Where did you first learn to harbor ill feelings toward that person?"

"Sometimes from someone older than me," says Magnus.

"I hear it from my mother," says Mardea.

"Sometimes I hear it at choir practice or at school when the big girls talk. I think my big brothers and sisters are the ones who make me hate some people. I hear them say bad things about those who fought in the war and killed people," adds Cindy.

I explain that little children have no prejudices. Their minds are born free. A baby can be held in the arms of a black or white person without feeling any difference, because a very young mind is free. But as the baby grows up, he or she starts to see differences—for example, that his brother wears shorts and his sister wears a skirt. Then the child starts to see differences in food, families and friends.

Millions of people have died because of prejudice. This is why we must learn to understand what creates it, at its root, inside ourselves. Besides looking at what other people say and do, we also have to look at the way we ourselves think and act—and understand ourselves, too. This is how we can overcome prejudice and stop millions from dying in the future.

At this point I read the story entitled "The Roots of Prejudice," in Dr. T's book *Why Is Everybody Always Picking Us? – Understanding the Roots of Prejudice*. While reading the story, I apply a teaching technique that Jean taught me. The children sit close together around the table, as if we are in a workshop. I sit at the head of the table, facing all of them, while I read. There is magic in the air; I can hear a pin drop. I really would have loved to ask one of the children to read, but we don't have a photocopier yet. It is great to have the children sit close while I read.

This story is about the Rock Tribe, a group of people who lived long ago in caves. As this tribe grew, their elders created activities which they expected all members to perform. Their superstitions included such strong and mysterious forces around stones that anyone who did not worship a pile of rocks would perish. Every month, members of the Rock Tribe had to dance to the rising sun to frighten away evil spirits. They had to paint their faces with a specially designed pattern to show that they all belonged to the Rock Tribe. These activities were carried out time and again—so often that they became a custom and gave the members a sense of belonging. Their repetitive ways of life became a habit—something they did often, without thinking.

The Rock Tribe elders passed these customs to their children. When those children became elders, they passed the customs on to *their* children. From one generation to the next, these customs became more and more firmly fixed in the minds and hearts of Rock Tribe members. Finally, the original superstitions had grown into very strong beliefs.

If a member of the tribe did not carry out a particular custom, he was punished. Over time, the customs supporting their beliefs became honored traditions. These traditions grew into rules that, in turn, developed even more strongly into laws. Their laws became the foundation of the tribe's heritage—a birthright, something members valued and honored forever, as a legacy to leave to *their* children and their children's children.

After reading the story, I point out to my students that as the tribe grew, no one ever stopped to ask why they performed these practices or lived by these laws. Their thinking became *conditioned*. This means that they were programmed to think and to act in certain ways.

These traditions and beliefs became a part of their unquestioned culture. The tribe grew in population and its territory became identified as a nation. The nation developed pride that caused a feeling of patriotism among all members. This patriotism bonded each tribe member to others in the group for centuries. All this was done to ensure the survival of the Rock Tribe.

I ask questions to see if my students have grasped the meaning of this story.

"What are some of the repeated practices that are performed by the Rock Tribe?"

"They used to put rocks together and pray to the rocks," answers Magnus.

"Why?" I ask.

"Because their big people said that if members of the tribe did not worship the rocks, they would die," explains Mai.

"Why did they dance to the sun every month?"

"They believed when they danced to the sun, evil spirits would be scared," Wodokueh explains with a big smile on her face. I infer that her smile comes from the supposed stupidity of people dancing to the sun to scare away evil spirits.

"Why did members of the Rock Tribe draw on their faces?" I ask.

"That way, people from their tribe would be able to identify each other," Cindy explains.

"How did these practices become habits and beliefs?" I ask.

"Members of the Rock Tribe did these activities over and over again," Emmanuel explains.

"How did their habits turn into customs and traditions?"

"They passed them on to their children and children's children," Natorah explains. "Their beliefs were stuffed into their heads."

"You're right," I say. "The Rock Tribe put these activities in their hearts and carried them wherever they went. So their activities became traditions. And how did the Rock Tribe's thinking become automatic, programmed—conditioned?"

"The Rock Tribe's thinking became automatic because they carried out their practices every day and every time in the same way. They were very used to these activities. It was not hard for them to do it again and again," Janet explains.

"Did they stop to ask why they were living by the Rock Tribe's laws?"

"No!" Magnus shouts. "No member of the Rock Tribe asked why they had to do all the things they did. Everybody was doing it, so there was no need to ask. The children saw their parents doing it and they learned to do it, too. They did not want to disrespect their elders, so they followed their ways," Magnus concludes.

Feeling gratified that their inquisitive minds are fully engaged, I ask, "Why did tribe members live by all these traditions and laws? What did these practices give them?" I ask these inquisitive minds.

"They wanted to feel like a Rock Tribe member. They did not want to feel that they were different. These activities made them one people. They would be able to spot a different person right away because a stranger would not know these things or might know different things that the Rock Tribe members did not know. Rock Tribe people would know foreigners quickly," explains John Pius.

"Do you think if you'd lived back then, you too would have felt safer, more secure, having traditions and repeated practices to help you survive?" I inquire.

"Yes, I would not want to die. If everybody was doing these things, why shouldn't I do the same?" little Mardea says perkily.

"I would not have prayed to the rocks but maybe I would have danced to the rising sun so that I, too, would not die," Cindy adds.

Attempting to bring the story into present time, I ask, "Do you think we still live in tribe-like situations today?"

"Yes, we do," explains Thomas Johnson. "Bassa people live in Grand Bassa County and do things Bassa people do. Kpelle people live in Bong County and do things only Kpelle people do."

"Can anyone give me an example of what Bassa people do?" I ask them.

"Bassa people send their girls to the Sande Bush (traditional schools for girls) and their boys to the Poro Society (traditional schools for boys.) Bassa people like to swallow dumboy" (a local food made of cassava that is a common diet for Bassa people.)

"Do you belong to any groups or organizations that are tribe-like? Do you think Unity Party and Liberty Party are like two different tribes?" I ask.

Janet says, "Unity Party people are behind Ellen Johnson Sirleaf (the current President of Liberia, first female to be elected in Africa) and Liberty Party people are behind Charles Walker Brumskine (Sirleaf's election opponent.) They wear different T-shirts, their offices are different and only Unity Party people come out to meet Ellen. This is the same thing the Brumskine people do with their own leader."

"Do you think the tribes we have today contribute to our survival?"

"Sometimes yes, but sometimes no," says George Brown. "Someone can kill you because you belong to a tribe. Many people die because of the tribe they belong to. My father said that because Bassa people stood together, they were able to drive the rebels from Buchanan when they came together against them. It saved the Bassa people."

"Bassa people and Kpelle people have problems because they are two different tribes," Thomas interjects.

"Can you think of a way that tribe-like organizations create war and prevent peace?"

Cindy begins. "For example, if a Kpelle man kills one Bassa man, the Bassa people and the Kpelle people will fight, and innocent people will die. This can bring big *palaver* (trouble) that will kill many people."

I continue my probe. "Do you think that living in tribe-like situations can give us the opposite of what we need?"

"Yes," replies Cindy. "For example, many Baptist people don't like Methodists and this can bring palaver."

"The world we are living in today," I tell the children, "is getting smaller. You can live in Buchanan and talk to someone on the phone in Monrovia or America in a matter of moments. A person can literally travel around the world in a day. Because people can move from place to place so easily, people now depend on others from all over the world for survival. But by living in tribe-like situations, we separate ourselves from other people. Isn't this the opposite of what we want—to live with other people in peace?"

To help the children consider this new concept, I talk about the basic necessities that we have traditionally fought over.

"What does it mean to survive?

"There are two kinds of survival—physical and psychological. We survive physically when we have enough food, enough water, clothing to keep us warm, and a place to live. Ancient tribes like the Rock Tribe helped their members survive physically by guaranteeing them these things. We survive psychologically when we *feel* safe and secure. Rock Tribe members were required to identify with their group and follow specific customs and beliefs. This dedication to the group made it more powerful—better able to care for its members—and gave members a sense of well-being.

"When the Rock Tribe grew, it began to encounter members of other tribes, including one called the Sand Tribe. Since both tribes needed food, shelter and clothing, both the Rock Tribe and the Sand Tribe started to perceive each other as enemies. The Rock Tribe believed that if the Sand Tribe came into their territory, it might change their traditional way of life. The Sand tribe thought the same about the Rock Tribe. As a result, the tribes began to fight. This condition created conflict, not only between the two tribes, but among other tribes as well. The tribes wanted to ensure that their traditions, beliefs, and customs were upheld. The Rock Tribe felt the best way to worship was to kneel down before a pile of rocks, and the Sand Tribe believed the best way to pray was to go to the creek and look up at the sky. The two tribes fought over the concept of how to pray."

"Do we still fight over enough food, enough land and enough clothing today?" I ask the students.

"Not really, sometimes mainly for food but not for clothing," Janet says.

"Yes, people are still fighting for land and food. Our Social Studies teacher said so," Mai explains.

"My father also said so," says Magnus.

"I have not seen people fighting for food in Buchanan," Aminata argues.

"Liberia is bigger than Buchanan," Wodokueh teases. "Maybe his father saw people fighting in Nimba, which you have not seen in Monrovia."

"Okay," I say, wanting to encourage my students and quell the rising confusion, "remember all questions are good questions. And no answer is wrong. We must respect everyone's view to get to the roots of prejudice."

As they settle, I ask," Do you think science has developed tools and technology that now give us the ability to create plenty of food, clothing and housing for our physical needs?"

"I think science has helped other countries but not Liberia," Thomas Johnson answers, in a tone of disgust.

"No, we are not able to create enough food, clothing and housing for all," Mai responds.

"Yes, science has helped us", says Mardea.

Pius questions her. "My mother says that people sleep outside in Monrovia, so why do you say science has helped us?"

When she starts to respond, Cindy jumps in. "If science has helped to create more food, then why are we eating bulgur wheat rather than rice in Liberia, still?"

I intervene. "We have been talking about physical conflict issues, such as food and clothing. Do you think science has helped us resolve *psychological* conflict too, or do you think science is unable to resolve the different ideas people have about how life should be?"

This question triggers an outburst.

"Science cannot help us solve our psychological problems."

"Science cannot change tribes and the type of church people belong to."

"Maybe science is doing that in other countries, but we don't know."

"Do you know of any country that science is helping in this way, Mr. Davis?"

"What about America? It seems that science can solve their psychological problems."

"So why does George Bush want to catch Saddam? America has problems too."

"You don't know that Saddam killed American people."

"Last night many of Saddam's people died too, so how is science helping America solve that problem?"

"They have big planes and bombs, the Americans."

"Why can't they catch all the bad people in Saddam's home, since they have all these big planes and bombs?"

I congratulate my students on their intelligent thinking. Then, I switch the questions back to the Rock Tribe.

"Was it fear of the Rock Tribe that created conflict between them and other tribes?"

"Yes, the Rock Tribe was too scared that other people would wipe them away," Aminata declares. "Fear made them confused about other people. The Rock Tribe was fearful among themselves, too. That is why they would not allow anyone to do anything that's different."

To personalize the concept of fear, I ask "Do you think fear creates conflict between us and people around us today? If so, how?"

"Yes, fear creates conflict today between us and people around us. I am afraid to allow anyone from Baptist School to come around to tell me that Catholic School is not good. We are the best and I don't want to see anyone from a different school say something different about us," Cindy says with passion.

"I don't like Moore Town community," says Thomas Johnson, spitting out each word. "So many ex-combatants live there." His eyes grew dark as he spoke, making it easy for me to feel his hate for the community.

The best way to understand the meaning of prejudice is to experience it first-hand. Just before closing, I say, "We need to look at prejudice—to examine it—in the same way that doctors examine sick people. We will find all the diseases that prejudice is made of.

"We have four ways to do this examination. First, we are going to *think* about prejudice and what it means. Then we will *recall* how it has personally affected us or people we know. Next, we need to *observe* prejudice as it happens in our brain. This kind of observation is called "insight." And finally, we will *talk with one another* about the prejudice we observe. I ask the students to *think* about a threat they feel and what this threat means to them.

Janet speaks up. "Last year I had a Bassa teacher. Now we have a new teacher; he is Kpelle. I don't like him. He is a bad man."

"What does this threat mean to you?" I ask.

"I may not pass this year if this man remains our teacher."

"Now it is time to *remember* how the threat has personally affected you or people you know."

"If I don't pass, my father will be disappointed. My father will kill me if I fail this year."

"Now it is time to *observe* the threat, I tell Janet. I ask her, "Do you see prejudice happening in your brain?"

She thinks and responds. "Looking at the threat, I don't think the man is really bad. I don't know him and he has not done anything to me even though he is Kpelle. Maybe I should just forget about this man and study my lessons. After all he has no power to give me a 70 when I earn a 90."

Janet has talked about her prejudice with all of us, and has reached a conclusion that helps her in her life.

I engage the students in an activity in your curriculum, Dr. T—the one called "Words We Use When We Are Prejudiced."

"One way to recognize when we are prejudiced is to examine the words we use. Sometimes our words give away our prejudices. What are some of these words?" I write a list of their words on a flip chart.

When they reach a lull, I say, "Now, I want each of you to take turns changing each of these words and phrases into a full sentence."

Sometimes the same students who suggested the first part, suggest the second, as well.

Some of their examples:

- He is *stupid*.
- He is a *Kpelle* boy.
- She is my *dumb* sister.
- The shopkeeper near us *does not like to spend money*.
- They *ought to* change their ideas.
- *Catholics* think they know it all.
- That is a really *dull* idea.
- They *should have* asked me.
- Can't you *do anything right?*
- *No one can possibly understand* how I feel.
- They think anyone who believes that is a *fool*.
- Newspaper people are *really liars*.
- You will *never amount to anything*.
- The boy's father was *a big drunkard*.
- Mano and Krahn people will *never live in peace*.
- These people from Bong County like *wearing red*.

At the end of this exercise, we place the chart at the back of the class. We will continue to add more phrases to it as time goes by. I re-emphasize the main points of our lesson, and we close for the day.

Back home in my bed, I put my own life in perspective. I think of all I had taught the children today about prejudice. In this short moment of contemplation, I recognize that I have my own personal prejudices. I look at how I have acted in my interactions with people from different backgrounds.

Traditionally, people have a long-held antipathy toward prejudice. They don't want to recognize that they have prejudices. So, without self-recognition, how can one deal with, or end, prejudice,?

I am happy that I recognize my personal prejudices. With this recognition, I am dealing with the problem intelligently. And in this way, I can truly help Liberian children, children of the world. Prejudice fragments people. How can a fragmented being help to make others whole? How can one give what he doesn't possess?

Reflecting on my personal prejudices brings me back to the root of the matter. I believe the faultiness of our reasoning process is what triggers prejudice. Unfortunate social effects stem from this central error. Instead of perceiving themselves prejudiced, they take pleasure in pointing guilty fingers. The fact is that all of us are prejudiced. It is difficult to grow up in this world without having to accept many ideas and practices before we are mature enough to know if they are true. Who can give a long philosophical explanation to a four-year-old child about a problem? We simply share with others the knowledge or opinion we have already taken in and accepted.

Everybody seems to develop a philosophy of life these days. Many of these philosophies are hazy around the edges. Even though we may think of ourselves as Christians, Muslims, Pan-Africanists, artists, agriculture experts, or football enthusiasts, as soon as we carry one such identity card, there is a danger that we will start to perceive ourselves as different, better, or smarter than others. Whatever our philosophy of life, the truth remains that our thinking eventually affects our ways of perceiving reality, and therefore our ways of reasoning and acting. Whether we believe or disbelieve that white people are more intelligent than black people, that democracy is inferior to communism, that one must defend his country with every ounce of his blood or that it is not good to join the army—such beliefs will profoundly influence our reactions, attitudes and views about a thousand separate issues.

Reasoning intelligently is a painstaking process. Some people don't like to use the logical parts of their brain. Reasoning intelligently deliberately casts off the restraints imposed by conditioning.

Many theories have been put forward as causes of the Liberian civil war—including unemployment, abuse of human rights, political patronage, illiteracy, lack of development and tribalism, among others. While it is true that all of these factors may have contributed, the heart of the Liberian conflict—and the fundamental cause of all human conflict—is psychological conditioning.

One type of prejudice affected me for a very long time. I am married to a Congo girl. The Congos are descendants of freed slaves. As a boy, I was brought up to believe that of all Liberians, the Congos were the most civilized and educated. Because of this conditioning, I also believed that Congo people were superior to indigenous Liberians.

Emily entered my world when I moved to Monrovia to enter college. I was working as a stock boy in a Lebanese store in Vai Town. She had come to the store with her friends from the University of Liberia, trying to purchase flour for what I assumed was a party.

They were loud and flippant, but Emily was gorgeous. I stole glances at her as I stacked bags of onions in one corner of the warehouse. She suddenly turned toward me and we shared brief eye contact before I turned away, embarrassed in my stock-boy apron and caught in my voyeurism. By some miracle, she returned the following day to buy more flour bags. In an act of rare gregariousness, I asked for her name and home address.

We saw each other regularly for about a month. My contract expired and I got laid off. I was so depressed I stopped visiting her. When we met downtown on Broad Street one afternoon, I gave her all sorts of excuses about why I hadn't seen her, and lied that I would see her the next weekend.

To my conditioned way of thinking, Emily was a good girl and I was just a poor boy who would end up making her feel bad. Congo girls and country (indigenous) boys did not mix. My family has always been poor. My father worked as a tapper, a low-end agricultural job, and my mother used to sell fish in the local market in Sergeant Kollie Town in Bong County, but now worked as a maid for some people who share similar blood with Emily. Though my heart ached, I would be lying now if I did not admit that I felt relief to get what I thought was the inevitable over with.

But I knew I loved Emily, and this realization frightened me more than the kind of family I had come from, or the kind of work my father did for a living. Yet my conditioning told me nothing would materialize from a relationship like ours. I knew it from the moment we kissed. As she comforted me on the loss of my job, I was busy reminding myself that it would be just a matter of time before I lost Emily, too.

Nonetheless, after four years of dating and two years of living together, even though my conditioning about our backgrounds continued to run me, we married. However, trouble brews when any of us continually believes something that isn't true, and the damage can be immeasurable.

For several years of our marriage, we shared many misunderstandings because of my conditioning. The source of our confusion was the fact that I hated to take suggestions and advice from Emily when we had a family problem. I always held the notion that her suggestions were an imposition of her Congo values on me.

A constant refrain ran through my head: "Why does she think Congo people know all the answers to problems? I will not allow a Congo girl to control me only because she feels that she is more civilized or comes from an educated family." I realize now that her suggestions and advice were always based on intelligence, but I felt at the time, that if I accepted her suggestions, she would see me as a country boy, or an inferior.

It was not until I started learning about conditioning and its effects that I realized that it was my conditioning that had made me act the way I did. Now when Emily suggests anything, I look at her point of view, independent of her background, and make rational decisions. I am not saying that we don't have normal differences, but I handle our differences with reasoning—not based on our backgrounds.

Because of this new way of thinking, I have discovered to my utmost surprise, that at no time during those years had Emily tried to look down on me, dictate to me, or feel superior to me. Everything she had suggested was in the interests of our family. The fact is she had always respected me, had always been proud of me, and had agreed to marry me because she believed I was ambitious.

I don't look back on those days with regret now, but with acceptance that I was ignorant then—not stupid, just ignorant of the facts. I am happy that I am living and interacting with my wife intelligently. We are on our way to celebrating our first ten years of marriage soon, and we are blessed with four beautiful children.

With my education and fresh insight, I have come to know that there is a tendency for some people to see themselves in a gracious way while seeing others as inferior, or as the "enemy." It is even more shocking to travel and learn about the attitudes of peoples of the world. Like the day when a Guinean driver came to pick me up at the Conakry International Airport, but refused to recognize me because I was dressed in an African suit. The Guinean was conditioned to believe that Liberians don't like to wear African clothes, and even though I was there with a banner of the organization that we both worked for, he deliberately left me at the airport. When we met the next day at the hotel where I was living, he said he had thought I was a Nigerian.

For me, reason alone is what will help us find our way across the minefields of bias, prejudice, superstition, selfish rationalization, fear, hate and ignorance. What is important to me now—rather than being right or winning—is the truth. I want to be an independent thinker, someone with an open mind, regardless of the majority's direction.

So here I am, helping to educate a new generation of Liberians about how to think intelligently. Many of our most fervent assertions involve probabilities, not certainties. Regarding some of our beliefs, it is very easy to be mistaken. Helping our children to think intelligently, to recognize personal mistakes, to be more willing to listen to all sides of a discussion, and to reason with evidence—these are goals worth achieving.

I will stay in touch,
Marvin

Lesson 2

What We Are Taught to Believe

"The kind of psychological conditioning that trains the mind to feed on our destructive, fragmentary and competitive way of life, will continue to create and sustain conflict for generations. Understanding our psychological conditioning is the greatest challenge to human existence in the 21st century, because it lies at the root of all human conflict, and it creates prejudice."

— *Marvin Garbeh Davis*

Dear Dr. T and Jean…

From your work in understanding the roots of human conflict, I am sure you know that learning about prejudice can be disturbing. When we read news reports of devastating clashes between cultures, nations and races, it becomes painfully clear how badly some people have been treated because of their family upbringing and beliefs.

In Liberia, children have not been able to watch television for more than 15 years. In Buchanan, we are blessed with two community radio stations. Many children listen to the news, even though hip-hop music is at the top of their listening list. I ask them, "When you hear the news about fighting among different people, what comes to your mind?"

"I feel sorry for small children when big people kill them," Martin laments.

"Why can't they just forgive everything and live together?" Janet asks.

"I wish all of us could just be one people," Aminata declares.

They speak with such clear hearts that I ask for more: "What are some things that affect you when you listen to the news?"

"Sometimes I don't understand all the things I hear on the news, but I feel sad when I hear people died," Ben says.

"I get really angry when I hear that many people are running away because of war," Marion declares.

During our civil war, some people were killed simply because they belonged to a particular tribe, came from a particular place, or worked for a particular company. Others were killed because they could not speak a Liberian dialect, even though they were Liberians. A man lost his son because the killers assumed from his last name, Krahn, that he was connected to people from the southeastern part of Liberia. In reality, his surname is used by people from three different counties. Killers murdered another man because they assumed he was on the side of the government. Why? Because he taught in a public school.

As these stories race around my brain, I realize that if we study these reports, if we think about how all these innocent people died in the Liberian civil war, and if we consider the parallels in the many other conflicts around the globe, perhaps we can reach a new level of understanding that will help the students appreciate where prejudice begins.

So I say, "A good way to begin to understand prejudice is to use our scientific minds. Like our prehistoric ancestors, we want to survive. Scientific thought allows us to make correct predictions about storms, earthquakes, heavy rainfall and drought. Scientists help us protect ourselves from natural disasters, and survive. Similarly, we need to learn to predict prejudice and conditioned thinking—to protect ourselves against man-made disasters."

If we treat prejudice as a science project, we can learn to protect ourselves from ignorance, fear, hate and the daily pressures brought about by our conditioned ways of looking at the world. By examining prejudice in ourselves, we can discover how to survive at the highest level of understanding—learning how to get along with other people, especially those who come from different backgrounds.

First, we must attempt to define prejudice. I want the children to both visualize it and feel it, so we use an example:

"If you throw a punch and hurt someone, will you feel pain yourself?" I ask.

"Yes, if you point one finger at a person, three are pointed back at you," James says.

"If you bend down to look at someone's butt, someone could be looking at your butt, too," says Thomas. At the mention of the word "butt," all the children look wildly at one another, because it is a rude word by Liberian standards, and children are not supposed to use it in the presence of adults.

"Thomas," I say, "don't be afraid. Go ahead and speak, any time." The tension in the class recedes.

Timothy formalizes Thomas' words: "Science says that to every action there is an equal but opposite reaction."

I am surprised, because he is only in the fourth grade. "How did you know this, Timothy?"

He responds, "My brother says this every day, when he hits me back for saying something bad to him."

"Do you think prejudice is like that? Does it hurt everyone?" I ask Thomas.

"I think so," he responds, "because if a Bassa man has something against a Kpelle man, the Kpelle man will also have something against the Bassa man."

"Yes, prejudice is like that," I concur. "It hurts everyone—not only the bullied person, but the bully too."

"Do you think human beings sometimes act before thinking?" I ask.

"Yes, sometimes people act before they think," says Mai.

"You want to give us an example, Mai?" I suggest to her.

"Last week I came home and saw a pot of water on the fire, but the coals under the pot were off. I hurriedly put my hand in the water. It burned so bad. I think I should have asked my mom to find out how long the fire had been off, and how long the water stayed on the fire. She would have told me and I would not have rushed my hand into the boiling water. I acted before I thought."

Pius adds: "Our mother might have turned off the fire because the water had already boiled. That way she could save her coals for another time. You really should have asked her."

"So how did you feel afterwards?" I ask Mai.

"I felt embarrassed," Mai says.

"No, you felt stupid afterwards," Pius injects.

"Don't insult me, Pius." Mai points her finger at Pius.

The word "stupid" is one that we use in situations like this. We talk about how the word hurts, and can instigate a fight. My students are discovering that this way of talking things out allows everyone to think, observe and make decisions on their own.

When I taught computer skills in Banjul, a student was chewing gum in class. Because this was against my rules, I asked him to go outside and throw the gum away. He not only left the class, but went home to tell his father, and made sure to emphasize the fact that I was a Liberian. Instantly, the father jumped into his car and tore back to the school.

Storming into the principal's office, he screamed, "You brought this man all the way from Liberia to threaten our children? Does he think that this is Liberia? Does he assume Gambians don't have the capacity to make war? I will show him some sense."

The principal then told the man to come and meet me in the faculty lounge to hear my side of the story.

"Are you Mr. Davis?" the man asked me.

"Yes, sir, I am. I hope you don't mind sitting down so we can talk."

Reluctantly the boy's father pulled up a chair. Then I asked him what the problem was.

I listened to him for a few minutes. When he was finished, I calmly explained what his son had done in class and why I don't allow gum-chewing. The lines of anger in the father's forehead loosened, his menacing squint relaxed and his tight lips softened. When I further explained that his son had left the school without anyone knowing and he fully realized that his son had misled him, he tensed up again, threatening to punish the boy. I tried to talk him out of it.

As we grew to know each other, this man and I became the best of friends. During one of our future outings, he told me that he had come to school prepared to fight, if I'd dared to utter one rude word to him. "I had my pocketknife ready, and I would have made you feel pain," he said. "You see, I had never met a Liberian before, much less ever visited your country. My judgments were based on the BBC news and rumors that drifted here from the civil war. For me, all Liberians were barbaric."

Often, we have information that simply is not true, and usually we never stop to question it. The kind of psychological conditioning that trains the mind to feed on our destructive, fragmentary and competitive way of life will continue to create and sustain conflict for generations. Understanding our psychological conditioning is the greatest challenge to human existence in the 21st century, because it lies at the root of all human conflict, and it creates prejudice.

The first step in freeing ourselves of prejudice is learning to question everything we see and hear. To get to the truth of any situation, it's crucial to ask, "Who? Why? What? When? How? Where?" These questions are part of the scientific method.

Prejudice is based on judgment. How do we see things? Do we believe that our words are facts, when in reality, we are only parroting thoughts, feelings, other people's opinions, or unverified readings? Prejudice is judgment, based on uninformed thoughts or feelings.

"What do you think of ice-cream?" I ask.

Many of my students will have heard about ice-cream, but I am not sure if any one of them has eaten any. There is no ice-cream shop here, and even if there were, most would not have had the opportunity to taste it. It's thus a good subject for examining their prejudice.

"I think it is sweet," Janet declares.

"Why do you think it is sweet?" I ask her.

"I saw a boy eating one in Monrovia and licking his lips as if it were full of sugar," Janet responds.

"I think it is too slimy," Pius concludes.

"Why do you think so, Pius?" I query.

"I have seen people eating it in the movies and shooting out their tongues as if the thing had okra on it," he says.

"Have you ever eaten ice-cream?" I ask Mai.

"No, but I have heard stories about it. When I read an ice-cream story, I thought it must be delicious. I feel the way I feel because I have heard people tell me about ice-cream."

"I have not eaten ice-cream but *they say* (in Liberia, stressing this phrase means rumor or gossip) it is very sweet," Thomas adds.

"So," I summarize, "each of you is able to express an opinion about ice-cream, even though none of you has actually had first-hand experience.

Louise," I say, moving from a fairly neutral subject to a case that's much more personal, "will you stand in front of your friends at the head of the class, please?" When she obliges, I turn to her classmates.

"John, what do you think about Louise?"

"I think she is not as strong as I am," he says.

"Come and try your luck, little man," says Louise.

"John," I ask, "is this not prejudice? Do you think this is a fact, or just the way you feel and think?"

"I strongly feel so," John insists. "Compare our muscles, Mr. Davis."

Janet steps in. "Maybe John feels that since Louise is a girl, he thinks he is stronger than her."

"Girls can be stronger than boys," Amanita adds. "I have seen girls beating boys many times."

With no rancor or judgment in my voice, I say, "John, based on no real evidence, you have concluded you are stronger than someone else. This is a sign of prejudice. You're making decisions that lack intelligence in this matter, without knowing whether you are really stronger than Louise. Bigger muscles don't necessarily make you stronger.

"This is the same as calling someone 'stupid' or 'foolish'. In the case of Pius saying that Mai felt 'stupid' earlier, she was *assuming* that Mai felt stupid without knowing the facts. That is prejudice too. If you judge a person or group of people as less than you, just because they appear different from you—that is prejudice. Prejudice arises when we judge people because we don't understand their thoughts or actions.

"What could make you hate someone you've never seen?" I ask them.

"Maybe because of what you hear others tell you about that person," Marion says. "You might hate him because of the place he comes from or the school he or his team supports."

"Maybe you've heard that this person bullies people."

At this point, we discuss the following concepts:

Most bullies become bullies because *they* were once bullied. Once we have been bullied and feel like a victim, it's human nature to want revenge. When we want revenge, it's usually because we're afraid of something. When we're afraid of something or someone, it helps to stop and think about what is frightening us. Just pausing for that one moment stops the fear, stops the prejudice—stops the train of hatred, anger and conflict in its tracks. When we can prevent conflict—in our minds as well as in our relationships—we can create peace.

"What's something *different* about someone you've seen that would give you strong feelings about that person?" I ask them.

"You can get a strong feeling about someone based on the clothes they wear, the tribe they belong to, or the family they come from," Mai explains.

"How would it make you feel to know that someone you know hates you just because you are different?" I ask.

"I would feel very sad, or get vexed or just decide not to have something to do with that person again. I'd watch out for that person," Cindy says.

"Can you think of a time someone tried to hurt you, or bully you, because you were different?" I ask.

Janjay stands up. "Some boys tried to hurt me when I went to play marbles with some of my friends in their community. A particular boy threatened to beat me up if I did not leave the playground immediately. I left right away, because I suddenly felt like a stranger in their place."

"As a result, do you now have feelings of prejudice towards that person?" I ask Janjay.

"Yes, I do. I have plans to pay them back when they try to come into my community to play. I think those boys are too selfish."

This is how prejudice grows. A fight begins and no one stops it. One person hurts another, and the victim seeks revenge. And this is how prejudice festers inside us, rotting our original good intentions. Though prejudice happened in the past, we hang on to it, and let it grow, making us unhappy for a very long time.

I say, "The next time you notice a feeling of prejudice creep up inside you, think about what gave you that unhappy feeling in the past. Then ask yourself: Do I want to hold on to this unhappy feeling? Do I really want to seek revenge? Or do I want to forget it and move on?"

Prejudice can slowly but steadily lead to a hostile attitude toward a person or group. We can be taught to think in ways that make us dislike or even hate another person without understanding why. All around the world, little confusions and disagreements take place every day. How much prejudice is at the root of a disagreement that turns into a war?

I organize the students to engage in a role-play which I had earlier typed up and copied. Role-plays are situations in which students are asked to play a certain part, a certain role—to pretend to be someone else and to stand in that person's shoes for a while. This one is about a pupil who has just enrolled in a new school. I distribute the copies and ask for volunteers to take on the roles of Chandell and Petrol.

Chandell: "Have you seen that new kid who just came to our school today? She wears the weirdest clothes and has a strange mark on her forehead."

Petrol: "I thought she was visiting for the day. She's going to be here forever? Oh no. Whose class is she in?"

Chandelle: "I don't know. But she doesn't wear any makeup and she doesn't say a word. Someone told me she could hardly speak because she's just learning the language. Can you imagine?"

Petrol: "If she can't speak the language, what's she doing in this school? How stupid can you be, not to know how to say hello and goodbye?"

Chandell: "If I were she, I'd just pack my bags and go back to where I came from."

I thank the students for acting. Then I ask, "What's the first sign of prejudice that you recognize in this conversation?"

"Chandell talks about the new student in a demeaning way," James answers.

"What words or phrases give Chandell away?" I ask.

"Chandelle says clothes the new student is wearing are *weird*, and calls the mark on her forehead *strange*," Pius says.

"Do the speakers know the person they are talking about?"

"No, she is a new student in the school and this is her first day in school."

"Do they have any experience being with that person?"

"They have no experience with the new person. In fact, they don't even know her name."

"Are they judging this person before meeting her?

"Yes!" the students cry in unison.

I then ask them, "Have you experienced this kind of prejudice recently? What was the situation?"

Janjay says, "I went to play football with my friends when we moved last week to our new home. I heard many of the boys saying I would not play because I don't look like a footballer. I was thinking, 'How should a footballer look?' I felt very bad that day and went home."

"What would you say to Chandell if this person shared these feelings with you?" I ask.

"I would try to meet this new student and find out the student's name," says Marion.

"I would try and make friends with her," adds Cindy.

"It would be better to introduce yourself and volunteer to take her around the school campus," suggests Ben.

Amanita chimes in. "I might try to find out who the girl is. Maybe she could be a good friend."

"Yes," I say. "Usually, strangers love to find someone to talk to. If you open up first, you may discover that this person is more like you than not."

For the final event of the day, the children engage in an activity called *Bag of Fears*. "Call out a fear you may have," I say. "Then think of any thought or action that might have caused such a fear."

Their responses are straightforward:

Fear: I'm afraid I'll make a mistake.
Cause of Fear: My father scolds me when I make mistakes.

Fear: I don't want people calling me stupid.
Cause of Fear: People say only stupid people make mistakes.

Fear: I'm scared of getting a bad grade.
Cause of Fear: My mother punishes me when I do.

Fear: I don't want to be dull.
Cause of Fear: My father says only dull people make bad grades.

Fear: I am afraid people won't like me.
Cause of Fear: It hurts not to be liked.

Fear: I am too fat.
Cause of Fear: People like to make fun of fat people.

At this point, I conclude. "As we have all learned, prejudice began long ago with the formation of groups or tribes who protected their territories and their rituals. They discriminated against any outside individuals for being different. Inside the tribes, members had to deal with prejudice, too. Anybody who acted differently, or who disobeyed tribal rules, was punished.

"Not only in Liberia, but all over the world, small conflicts happen every day. Maybe someone has called you a name or tried to bully you because you were somehow different—like the man in Banjul who tried to hurt me because I was a Liberian. I still feel the pain of it—not physically, but psychologically—inside, in my feelings and my memory. When I talk to you about it, some of that pain is released.

"What's wrong with being different? If someone told you that there was a new cinema in town and that it had beautiful movies, something really different from the others in town you had seen or been in before, would you instantly hate it? Wouldn't you want to go and see this much talked-about cinema? Wouldn't you be proud to tell a friend that you were among the first few people to enter? With the tempting possibility of seeing such exciting new movies in this specially designed theatre, why would this fresh difference be unappealing?

"Why would someone who dresses differently, speaks differently or thinks differently be less exciting than a trip to this new cinema in town? Do you think there is some kind of prejudice at work here?

"You and I can be taught to think in ways that make us dislike, or even hate, another person without ever understanding why.

"Feelings of hatred among people have caused tremendous suffering and pain to many generations over thousand of years. Similar feelings continue to cause pain and suffering to people in our world today. If we can simply learn to understand how our conditioning prevents us from being the peace-loving people we truly are, do you think that you and I can change this?"

I will give you details as things progress,
Marvin

Lesson 3
Our Mechanical Brain

"It is the hushed but destructive side of conflict that I seek. I wish to explore the root cause of all human conflict—at its primary level, where seeds can be withdrawn before controversy sprouts. How is conflict fundamentally created through conditioned beliefs in our brain?"

— *Marvin Garbeh Davis*

Dear Dr. T and Jean…

I have been thinking about the human brain a lot these days. I want to increase my knowledge of the brain—its construction, development and function. Not because I think it will increase my intelligence, but rather, to familiarize myself with the organ created for the *organization* of intelligence.

The brain is the only thing in the universe that can regard itself. Rocks can't consider rocks just as hands cannot consider hands. But the brain, as you have pointed out to me, can observe itself. So even if a person lives in isolation, one part of the brain can inform another part. The brain not only perceives, but also remembers. And the most amazing feature of this incredible organ is its ability to perceive relationships—between places, things and people.

One can be a teacher without going to a university. But the person who goes to a university to be trained to be an educator will know more about teaching. A person who understands both the mechanics of driving and the mechanics of a car is more informed than a teenager who is taught only how to start the ignition, turn a steering wheel, step on the accelerator and brake.

In short, we all want to think more intelligently. Our body's thinking engine is the brain. But for the brain to do its work, it must be fed. It must be programmed. It must receive, filter and sort out information.

The first mental activity we are engaged in, even before we leave the womb, involves receiving information. We have an incredibly intricate system of nerves that exists purely for this purpose. In the womb, information comes from the skin. We are able to feel moisture and temperature. As the ears and eyes are formed, we are able to hear and see. Then our nose allows us to smell.

We will never stop taking in information, not even when we are asleep, unless we become totally physically handicapped. Even then, the level of information we take in might only lessen. Our consciousness cannot possibly come into operation unless we receive information about how things feel, sound, look, smell, or taste.

And what does our brain do with this huge database of information? Miraculously, it stores it. In the world of computers, people say, "Garbage in, garbage out." The same is true of our computer brain.

We've all been frustrated when a television screen suddenly erupts with a haze of diagonal lines. When that happens, there's a good chance that something mechanical has gone wrong. Prejudice is like that. It is a mechanical difficulty in the brain. A thought can get programmed into our heads and create a groove, where it becomes ingrained. It happens to us all.

Suppose we were told that conflicts could only be resolved by fighting and hopefully winning. Would we have stopped to question whether these words were true? Whether they were based on facts? The words placed strong images in our brains, images that might try to run our future reactions, but were they truly anything more than an unverified thought?

An image repeated becomes a message reinforced. A feeling surrounds the message. Together they create a *think/feel*—a thought associated with a feeling. One day, we see the person who made the comment that set us off in the first place, and our *think/feel* kicks in. This think/feel triggers the fight or flight system in the old brain, the brain that has been passed to us from generations of ancestors.

This is where the real problem lies. This area of the old brain interprets the images as real, as an actual threat to one's well-being. It is this area of the brain that holds the conditioning in place, and it is this part of the brain that reacts with tremendous force in defending itself from what it perceives as a real threat to its survival. And it will defend itself to the death in carrying out its purpose— to survive—even if the image, and hence the threat, is not real—just a conditioned response.

This is mechanical, automatic and robotic. None of us can stop the *think/feel from* triggering the image. It is projected on our brains just like a movie projector throws pictures on a screen. This triggers the "fight or flight" system in our brains that sparks a fight, all based on an image which may be real or which may be fictitious.

It is this hushed but destructive side of conflict that I seek. I wish to explore the root cause of all human conflict—at its primary level, where seeds can be withdrawn before controversy sprouts. What are the fundamentals of conditioned thinking that encourage our brains to create conflict?

I ask my students, "So if you fight and someone wins, is the conflict over?"

Janjay offers, "Sometimes, you really think it is over, especially if you are the winner. I had a fight with a boy in our community and I won. He went home with a bleeding mouth and all the children mocked him, and some of the boys raised my two hands in victory. For me, the conflict was over. The fight decided who was right and wrong, strong and weak.

"But two days later, the boy told his older brother who had traveled to their home village. The older brother decided to make me pay for what happened to his little brother. I was not aware of all this. On my way home from school, the older brother attacked me. He jacked me up by my shirt collar and asked his brother to punch me in the mouth. He wanted to make sure I sustained similar injuries, so he held my hands while his younger brother punched me in the mouth. A woman passing by heard me shout and came to my rescue. I went home with two buttons off my uniform shirt and a swollen mouth."

Winning a fight does not mean the conflict is over. The belief—that the only way to resolve a conflict is by fighting—is not real. The image is not happening in the real, outside world. It is happening in only one place—inside our brains. We believe what our brains have told us is factual, but instead we have been judging. And all the time we've been judging, we have not been understanding.

When I was a boy, my mother told me that Kissi people ate dogs. "I don't want you to eat dog meat because Bassa people don't do that." One of my school friends was a Kissi boy. We walked to and from school together, played ball together and sometimes ate at my home together, but my mother made sure I never ate at my Kissi friend's house. I believed my mother, even though I never saw his parents kill or cook dog. When I passed this information to our friends, they too decided not to eat at the homes of Kissi children. For a long time afterwards, even though I have never seen a single Kissi person kill or cook a dog, and even though I was sure that there was no dog meat in their food, I could not eat in their homes.

I know all of us have such issues. Our parents, pastors, teachers and coaches mentor us; we believe them unquestioningly, and try to run our lives according to their advice. But we must think and act like scientists, who know it's important to remain fair and impartial when exploring the cause of any problem. If, without examination, we label any person, place or thing "bad", we are being prejudiced.

Learning about prejudice requires a mind that can learn to think without judgment. Most of us have been victims of prejudice at one time or another, and have felt its intense sting. Whatever the degree of our pain from intolerance, we must strive to *understand* how it happens. Once we know the brain's path to prejudice, we can prevent it.

I ask my students, "Have you been told by your parents, teachers or older family members not to do certain things?"

"Yes," Janjay responds immediately.

"You want to tell us your story, Janjay?"

"Yes," he says. "During the war, my father was beaten by a rebel soldier who belonged to the Gio tribe. He was beaten so badly he could not walk, and my mother had to bathe him. Since that day, my father has not wanted to do anything with people from the Gio tribe. For him all Gio people are bad people, because of the one boy who beat him. Now, he tells my older sister and me that unless he dies, none of his daughters will ever marry a Gio man.

"We used to live in Corn Farm (a community in Buchanan) when we returned from the displaced camp," Janjay continues. "One day, there was an empty room in the house we rented, and the people who moved in were Gio people. Actually, the man was Gio, but the woman was Bassa. As soon as my father discovered that the man was Gio, he moved us to the Bassa community where we live now. To this day, when I see a Gio person, I am afraid. I don't want to come near that person. There was a friendly Gio boy in our class last year, but I would not get near him. I used to think my father was walking behind me and if he saw me talking to this boy, he would kill me."

"Thank you very much, Janjay, for sharing your story," I reply. "Prejudice is a difficult habit to break. Does anyone else want to share a story with us that has to do with prejudice?"

Mai responds. "My parents' home is next to a family that has a car and a video player in their home. They are the only ones with a generator in our area. My father does not like the man and his family. He has not told me so, but I can see the anger on his face when he talks about this family. When I see his face like that, I know he is serious and I get scared. My father tells us the man is too proud, that he thinks that because he has money, he is everything. So he does not want us to have anything to do with this family. My father has told us not to ride with the children, even if the man offers us a lift. But the man's children go to the same school with us, and they are nice.

"Last week when my father went to our village," she continues, "my little brother and I crept over to the home of this family. We wanted to watch some movies. So we went to the big window in front of the house to watch from the side. The man who has the house came outside and saw us, and we decided to run. He was calling us to come back and enter his house, but we ran away anyway."

"Do you believe that all Gio people are bad and beat people?" I ask Mai.

"Yes, Gio people beat people during the war," answers Mai.

Ben retorts, "But so did Kpelle, Bassa, Krahn and all the other boys who were soldiers."

"Do you think we should hate all Gio people because one Gio person did something bad to us?" I ask.

"No, not all Gios are bad," says James Dennis. "I have lived in Nimba, where my father used to teach during the war. We lived in the house of a Gio family, and their son who was my age became my best friend. I cried the day we left to come to Buchanan."

"It's hard, isn't it," I say, "to leave best friends? And harder still to hear them being called bad names when you know it isn't true. Every time someone says something bad about someone you know, maybe because of a difference in tribe, church, school, cultural beliefs or nationality, their words dig a new hole in the field of your thoughts. They plant a seed there that grows in your mind. It happens in four stages.

"First, you hear this message—this bad thing about someone or a group of people you know—which creates a picture in your mind. For example, Janet's mother tells her that Bassa people are mean. You see Bassa people with nasty faces, being brutal to others.

"Second, the message is repeated over and over again. It's like Janet's mother's words water the seed she planted earlier in Janet's mind. The picture grows in size, like weeds in a garden: more, cruel Bassas threatening to harm her and her friends. It replays and replays.

"Third, those mean images causes negative feelings to swell up: 'I hate Bassa people because they are mean.'

"In the fourth stage, a program in your brain labeled 'Fight or Flight' gets triggered. As a result, you feel you'd better defend not only yourself, but everyone in your tribe. You have to either fight that Bassa person, or run away in fear.

"What happens to you when you see a Bassa person?" I ask Janet.

"I see a very bad person, someone who steals, lies or can hurt others."

"So what does your mind tell you?" I ask.

She responds, "Watch out, Janet, you are meeting a bad person."

Without any investigation, Janet has a bad feeling in her head for Bassa people. Hence, the moment she sees one Bassa person, the bad feeling pops into her thoughts, just like that—automatically and unconsciously. She is not able to control it. The image and feeling are programmed into her brain, triggered by the appearance of a Bassa person and projected towards the person like a movie projecting on to a screen.

What is important for us to realize is that this image is not real.

It is just a picture in the brain. We don't need to be afraid, or fight, or run away if we can understand that the image is not real, even though a part of our brain is reacting as if it were real. The key is in suspending the fight or flight reaction long enough to see how falsely it is reacting. If we can just see it as it is happening, we won't act out that imagined distress as we did in the past. It is like waking up from a dream, and now we can see what is real.

A little girl named Joan came to the Peace School, and after the usual, short interview, I registered her. She stood for a moment in my office, which was not very normal for the children to do, so I invited her to sit down.

"You want to tell me something before you leave, Joan?" I asked.

"Do you speak Bassa?" she asked me.

"Yes, I understand and speak Bassa," I replied.

"My father says when people travel out of this country and come back, they don't like to speak Bassa. They always try to look down on other people."

"So he did not want you to come here?" I asked.

"Yes, but my mother thinks you are a nice man," she responds.

"I will not look down upon you or any student here in the Peace School, and no one else will either," I assured her.

A week after this conversation, Joan's father came by to see me. When I heard him introduce himself to the secretary, I immediately left my office to meet him in the doorway.

I spoke to him in Bassa and showed him a seat in my office. We talked for several minutes in Bassa, and I explained to him what the Peace School was about.

"Thank you very much," he said while we walked together outside my office. "I want to ask a favor, Mr. Davis. Could I send my niece to the Peace School, too?"

"Yes, we still have space," I said. "Send her tomorrow."

The next day, Joan came to school. "My father says he loves you," she smiled. "He thinks you really acted like a gentleman and he has decided to be your friend."

Sometimes we think that what we see is what is actually happening in the real world. But sometimes, this is a vision that happens in only one place: our heads. That is what we move and act on, believing that what the brain has told us is factual. But instead, we have been judging. And once we judge, there is no space left to understand.

Understanding is one of the most important goals of scientists. To continue our exploration of how prejudice works, we must do everything in our power to use our minds to follow a scientific method that promotes understanding, so we can actually become *aware* of how prejudice works mechanically in our brain. It is this awareness in the moment that allows us to respond separately from our conditioning, from our prejudice, so that our past habits do not inhibit us. It is this awareness of the fact of what is happening that can free us from conflict.

To keep our minds in a mode of operation that promotes understanding, I give my students some simple goals:

"*First, remain cool.* In our everyday life, we hear people say that it is always good to be able to think in an objective way when we find ourselves in a difficult situation. Do you think it's possible to understand a situation when we are so angry that we cannot speak? It is good to thoroughly examine the source of our anger. Use that anger button to turn on your 'inner scientist' button. Take the time to understand the person or situation thoroughly, from all perspectives, as a good scientist does. It is difficult to make a good decision when we are upset or in a hurry. At those times, we are never able to examine all points."

Jimmy, one of our pioneer students in the Peace School, said one day, "You know, before I came to the Peace School, I would get so mad at my younger brother for calling me stupid, that I would slap him, every time. But since I've come here, I've learned to cool off when he insults me."

"And what happens when you cool off, Jimmy?"

"My temper goes down. When I look at my little brother, I realize that he is very little— just a small boy who does not understand what he's saying. Besides, when I replay the problem in my mind, I sometimes see that I have acted stupidly. So, I don't slap him. And my mother never throws anything back at me for beating him, so neither one of us gets hurt."

Second goal: "*Question without assuming.* Instead of jumping to conclusions, it is much better to become the scientist who questions the facts. Before putting that scientist's cap on our heads, without really having any concrete clues, we blurt out, "This is wrong!" "That is right!" "This is bad!" "That is good!"

Jemima, one of the active girls in the Peace School, said, "One day, while on my way home from school, I was thirsty. I did not have money to buy water, so I hoped that I would be able to stop by the home of some nice neighbor and ask for some water. I saw a group of women pounding cassava. I thought they were Bassa women, since people say that Bassa people love pounding cassava.

"But when I spoke Bassa to them, the women replied in English, saying, 'We are Grebo people. What do you want?'

"When I answered, 'Water,' one of the women handed me a cup of water."

In this situation Jemima assumed that because the women were pounding cassava, they were Bassa. She had learned that Bassa people love cassava. So she jumped to a conclusion without having any facts about the people beating the cassava.

Third goal: "*Test your findings to see whether they are factual.* When you hear a rumor about something or someone, do you immediately accept it as true? It is important to explore information and test it yourself before reaching any conclusions."

There is a saying: "Where there is smoke, there is fire." In Liberia, this means that when we hear any news about somebody, especially anything mean, there is some truth in it. Therefore, some Liberians will believe anything, because, for them, there is some level of truth in any falsehood.

After staying away from my country for seven years, I returned to my hometown, Buchanan during the elections of 2005. The first thing I heard people say was "Oh, oh, see that man in the little car with the tinted windows? He's a heart man." 'Heart men' kill other people and sacrifice their body parts in fetish practices so that they can get top civil service jobs.

Some said, "You know why he's recruiting children for his programs? He's come to buy children to sell in Europe and America."

Still others said, "He says he's running a nonprofit organization, but just wait. He's really come here to seek political office."

One evening, after giving some students a lift home, I stopped in at one of my neighbors to introduce myself, as I had been doing since moving back to Buchanan. Upon entering their house, I heard a woman in the kitchen say in Bassa, "What has that society man (heart man) come to do in this kitchen?"

I replied in Bassa, smiling, "I am your son, not a heart man."

If this woman had the power to ask the ground to open and swallow her up, she would have done it in that instant. She said, "My son, that is what people are saying around here."

Many people think prejudice comes from the outside. At first it does, but like a virus, it worms its way in—and then lives and grows inside us. While we may collect all shades of prejudice from outside, the prejudice we project comes from within. Although our ancestors may have planted the seeds of prejudice in us, it now lives and breathes within us. We become a giant weed of prejudice.

As we spew out our prejudices, we struggle within, where an intimate and excruciating war simmers. Our eyes see people dressed differently and our ears hear them speaking foreign words. Our thoughts rage: "He's bad, but I'm good." Or "She's wrong, but I'm right." Or "Their culture is disgusting, but ours is beautiful." And "Why can't they just learn to be like us?"

Mai Tarr, one of my students, tells me that she has a friend who likes playing football with the boys. Mai's mother says to her, "Don't play with that girl, she likes boys too much. I don't think she will ever finish grade 6."

"I really like the girl," Mai tells me. "She's friendly and she challenges the boys in their own game. But I don't want to disobey my mother and I don't want to lose my friend. So when she is playing with the boys, I just sit and watch, waiting to run away when I see my mother coming towards me. It really hurts me to act in this way. I feel I have a blade cutting through my heart."

As the prejudice within spills out, we behave negatively toward someone we perceive as 'bad', and act superior toward someone we perceive as 'stupid.' But is that person really bad? Is that person truly stupid? Or are these simply pictures in our mind?

Why have some people created a list based on race, color, gender, social class, occupation, appearance and ability? It only creates an 'us versus them' situation. By creating separation, we fictionalize a reason to treat others with disrespect or hatred.

Negative messages programmed as images in our brains prevent us from seeing the similarities we share as human beings, the common connections that bind us, and the countless personality traits that intertwine us in our humanity. Instead, we focus on the small things that divide us, spinning our lives in a web of conflict.

Programmed images are part of the basic structure in our brains, which are triggered by such words as "stupid," "foreigner" and "inferior." The careless use of such powerful image-provoking words can culminate in the worst outcome. For when prejudice lives inside us, and we transfer it by acting prejudiced toward another human being, we set the stage for conflict. From there, it's a small succession of steps to war.

When we hear or read a news story that is shocking, our natural reaction is to push it away, to refuse to think about it, to protect ourselves from imagining it. We want such horrible news never to have happened. But it is better to learn from situations—even if they are terrible.

It is difficult to look at the suffering that prejudice has generated in the world, because often as not, it reminds us of our own, similar wounds. I say to my students, "Perhaps someone has perceived you as 'different' and, as a result, picks on you. If you have felt the pain of such bullying, you already have a good reason to want prejudice to end. Whatever your reason, learning to understand it will help you end it—even before it begins. By learning to stop prejudice before it begins, you will be helping to both avoid current conflict and prevent future conflict."

Our brain is capable of amazing feats. In the better world we all want to create, there is no need for any group of people to feel superior to any other group of people, because basically we are all the same. One of the ways to feed the creation of this new world is to learn to accept the unique individuality of our children, instead of regarding them as extensions of ourselves and conditioning them with our old tribal beliefs that have been creating conflict for centuries.

We need to bring about new human beings, brave new children who have a chance to be free of the conditioning that has created conflict here in Liberia and in the world, for conflict is conflict. No matter where it exists, it has the same root in creating prejudice, the prejudice that poisons the world with fear and hate. We must educate our children and give them the priceless opportunity to learn about themselves. First, we must educate ourselves about the limitations that we have been conditioned to encumber them with. Once we have cleared up our misconceptions, we can embrace open-mindedness. We must then give them the gift of honoring the fact that they are independent, thinking, human beings, capable of going beyond, and improving the world.

It is these milder, common forms of parental narcissism that Kahlil Gibran addresses in his classic, "On Children". I see these as the finest words ever written about child rearing:

> Your children are not your children.
> They are the sons and daughters of life's longing for itself.
> They come through you but not from you.
> And though they are with you yet they belong not to you.
> You may give them your love but not your thoughts,
> For they have their own thoughts
> You may house their bodies but not their souls,
> For their souls dwell in the house of tomorrow,
> Which you cannot visit, not even in your dreams
> You may strive to be like them, but seek not to make them like you.
> For life goes not backward, nor tarries with yesterday.
> You are the bows from which your children as living arrows are sent forth.
> *Kahlil Gibran, 1883 -1931*

Sincerely yours,
Marvin

Lesson 4

The Prejudice Within

"What happened in Liberia has happened everywhere—and for millennia. Conflict is conflict, no matter where it happens. If we are to survive psychologically and socially, we must understand conditioning—the prejudice within."

— *Marvin Garbeh Davis*

Dear Dr. T and Jean…

There are two seasons in Liberia: the rainy season, from April to September, and the dry season, from October to March. As it is now July, it's pouring. Being one of the counties near the coast, Grand Bassa gets a lot of rain, and Buchanan, its capital city, is rated the highest of all.

Buchanan's main avenue, Tubman Street, named after Liberia's longest serving president, William V. S. Tubman, is now muddy. The potholes have increased, and driving along the street is more difficult—taking a heavy toll on local cars. Mainly because of bad shock absorbers, many autos are parked in repair shops around the city.

The rain has been relentless today. For several hours I have been hoping it would stop, but the showers only increased. I am beginning to worry about the children, because in half an hour, Peace School classes are supposed to start. Many of the students live far from the Common Ground office. If it continues to rain, many—if not all—might not come to class.

Looking through the windows of my office, I watch the sky turn darker. My concern about attendance intensifies. I begin talking to myself. "I wish I had a pick-up to collect the children from their communities and bring them to the Peace School today. Or money to buy each of them an umbrella. Then those who are willing to come could walk in a downpour."

I leave my desk and walk to the main entrance of our office building. Standing in front of the office, I see a group of naked children running in circles in the gutter that divides my side of the office grounds from the main street. The youngest of the children stands with his back facing the road, tossing pebbles in the gutter while his friends run around.

The bigger ones hold each other's waists and sing as they move in circles. I don't understand the meaning of the song they sing, but the last line says something like "If the rain comes again, I will plant my rice, but today I will take my bath." I return to my office hoping that the rain will stop.

The deluge gradually lessens. I leave my office and stand again in front of the main door. The children who were playing in the gutter have gone home. People are stepping into the main street. Across the road, a group of women who had abandoned their roadside markets and stalls have started crowding up the road again. People who had been waiting in empty stalls and under roadside house roofs for the rain to stop have started their journey either up or down Tubman Street. Less than an hour ago, the roads were so empty that a stranger would have thought the city a ghost town. Now the streets have come alive; motorcycles are transporting people, fish sellers are advertising their fish, wheelbarrow boys are moving up with their wares.

It is amazing how much Liberians fear water. A Sierra Leonean friend of mine once said to me that Liberians are more afraid of rain than cars. When I think about how often pedestrians jaywalk across Tubman Street, and how hurriedly they flee the streets in a downpour, I tend to agree.

Up Tubman Street, near the welcome monument, I see a group of children walking toward me. They are all in colored clothes, so it is difficult to tell if they are coming to the Peace School. As they get closer, I see that each of them has a plastic bag. "I wonder what all those children are carrying," I ask myself. As they draw within two hundred meters of me, I recognize three of them: Mary, a little girl living with her mother near the coconut plantations community, Mai, another girl living with her aunt around the pipeline community, and Janjay, who lives with his grandmother in the town community of Jecko. Soon I spot nine children and my heart leaps a beat in relief.

"Good afternoon, Mr. Davis," they greet me in the sitting room.

"Good afternoon," I respond. "I am sorry about the rain today. Come in, please."

"Ernestine," I ask my secretary, "Will you please bring a towel and help the children wipe themselves dry?" As they remove their drenched shirts, I glance at the contents of their plastic bags, and see their Peace School T-shirts. They have sacrificed their ordinary clothes to make sure that they could wear a warm T-shirt in class. I flashed back to how I, as a boy, would put my uniform in a plastic bag and walk to school in my casual clothes, change into my warm shirt and then put my wet clothes in the plastic bag. Since my father was a tapper, he could not afford to buy me an umbrella during the rainy season. None of the other schoolboys from the laborer's camp had umbrellas either. But we all had our treasured plastic bags for these rainy days.

We have eleven students in class today: seven boys and four girls. I have a feeling some will come later, now that the rain is simmering down. I thank the children for making the effort to come in the rain, and I begin the lesson. Today, we continue our discussion of prejudice—prejudice within.

"I would like each of you," I tell the children, "to think of one way in which you may be prejudiced. And to remember where that prejudice possibly began."

Timothy, the tallest boy in this section of the Peace School, raises his hand. One of the first things I noticed about him were his eyes, for his glasses have frames so old that I expect the handles to break whenever he pushes them up on his nose. Ever since he told me he got his glasses through a donation from an international non-governmental organization, I have been pondering who I might speak to, for help to change them. He is fourteen years old, but barely talks in class, so I am happy he volunteers to contribute today, especially right at the outset.

"I don't like Bassa children in my school," says Timothy.

"What do you mean you don't like them, Timothy?"

"I don't want their friendship."

"Why don't you want their friendship?"

"They always say bad things about Kpelle people," he says.

"You want to tell us some of the bad things the children in the school say about Kpelle people?"

"One of the boys in my class called Joe says that the meaning of Kpelle is stupid."

"Can you explain this better for me to understand, Timothy?" I ask him.

"This means that if you are Kpelle, then you are stupid."

"So," I ask Timothy, "do you believe that any prejudice you have about Bassa children began from something someone did or said to you?"

"Yes," Timothy says.

I ask all the children, "Why do you think Timothy does not want to be friendly with Bassa children in his school?"

"Because they are mean to him," Patience says.

"Timothy does not like them because they say he is Kpelle, and that Kpelle people are stupid," Janet adds.

"Prejudice is a way of thinking that is usually out of focus," I say to the children, "like looking at your shadow. When we are prejudiced, our judgment slants the way we see things. This certainly must be true of the children who talk this way to Timothy."

"I want to say something," Janet says. She is the most active girl in this section.

"Go ahead, Janet."

"If we sit in our living room and the lantern is burning, my small brother and I will go in front of the wall and look at our shadows. I can be very short and fat if the lantern is close to the wall, but if I back away, I can be very tall and skinny."

"This is how prejudice works, Janet. You only have to look at yourself again to know that the shadow on the wall is not the way you really look.

"There is a place inside each of us," I tell them, "that holds on to any bad thing you hear about somebody. It may be in your head, your chest, or maybe your stomach. It is a place where you make all your decisions. For instance, if someone tells you that your next-door neighbor is bad, that 'bad' goes to your head, your chest, your stomach, your heart, or whichever special place your body decides to keep it. It is from this place that you act the way you act. But you can create a different place inside you—a stopping place—where you question your thoughts.

"Today, let's each of us put up a sign in that place that makes us act automatically from prejudice. The sign should read: "All rumors stop here." And in your stopping place—the place where you look at any information that you suspect may not be real or true—let's put up another sign that says: "I can stop prejudice *before* it starts.

"Prejudice inside us creates conflict inside us, and it can also create conflict outside us.

For instance, if you think that someone is stupid and that you are much smarter, you create conflict in your mind. When you have a lot of conflict going through your mind, there is no room left for clear thinking. This conflict builds up inside you.

"Whatever builds up inside, explodes, and usually at the wrong time, in the wrong place, and against the wrong people. If you simply *think* you are smarter than another person, the way you feel will come out—in your words and your actions."

Janet raises her hand again. "You know, Mr. Davis," she says, "I don't like to keep thoughts against people inside me."

Sometimes I wish I could stop Janet from talking so much, but other times I feel it is because of her contributions that other children talk and we learn more. In Liberia, teaching is a serious business, especially when working with young children. Creating a congenial atmosphere draws children out. I like to believe we are getting there, so I encourage them.

"It is very good for you to express yourself, Janet. So tell me why you don't like to keep things inside?"

"You see, Mr. Davis," she starts to smile, the little captivating gap in her teeth slowly emerging, "if I keep mean things inside me, I have to blow up one day soon and sometimes I blow up for the wrong reason and in the wrong place."

"It happens to all of us, Janet. I sometimes blow up like that in a wrong way when I have kept feelings inside for a long time. And what's worse is that when we do this, we act out of prejudice and inflict pain on other people."

Marian says, "I always try to wear a different color skirt or blouse that is not red when I know my friend Janjay and I are supposed to go for an outing."

"Why do you choose a different color, Marian?"

"Don't tell me you don't know, Mr. Davis!"

"Please tell me, Marian. It is always good to learn new things."

"Kpelle people like to wear red clothes," Marian says. "That is why I never wear red when I go out with my friend Marian. She is a Kpelle girl, and I don't want anyone to think that I am Kpelle too."

"Do you perceive this as prejudice, Marian?"

She does not respond, so I ask her to think about it.

"And what about you, Timothy? How do you act toward the boys who say mean things about you at school?"

"When it is one of those boys who always call me all kinds of names at school, I will never share my lunch with him. They can go on their knees begging, but I will not give them anything. And if they were dying I would not help them," Timothy explains, his face scrunched up with his angry memories.

"And what do the boys do to you when they have their own food?" I ask.

"I don't bother with them, because I already know they will not give me anything. I only stay around those who I share with."

It is simple but true: When we act with respect toward another person, that person will act with respect toward us. When we live together in mutual respect, there is no conflict. When we act disrespectfully, then the opposite is true. What happened in Liberia has happened everywhere—and for millennia. Conflict is conflict no matter where it happens. If we are to survive psychologically and socially, we must understand conditioning—the prejudice within.

In this world, we have created many kinds of prejudice. Some allude to skin color, sex, age, race, nationality, culture, belief system, social class, physical disability and body size. All these distinctions divide human beings. They don't allow us to see and think about all the ways we are the same, the common things that bind us together as human beings. All these distinctions are programmed images, fixed in everyone's brain.

Raindrops begin pitter-pattering on our classroom roof again. I walk toward the windows and look at the clouds. There is an impending storm, but I want to close today's lesson with an activity from your curriculum, Dr. T.: the one called "The Need to Be Right."

As I hand them each a piece of paper, I ask, "What do you need to be right about? Please write it down."

After about five minutes, I ask, "Who would like to volunteer to read what they've written?" Two boys and three girls put up their hands. The rest decide to share only with me, and hand in their papers later.

Janet: "I feel the need to be right about my school. It is the only Catholic School in Buchanan and it is the best."

Timothy: "For me I just like my Baptist Church. I don't care about other churches."

Marian: "I love my Buchanan. I don't like to hear people say bad things about this town, especially when they come from a different town."

Theo: "I feel that my school uniform is the best in town."

Mai: "I feel strongly about my dance style."

The rain has started falling heavier, so I try to wrap up quickly in order to have time to drive the children home.

"Everyone has a need to be right," I tell the children, "but sometimes insisting on being right causes conflict. Can you see this?"

At this moment, especially when it is time to pinpoint the essence of the day's lesson, I make sure all of the children are sitting quietly. Once I am sure that they are fully engaged, I continue.

"Insisting on our rights can sometimes be a sign of prejudice. The Liberian War lasted for more than fourteen years. During this conflict, the parties held dozens of meetings, both inside and outside Liberia, to find ways to bring the war to an end. There were many times when they could not agree on any terms, because each of them insisted on being 'right'. Nobody wanted to bend for the other. Both sides stuck to their views. They could eat together, and drink wine together, but they could not reach any decision for peace together.

"Sometimes it is good to be right, but it is more important to *understand* what right is. More importantly, there are times when there is something better than being right."

As a result of the "heart man" business, the town of Buchanan lives in the grip of fear. In order for the children to continue coming to the Peace School, I have started driving them to the intersections nearest their homes. I make two trips: first, up Tubman Street towards the Atlantic Ocean, where most of our students live, and second, down Tubman. Each day, I spend time visiting one of the student's parents. Today I decide to take Timothy home so I can meet his father and aunt. They live in one of the most impoverished communities in Buchanan.

"So, do you think your father will be glad to see me at his house?" I ask Timothy, as I turn off Tubman on to the narrow road that leads to Gwenigale, a town community, near the Christian Mission Church.

"Yes, he will be glad." He sounds very sure, which makes me look forward to the meeting.

Within three minutes of driving down the narrow stretch of road, Timothy says, "You can turn right around the breadfruit tree, Mr. Davis." A few seconds after the engine grinds to a halt, the car is surrounded by children..

"Hello, Uncle, hello Uncle," the children greet in chorus as I step down from the car. I follow Timothy as he leads me to his home. It is a small mud house, draped in a combination of very rusty zinc and tarpaulin, no doubt to fight the many leaks. Sitting on a small bench in front of the house, a man dangles a green, plastic cup from one hand and in the other, holds a bottle, probably full of palm wine.

"Hello Papa," Timothy says to him. Pointing toward me, he says, "This is our peace teacher, Mr. Davis."

"But Timothy, why are you always making me ashamed? You know we have nothing, and then you bring this big man to our house," Timothy's father says angrily.

I interject. "No, Pa. I am the one who asked Timothy to bring me. I am sorry. I should have told you before, but don't worry. I just came to see *you* today." He calmed down.

The man stands up and we exchange handshakes. "Timothy, please bring one bench for the teacher." I say my name, and the man introduces himself as Mr. Johnson.

"Mr. Johnson," I say, "I have come to introduce myself to you, because we have not met before. I also came to say thanks for allowing Timothy to come to the Peace School."

"What can we do, sir?"

"Please call me Marvin," I reply, trying to make the atmosphere more congenial. "By allowing your son to join the Peace School, you have already started doing a fine job."

I study Mr. Johnson as he swallows the full contents of his cup. Probably in his late fifties, he is thin but muscular, bones solid after many years of working for the Liberian American Swedish Mining Company Railroad, digging and laying rails. His scruffy hair is dashed with gray, his face speckled with a week's growth of beard. His clothes, old and torn, look in need of cleaning. But this is the least of his concerns.

The burdens of war have turned him into a sad, weather-beaten man. His wife died from a cholera outbreak at Besama, a displacement camp outside Buchanan where they had gone to seek refuge from rebels of the National Patriotic Front. Another son was killed fighting in a different warring faction. He rubs a soot-smeared hand across his face and gulps down another mouthful of wine.

"I want my son to live in peace," he says. "The war, we thought it would bring us peace and freedom. But it only brought us death and pain and the loss of my son. We say we are alive, but we are dead. We pray for peace, not for us—we are already gone—but for our children, so that when they learn their ABCs, they can live in peace, and work and raise their children in peace. That is all I hope for," he says. He shakes the last few drops out of his bottle into his cup and takes another gulp.

"My son," he continues, "you are doing a good job. Everybody's talking about jobs, money, light, water, schools, and hospitals. It is good to talk about these things. But didn't we have them all before? We had, but where are they today? If we get them all back and don't learn to live with each other, we will destroy them again. But right now, that is not what I am thinking about. I am waiting for my time to join my wife and son. This is now your problem, you, the book people. They say you started the war, you book people. You must teach the people to live in peace again."

This is a common feeling among Liberians, especially those who cannot read and write.

For them it is the intellectual elite who brought the war. The man had said it all. There was nothing left to say. I stand up and we shake hands again and I ask to leave.

"I am sorry I did not give you anything to drink. If only it were during those days, those days when Johnson was a man, I could have offered you a large beer. But you see how we are managing here, my son. We can barely get a cup of bulgur wheat."

"It is okay, Mr. Johnson," I tell him. "Maybe some day, things will be good and we will have a beer together." I am not able to see Timothy's aunt. She is still at the market, selling.

I am sure the heavy downpour has stopped her from coming home. "Please extend my greetings to your sister. I am sure when I come the next time, I will meet her."

I ask Timothy to walk me to the car. I push my hand into my pocket and take out LD $100.00 and pass it to the boy. "Give this to your father. You can have this for food tomorrow."

As I drive home, I begin to think about all the man has said, but what touches me most is the way his face twitched when he talked about not being able to get a cup of bulgur wheat for himself and his family.

Before I returned to Liberia, I knew people were suffering here. But I did not understand the intensity of the life people were living, and I had not bargained for the daily begging. On average, Common Ground Society receives three letters from people living in different parts of Buchanan. Some of the parents had first imagined that I would help pay the school fees of children registered at the Peace School. Thanks to you, Dr. T and Jean, and the Atrium Society for graciously paying the fees for one student.

It is even worse in the community where I live. Many people walk to my house and wait for me to get up for work. Then they begin to tell their stories, most often begging me to assist them to get food or help them with their children's fees.

It is a difficult situation. What bothers me most is that it is hard to make people understand that I do not have money. How can I convince people that I don't have money when I am the only one in the community who drives a car, wears a necktie to work during the week, and has light in my house on weekends? When I tell people that I am a social worker or a volunteer, many just laugh and walk away. Others think I am mean.

Back home in my bed, I think about Emily and my daughters in Gambia. I have been away for five months and miss everyone. When we finally agreed that I would come home, I toyed with the idea of bringing along our youngest daughter, Mardell Joy, but my wife flatly refused. "Who will take care of the girl when you go to work or travel back and forth to Monrovia? Who will cook for you and wash her clothes?" I had tried to convince her to let me bring the little girl, but being here has put the arguments into perspective and, as I consider the life I am now living, I know Emily was right.

As I lie pondering all this in my bed, the realization becomes clearer. I had wanted our entire family to come home on the same flight, but it was not possible. Our oldest daughter was in twelfth grade and had to be there for her West African examinations. Also, Emily was doing graduate work in the field of gender and development, and Mardell Joy was in the middle of completing first grade. "Besides all that," Emily said, "it would be a good thing for you to come here first, and prepare a home for me and the girls."

I wake up and glance at the picture on my study table in the room. I remember taking this photo on a trip to Dakar, Senegal. I lift it from the table and hold it in my hands. She smiles back at me. After nine years of marriage, Emily still looks pretty to me, an awareness that seizes me, compels me to switch on my computer, load my word processing software and start to write. I will email her the letter when I go to town on the weekend:

Dear Emily...

Sometimes, when you are so close to people you love, you can't imagine that in their absence you will miss them in a heart-rending way. This is how I feel right now. Now I agree with you when you say that it is important for people to make every single moment they share together meaningful. It is true: it is only the special moments we shared together that keep me going. I miss the girls too, and I feel terribly sorry that I am not there to help with caring for the family.

As you may be aware by now, Common Ground is up and running. The Peace School is going fine. It is difficult, but what more can we do for this country than help our young people understand the root causes of conflict? If our children can learn to live together in peace, then when we are old, we will be able to rest.

Buchanan is not the town we used to know. When I walk along its downtrodden streets, I can smell desperation all over the place. People are living in poverty here, extreme poverty. When I see young people walking down the street in the careless fashion of the times, while adults are neatly dressed, I don't imagine everything is fine. People are anesthetized in their breasts, walking corpses. But we cannot lose hope; it is the only thing that binds us together. I hope that our country will be fine again, that it will be a place to raise our children and live in freedom and justice. It is this hope that probably made me come home. It is also my hope that our generation will be the last to get a kick out of combat. War is a complicated, deadly and costly business. People have to figure out a saner way to run this planet. We must work with this generation to find that tool.

I miss you every night here in Buchanan, but tonight is the most tormenting of nights.

You are so far away, so impossible to physically feel, yet so close here in my heart. I am again looking forward to our shopping, our laundry, our housekeeping, and all our arguments. But one thing I can tell you right now is that despite everything that has gone wrong with us, and all the scars, I am a happy man knowing that you are my wife. And I will do my best to make you happy.

I will be in Monrovia this weekend trying to communicate with Jean and Terrence. If you receive my email, please write me immediately. I am looking forward to hearing from you.

Your husband, Marvin

P.S. Marvin Jr. joins me from Ghana next week. I hope that his presence will lessen the loneliness.

Thanks for everything, Dr. T and Jean,
Marvin

Lesson 5

When We're Asleep, We Can't See

"I know well from your curriculum on prejudice and your books on the barriers to peace, Dr. T., that one cannot achieve peace by *envisioning* it. Envisioning peace is just an ideal, and setting ideals has got us into conflict in the first place. People have been envisioning their own particular brands of peace, according to various, established, tribal, belief systems, and these have divided us, as they have divided citizens worldwide. These rigid, conflicting ideals have created our civil war.

"So now people again want to *envision* peace because we have conflict. But peace according to whose beliefs? It is imperative to understand what *prevents* peace, in order to understand what creates conflict. Ironically, we create conflict by going after an ideal of peace, the very thing we think will save us! What we need to do is to understand the reality of conflict. Then, putting aside all that prevents peace—that being everything that creates conflict—we can come upon the peace that has always been there. It is only envisioning the *ideal* of peace that prevents us from seeing it!

— *Marvin Garbeh Davis*

Dear Dr. T and Jean…

Buchanan is about 150 kilometers from Monrovia, the capital of Liberia. Though it is the second largest city in Liberia, there isn't much else to distinguish it. There is no bank, college, post office, or Internet café in Buchanan. To post a letter or find a courier service such as Federal Express or DHL, I have to go to Monrovia.

If I want to be current, I do my newspaper reading in Monrovia, because papers sometimes take several days to reach Buchanan, We have a local radio station that relays BBC news, but the station is often down, sometimes for several weeks at a time. The technicians live in Monrovia, and it takes days to get the necessary funding to transport them to Buchanan.

If a young person graduates from high school in Buchanan and wants to pursue a college education or a vocational or technical career, Monrovia is the only location. To learn how to drive, get a driver's license or even buy a car, one has to go to Monrovia. The other day, a school principal said, "Buchanan is in such short supply of everything that if a young man wants to marry or have a child, he has to move to Monrovia."

Buchanan is not the only city in Liberia that suffers this way. I have a friend who works as an accountant with an international, non-governmental organization in Nimba County, northeast Liberia. The other day, he said, "I'm happy I have a job, but I spend half my money trying to get to Monrovia—sometimes just to buy myself decent underwear."

Once in Monrovia, people face delay after delay. They sit or stand in long queues waiting for tellers just to get into their cubicles. A teller barely lasts fifteen minutes before disappearing again. One of the saddest things I know about the banks in Monrovia is that when a customer finally reaches the teller, someone else walks into the cubicle and the teller serves that person first. It is not only in banks that we suffer this problem. It happens in the hospital, at the airport, in restaurants, and any other place where people have to line up for service. The amazing thing is that I have never heard any Liberian speak against such treatment. The customer is always right, but in Liberia, being a customer is akin to being a beggar. I don't know if people are scared, don't know their rights, or are just happy to live with the status quo.

Driving from Buchanan to Monrovia takes about three hours during the dry season, but about five hours during the rainy season. When I was in secondary school, people used to make this trip in an hour and a half. That was decades ago, when the road was paved during the administration of William Richard Tolbert, Liberia's 19th president. After he was killed in the 1980 coup, Samuel Doe's government let the roads fall into disrepair. During the civil war, the roads were forgotten. When President Taylor became president in 1997, he let the roads become even more derelict.

The highway between Buchanan and Monrovia is crucial. It connects Buchanan to the world's single largest rubber plantation (Firestone), and to Liberia's only international airport (Roberts).

Monthly, I travel this highway two and sometimes three times. My trip is primarily to cash employees' checks on the first and last Fridays of the month, occasionally to attend to Common Ground Society business, or simply to handle email. Internet cafés in Monrovia are randomly down and often occupied. So I bide my time by going to an entertainment center, or fill my stomach with a sandwich and coke. Most often, I go down Carey Street to sit at a local tea shop called the Ataya to hear the latest political gossip.

But the real trouble starts when I finish sending my email. I have to take my car to the garage to have my shock absorbers changed. A pair costs U.S. $300.00. The mechanics take several hours replacing the old ones. The next morning, I go to JFK Hospital because my body aches after the trip. At JFK, the physician's assistant tells me that the pharmacy is out of drugs, so he writes a long list of medicine that I have to buy from a local pharmacy. I rest for a few days, write more emails, get some replies, wait in vain for others, and then I am on the way back to Buchanan. In Buchanan, I go through the same quandary. I take the car to a garage to have the shock absorbers repaired, go to the local clinic and stay in bed late for two more days before I can start to work again.

The whole journey is a nightmare for which I must prepare myself physiologically. Before I returned to Liberia, I used to tell my wife "Oh, I'll manage when I get there." But some things are impossible to prepare for in post-civil war Liberia. Who would ever expect that a simple thing like sending an email could cost so much, financially, physically and psychologically?

I can see why many of my friends don't even think about returning home. Who can blame them? If they are used to twenty-four hours of electricity, running water and the Internet, then living in Liberia is like going to live in the dark ages.

Life everywhere is a struggle, but in Liberia, especially post-war, life is hell. We sometimes pay for everything tenfold. "You came home at the wrong time," my cousin says one evening, as we are drinking tea.

"But the war is over," I say.

"Yes, but we are fighting a different kind of war. We are fighting against hunger, unemployment, and disease. If you survive the war and live through this period, then you will live well in the new Liberia we are all envisaging."

I know well from your curriculum on prejudice and your books on the barriers to peace, Dr. T., that one cannot achieve peace by *envisioning* it. Envisioning peace is just an ideal, and setting ideals has got us into the conflict in the first place. People have been envisioning their own particular brands of peace, according to various, established, tribal, belief systems, and these have divided us, as they have divided citizens worldwide. Rigid, conflicting ideals have created the civil war.

So now people again want to *envision* peace because we have conflict. But peace according to whose beliefs? It is imperative to understand what prevents peace, in order to understand what creates conflict. Ironically, we create conflict by going after an ideal of peace, the very thing we think will save us. What we need to do is to understand the reality of conflict. Then out of this, putting aside all that prevents peace—that being everything that creates conflict—we can come upon the peace that has always been there. It is only envisioning the *ideal* of peace that prevents us from seeing it!

This October, I am planning to celebrate the Global Peace Games in Buchanan. Over the past few weeks I have been writing for sponsorship. I have just returned from Monrovia soliciting assistance from the Lone Star Cell Corporation.

The aim of the Peace Games is to uphold, in a more practical way, the declaration that the world's children are the central focus of the International Decade for the Culture of Peace and Nonviolence. The Peace Games will be in commemoration of the International Day of Peace. This occasion is expected to bring together six soccer teams, both male and female, all under the age of 15, from various communities in Buchanan to participate in a Mini-Soccer Olympic Games at the Doris Williams Sports Stadium. As part of the peace games, various teams, including children from our Peace School, will parade through the major streets of Buchanan, attend an indoor program, and then proceed to the stadium where the matches will be held.

This year, we decided to celebrate the International Day of Peace through sports, because our organization believes sports is a medium that brings young people together, harnessing their abilities and strengthening their capacity for respecting diversity and building peaceful communities. We are convinced that such events will help teach young people to be effective leaders and productive members of society, able to make responsible decisions while coping with the many differences our diverse society presents.

Through the celebration of these games, we believe that we are sowing the seeds of harmony among children who have grown up with the horror of war. We will help teach young people to develop trust and empathy for one another, thereby changing the landscape of conflict in our country and enabling people blinded by hatred to see one another's humanity. Making young people an active part of the communities in which they live could help to create a new future for our rural communities, where the next generation can live together in peace and harmony. However, as you have said in your book, in order to bring about peace, they need to understand what prevents it.

Peace School is now in session, and we are discussing a new lesson. In this lesson, which continues to expound on the dangers that prejudice poses to humanity, we draw a relationship between being prejudiced and being asleep.

Being prejudiced is sometimes like being hypnotized. When someone is hypnotized, he goes to sleep and acts out what he is told to do. He reacts to a situation as if it were real—unaware that he has been hypnotized. If he is prejudiced, his brain goes to sleep and acts according to thoughts he has learned, based on what he has been told. He reacts to these mere thoughts as if they were real.

Whether adopted or developed, prejudice most often begins with attitudes and stereotypes expounded by a child's family or cultural environment. Along with beliefs and antagonisms, parental words, tones of voice and gestures are automatically transferred to the child, who absorbs and mimics them.

I ask my students, "Can anyone think of a prejudice that a parent, guardian, or other adult may have passed to you?"

Julia Cassell responds. "My mother told me not to befriend Bassa girls, because Bassa people always say that Kpelle people are stupid."

Many times we are scared to let go of our prejudice, because it is something we have always believed. If, as in the case of Julia, this is the only thing a significant adult in our lives tells us about a certain group of people, distrusting it would be the same as challenging or disobeying our parents. Julia is scared to let go of this prejudice, because her mother's instructions have become gospel. What else could she possibly dare to think of a Kpelle person?

Becoming aware of prejudice is difficult, because we tend not to talk about it with the very people who passed the prejudice on to us.

Here is an example I heard from Decontee, a very agile girl who loves sports and plays kickball, a very popular girls' game in Liberia: "I am friendly with a Bassa girl who is my teammate on our school kickball team. One afternoon, she passes by my house so we can walk together to the practice. After I return home, my mother calls me inside and she asks, 'What did I tell you about being friendly with Bassa girls?'

"I try to explain, 'But the girl plays on our kickball team, Ma.'

'I don't care if she is a superstar. You know that she is Bassa.'

'But she is nice to me.'

"Ma says, 'What do you know about being nice? This is how the Bassa people behave; they show you their white teeth and stab you in the back when you turn around,'

"I keep trying, and tell Ma, 'She has not said anything mean about me.'

"But Ma just gets mad. 'I am finished with you,' she says, meaning the conversation is over. Then she tells me, 'I don't want to see you play with that girl or any other Bassa girl again.'"

In this situation, the mother has expressed her personal prejudices by threatening so strongly that the child feels helplessly indoctrinated with suspicion, fear, and hatred, which she will continue to attribute to all Bassa people.

So I ask, "Do you think it's possible that when you feel fear, it can sometimes awaken you to a new realization? A helpful realization?"

To understand prejudice we must question our conditioning. Sometimes we are conditioned to be prejudiced, because someone—perhaps someone like Decontee's mother—believes that thinking and acting in certain ways is a way to be safe, predictable and orderly.

But in reality, acting in prejudiced ways is not safe or orderly. It is a failure to find out, or to challenge, whether what we hear is true. In essence, it is ignorance. When we act in ignorant ways, we are not stupid—we are merely asleep and need to be awakened. Ignorance means to ignore, to not give one's attention to what is actually going on.

It is time for us to wake up. Acting with prejudice is like acting in a bad drama, among bad dreams that have been played out for centuries, passed from one generation to another.

When I was growing up on the Liberian Agricultural Plantations, I was brought up to believe that Kissi people ate dogs. With this prejudice drummed into my brain, I started to behave in a superior way to all Kissis, including my Kissi friends. I never ate with Kissi people because my parents said eating dog meat was not human. I despised and looked down on Kissi people for several years.

When I realized I had a fear of being friendly with Kissi people, I awoke to a new realization. I could see that I had blindly followed my carefully-groomed conditioning. Because I was brainwashed, I acted superior to Kissi people, and as a result, they all interacted angrily with me. As I looked back, I could see that I had the facts wrong. Many Kissi actually refused to eat dog meat, while other tribes imbibed. By becoming aware of my prejudice, I have re-discovered so many people in my life and made wonderful Kissi friends, some of whom are very close to my heart.

In my interactions with people every day, I hear such biased thoughts as:

- Men are stronger than women.
- Women are smarter than men.
- Black people are not as intelligent as white people.
- To have peace, we must protect ourselves and fight.
- To be "good," we must accept what we are told to do.

I am sure that people have reasons for what they believe, but it is good to ask *why* a particular thought or feeling surfaces about a specific group of people. Exploring this simple question can lead to the discovery of having been caught in the jaws of prejudice for a long time.

One afternoon, as I was walking down Tubman Street, approaching Bassa High School, the only public senior high school in Buchanan, I decided to branch off the main road and walk toward the government hospital. Near the end of the road leading to the hospital, I saw a little boy crying.

Bending down, I asked "What happened?"

His sobbing was so loud, I could only make out, "Guh, guh, oy it me."

Quieting him down, I asked the question again.

Tears dripping down his cheeks, he repeated, "Gio boy hit me."

Some women were selling wares at the side of the road. "Could you tell me whether the offender was a Gio boy?" I asked.

"No," they all answered in unison.

So I turned to the boy again. "Who did you say hit you?"

Steadfastly, he repeated, "Gio boy hit me."

I decided to find out about the offender's family. While continuing my walk home, I discovered that the boy who was hit shared a house with Bassa people. The mother drilled into her son's head that 'Gio' and 'bad' walk hand in hand. If something is bad, it is Gio. So the little boy felt that if an older boy hit him, which is bad, then he must be a Gio boy. However, I learned that the offender was a Bassa boy who lived in the same tribe as the injured boy.

"Anxious feelings," I tell my students, "can cause a person to experience feelings of fear, tension and danger. If the anxiety grows strong, it can become a phobia, a kind of exaggerated, inexplicable, illogical fear of a person or a place." I give the children a personal example.

"I used to fly often, but now I am afraid of flying. When I get on a plane, I don't eat or drink. My stomach somersaults until I disembark. I don't even care how long the flight is: I will not sleep. Sometimes I drink a couple of glasses of beer in the terminal, hoping that this will help me fall asleep when I get on the plane. It never does. As soon as I get on the plane, the beer clears itself from my system.

"Once I am on the plane, I start to get weird feelings, as if the plane is heading into the ocean. But while I am thinking all these thoughts, there are other people on the plane, eating, drinking, reading, sharing a joke or two, and taking turns going to the lavatory. But I dare not leave my seat."

Janet, our celebrated peace student, says, "I'm afraid of wall geckoes. When I see one on the wall, I run away. One night, when my mother took my socks off my feet, I saw them waving near the wall and shouted, 'Gecko! Gecko!'"

Timothy says, "I'm afraid of centipedes."

When Julia says, "I hate frogs," all the students share their own fears.

The phobias associated with these fears produce exaggerated images in their minds. What these children and I see or fear is not real; it is merely a product of distorted thinking.

Similarly, an extreme fear of foreigners is a prejudice held by people who believe strangers are a threat to their safety and security. The brain turns the "foreigner" into "someone different," and this feared person becomes an automatic enemy. In fact, there is only one enemy—the one created in our brain.

At the high school where I teach in Buchanan, the English teacher recently traveled to Ghana for a master's program. He was replaced by a Nigerian. The children wanted to go on strike. When I met with them to find out why, their only answer was, "Nigerians are crooks."

One boy in the class told me that his father had been robbed by a Nigerian. When I asked what this had to do with the man teaching English, I found out that they were agitated simply because he was Nigerian.

A large part of our attitude is conditioned by opinions and emotions that we unconsciously absorb from our childhood environment. In other words, tradition makes us what we are. It would be foolish to despise tradition. But with our growing self-awareness and increasing intelligence, we must be able to understand that different people have different traditions and that it's respectful to honor them all equally. Thinking that our own tribal traditions are better than those of others can divide us and create conflict, for it is our own arrogance that separates us. If human relations are ever to change for the better, we must recognize that some of our accepted traditions may be damaging to both our dignity and our fate.

Shall we continue sleepwalking through our life and act only on images we are conditioned to believe? Shall we continue to create enemies that exist only in our brains? Shall we understand only what divides us, or shall we commit to finding similarities instead of differences?

Rather than a source of confrontation and animosity, cultural variety should be an inspiration to us. We must learn to respect, to understand and to admire all cultures. There is enough room to accommodate all our many diversified contributions, not only individual, but also national and racial. It is a waste of time to discuss who or what contributions are superior or inferior.

There is so much good in the worst of us
So much bad in the best of us
That it scarcely behooves any of us
To talk about the rest of us.

—*Edward Wallis Hoch, 1849 – 1925*

Take care,
Marvin

Lesson 6

The Bells and Knots of Conditioning

"Understanding psychological conditioning is at the core of learning about ourselves in relationships. What is that conditioning? How does it form our attitudes and behavior? How does it fundamentally create conflict in our lives? What is the nature and structure of that conflict as it resides in our thinking process? Reaching for these insights will bring inquiry into the roots of our disorder in a way that honors the place of intellectual capacity, therefore creating a world free of conflict."

— Marvin Garbeh Davis

Dear Dr. T and Jean…

July 26th , only a week from now, is going to be a happy day for our children, as it is Independence Day in Liberia. I have just concluded negotiations with the Buchanan office of the World Food Program, enlisting Common Ground in the Food for Training program. Personally I am happy because we have been awaiting the conclusion of this development for several weeks. We will be able to feed the children in the Peace School three times a week.

Today I received a phone call from the World Food Program office informing me that our first batch of food supplies will arrive during the weekend. Our thanks to the Atrium Society for buying plates, cooking pots and providing funding for additional ingredients to pay the dietician. Everything seems set for cooking. I am looking forward to announcing the news to the children.

July is a busy month for us. I am now in the final planning phase of the Independence Day Peace Dance and Rap Competition. I want to make the 26th very special not only for the children in the Peace School but for all the children of Buchanan. As a child before the war, I remember July 26th as a special day for youngsters.

At the Liberian Agriculture Company (LAC) where I lived as a boy, workers were paid a few days before the 26th, so that parents would be able to get something special for their families. Although the food was more than enough, my father would go to great lengths to make sure I had a new suit and toys for Independence Day, just like Christmas. We had bowls of rice and *fufu* (locally produced from cassava and commonly eaten by the Bassas and other Liberians.) Old and seldom-seen relatives brought other local foods. Music blared from all directions in the camp and children stayed up for their longest night in the year.

But during these past civil war years, many children have not had any opportunity to celebrate this joyful day. When I asked children at the Peace School whether there had been any programs for them during the last few July 26th holidays, their negative answers impelled me to plan the Independence Day Peace Dance for our young people and a Rap Competition for youth groups.

Early Saturday morning, a security officer from the office calls me at home. "There's a big truck parked on the roadside in front of the Peace School. The driver is asking for you."

"Does the truck bear a United Nations (UN) or World Food Program (WFP) insignia?"

"Yes. WFP."

"Hurray! I'll be there soon." Our supplies had arrived. Hurriedly I jump out of bed and drive to the office to meet with the team. In no time, the food is off-loaded: 15 bags of beans, 12 tins of oil, and 15 bags of bulgur wheat.

News travels rapidly in Buchanan. Before I even reach home, three of our students are already waiting. "Is it true? Has WFP supplied Common Ground with food?" they ask with eyes wide.

Having completed most of the plans for the week, I decide to visit my mother. I have not seen her since arriving in Liberia. In fact, I have only managed to see her twice in nine years. Emily and I had agreed that once the girls were here in Liberia, I would take them to see their grandmother.

My mother lives in Bong county, central Liberia, in Sergeant Kollie's Town, commonly known as SKT, less than a 15-minute drive from Gbarnga, the capital of Bong County. Gbarnga is the city where Mr. Taylor had his rebel headquarters for several years. From this town, he drove in a convoy escorted by forces of the Economic Commmunity Monitoring Group to Monrovia to take his seat as one of the five members on the council that evolved from the peace talks which brought together all the rebel factions.

So on the morning of July 12, a few weeks after my youngest daughter, Mardell, had joined me, we take off for Gbarnga to see my mom. There is no way of letting her know that I am going to visit her, so the whole trip is a big surprise. In SKT, I park the car near the church. As her husband is the pastor and she's a missionary, they built their house conveniently near the church. Here my mother had her three youngest children. Before the war, I had given my mother some money to change their rusting zinc roof.

However, the house is now a skeleton. Rebels have looted everything, including the nails. My mom and her husband have moved temporarily into a hut while waiting for assistance from the United Nations Refugee Agency (UNHCR) for a tarpaulin to roof their damaged house. I find a stool and sit with my back to the hut, staring at the carcass that used to be home to several people, but now hasn't the least hope of being rebuilt.

My mother comes outside and we hug. She is happy to see me, but I am sad that the fat woman I had known is now a skeleton. We start with the normal formalities.

"Where have you been all these years, my son?"

"Trying to find peace in other people's countries, Mom."

"I have been praying for you, my son. I am so happy to see you again."

"Thank God to see you too. I have brought our little girl to see you. This one was not born here, so I wanted her to come and see you. When Emily arrives, I will bring all the children to pay you a visit."

"That will be very nice." She holds Mardell by the hand, drawing her closer to her lap, but being frail, she does not dare pick up her rather plump little granddaughter. We are all silent together, and then my mother begins sobbing quietly.

"What is it, Mom?"

"I have been thinking about your father. I just can't believe that he is dead and gone. Here is a man who worked so hard to send his children to school, and now that the oldest one can speak like the white man, he is not alive to see him. I am really sorry about your father."

"Yes, Ma, so many people died in the war."

"But what did he do? He was not a soldier; he never worked for the government. He was just a tapper."

"War never chooses," I tell her. "It takes any life."

"I am happy that you are not crying, my son. You are a man. You see that if a man prays for life, he does not mean life for himself, but life he is able to pass on to others. For those of us who cannot read, that is the purpose of life. We have life given to us from the past generation, and we pass that life on through our children. If your father had lacked the power to have children, his life would have been useless.

"But look at you now, son. Your father must be smiling in his new home among his ancestors. The ability to have children is the most gratifying and greatest gift for us. So we pray to have many children. For those who do not have children, their lives are meaningless. If your father did not have you, how could he be remembered again? The happiness of the dead is dependent on their having children. Now you are a big man. Carry on with that life your father gave. He never had much, but he had a great heart and gave you life. Give that life and heart to your own children."

Since my return I have not discussed the death of my father, not even with my younger brother. I know our father died during an invasion that was codenamed Operation Octopus, designed to take Monrovia by force. He had run away with his family to Nimba, where he died in reprisal killings carried out by citizens of Nimba against the Bassa people. Nobody knew where he was killed or buried, whether he had been left to rot above the ground or at the mercy of some anonymous burial.

It is time to leave, so I take out the bag of rice, oil, fish and magi cubes I have brought for her. I squeeze some money into my mother's hands, and we are on our way to Monrovia from where we will travel the next day to Buchanan.

Back in Buchanan everything is set for Independence Day. Even more importantly, everything is set for Monday's first distribution of food to our children.

This is our last class before we close for Independence Day and its one-week break. Today is the big day; the children will be eating something substantial during their break, unlike the snacks and juices usually offered them for lunch. We have had a few absences for the past two weeks, sometimes two or three students on average. For a class of twenty, this has been significant, especially for an after-school program. But today, all the students are present.

We are talking about the bells and knots of conditioning and how they are linked to the prejudices we all have in our lives. I start the class by opening our flip chart and asking for volunteers to write things that make them scared. An equal number, three girls and three boys, stand up. The rest agree to write their fears in their exercise books.

Janjay: "I am afraid of snakes."

John: "I am scared of darkness."

Mariam: "I am scared of people who carry lies around about other people."

Betty: "I am scared of people with army uniforms."

Paul: "Fire scares me."

Trokon: "Dogs make me scared."

Knowing the importance of addressing their fears, I probe for more details.

"So what makes you afraid of snakes, Janjay?" I ask.

"A snake bit my uncle and he died," says Janjay.

"What happens when you see a snake?" I ask.

"I am too scared. I run away."

John says, "I'm scared of the darkness because many bad things happen in the night."

"What about you, Miriam?"

"I'm scared of people who carry lies around because they are very bad."

"And you, Betty?"

"The armed robbers who raped my sister during the war wore army uniforms," she explains.

I nod towards Paul. "I woke up in my bed to see my neighbor's house on fire one night," he says. "All those who were living in the house died."

And Trokon says, "A dog bit me once, and that's why I'm afraid of dogs."

All of us are faced with life-threatening situations, whether we are young or old, and we sometimes have to make decisions that may save our lives. When something threatens our lives our brains register fear first, and send messages preparing our bodies for one of two actions: flee or fight. This is natural in a life-threatening situation. Our brains want us to survive. The "fight or flight" response exists for our self-preservation. It is a healthy and natural response to real danger. Sometimes, however, the "fight or flight" response takes place when the danger is not real.

I share an incident with my students. "When I was a little boy, my father and I went to see a friend in a nearby laborers' camp on the Liberian Agricultural Company Plantation where we lived. On our way, we passed through the residential area on the plantations. From the garage of one of the bungalows, a black dog slipped off its leash, rushed toward me, and before I could reach my father, the dog bit me. For many years after that experience, I always carried a stick or picked up a rock whenever I saw any black dog. It did not matter whether the dog was near or far from me, whether it was barking, or wagging a friendly tail. I always armed myself.

"My reaction—to pick up a rock or to carry a stick—became conditioned. My brain always re-created a threatening image of the first black dog, the one that bit me. Since I felt I had to flee (to save my life) or to pick up a stone or stick (to defend myself), my automatic reaction in the present is based on that memory. Although another black dog may be friendly and harmless, my reaction remains the same. It is based on what my brain has learned and has never taken the time to question. No matter what our experiences are, for protection in a conflict when danger threatens, everyone's brain sends messages to get ready for either defense or flight.

"It is important to know this when we encounter someone different from us who triggers our old, negative experiences. Whenever we are in a scary situation, we *react* based on past fears. Our reactions are based on memory, and not on what we really see in the moment.

"Ivan Pavlov was a famous Russian doctor, physiologist and psychologist who won many gold medals and even the Nobel Prize for his scientific research. Perhaps his best-known experiment was his development of the concept of a conditioned reflex. Pavlov was very interested in how animals digest food, and had many dogs which he studied. He noticed that they drooled before receiving their meals. He decided that before feeding them, he would first ring a bell. Then he would give them a meal. Soon, the dogs salivated just hearing a bell in expectation of the treat to come. Pavlov had carefully conditioned the dogs to react in this way

"Then one day Pavlov decided to try something different. He rang the bell without giving them any food. But the dogs salivated nevertheless. So the next day, he rang the bell again, and the dogs salivated whether they had food or not. He decided to try other sounds, different touches and sights to stimulate them before a meal, and soon he was able to again tease the dogs to salivate without food. Pavlov proved that he could create a conditioned reflex and make the dogs salivate—by creating a link between the stimulus and the food."

When I was teaching at the Catholic School on the Liberian Agricultural Company Plantations, there was a nun who was very strict about the number of times the school bell was rung. The first bell meant first period was over; the second bell meant the second period was over, and so forth. The recess bell was rung continuously.

One day, visitors from the Catholic Archdiocese arrived at the school just before the end of the second period. Because of their tight schedule, they didn't want to wait until the end of the period to speak to the students. The nun ordered the bell to be rung. The janitor rang it several times. All the kindergarten students ran outside yelling "Recess!" It took the teachers several minutes to get them to the auditorium where the guests were supposed to speak.

The children had been conditioned to run outside for recess whenever the bell rang several times. It did not matter what the occasion or what time of day. Once the bell rang several times, for them it was recess. All of this reminds me of Pavlov's experiment with the dogs, except instead of salivating for food, the children are conditioned to obey a rule they never stop to think about. It is this kind of conditioning—to respond in a certain way toward authority—that is a major contributor to the creation of conflict, because it cuts off our own intelligent thinking.

When my little daughter, Mardell, joined me in June of this year, I went to pick her up at the airport. On our way to Monrovia, we stopped at a gas station to put some gas in the car. A young attendant put one end of a tube in a gallon tank of gas, and sucked the other end momentarily before turning it into the car. My daughter was amazed. She had never seen anyone sucking on gas the way the gas seller did.

"The man will die," she told me as I turned to get on the main road.

"Why do you think he will die?" I asked her.

"My teacher says if someone drinks gas, he will die. I have never seen anyone drinking gas before, Dad."

"The man will not die," I calmed her. "He was only pulling the gas through the tube into the car. We don't have electronic machines like those where you moved from. People sell gas on the street and have only one way to put it into a vehicle: by sucking just enough to get it moving. They jerk their mouth away and then quickly redirect the tube into the car." She put her head outside the window to see if the man was still alive.

Congo Town, a suburb of Monrovia where I lived and went to college, was much closer to the home of rebel leader Charles Taylor. Less than 200 meters away from my house at one of his bases, called Watanga, resided a group of young rebel soldiers. On my way home from school one day, I walked along the road beside a fellow I'd never met before. We shook hands and introduced ourselves. Peter Brown explained that he came from Nimba and had worked with Charles Taylor for several years in central Liberia, so had recently come to Monrovia to continue his work in the new coalition government.

My first impression was that the man was an ex-combatant. Two reasons for this conclusion: we were very close to the Watanga base, and young people from Nimba County formed the bulwark of Taylor's rebel army. All the time I was standing by him, I pretended to be friendly, while my stomach churned and anger filled my being. I wanted to hit him so hard that he would never get up again. But the young man I stood beside did not look threatening at all. He did not even look like a soldier.

So what was making me want to clobber him to death? It was the prejudiced feelings and thoughts I had for all those who fought for Charles Taylor's rebel army in the war. These feelings were based on repeated judgments, opinions and hearsay about how inhumanely the rebels had acted. Although I had never seen a rebel soldier in action, here was a man from Nimba who fit right into my conditioned picture of a Taylor rebel solider only because he came from Nimba and had come to Monrovia to work in the government.

A few weeks after this incident, Peter came for a visit. To my surprise, I found out that he was actually part of my own tribe—Bassa—and had gone to Carroll High School in Nimba in order to complete his studies. Moreover, during our conversation, I came to realize that we felt the same way about the war. Peter and I became very good friends until I left Liberia.

Even though I continue to harbor vestiges of prejudice against Taylor's rebels and people from Nimba, my reactions are quite different today when I meet an ex-combatant or anyone from Nimba. That experience taught me how prejudice can divide people and cause people to hate. Today I treat people on the basis of their humanity. When the bells of conditioning ring, like those that made Pavlov's dogs salivate, they ring up a realization that the brain is spinning through a cluster of old, mixed-up memories and reactions. This sudden awareness of those old knots in the brain brings insight and clarity.

In our daily lives, people often ring a certain bell that makes us react without thinking.

"What bell rings or evokes a reaction in you?" I ask my students.

"When someone calls me fat," Janet says.

"So what do you when someone calls you fat?"

"I get angry and I could fight the person."

"Why does calling you fat make you angry?"

"Some of my friends think that because I am fat, I can't run or play kickball. Some of my friends will not choose me to play knockfoot (a girl's game in Liberia) with me."

Trokon has an eye defect which makes people feel when he looks at them that he is looking at someone else. The children tease him. "When someone talks about my eyes, I feel ashamed," Trokon says.

"What do you do when someone mentions your eye?"

"I walk away. People think because my eyes are bad, I am stupid or can't think well."

Understanding psychological conditioning is at the core of learning about ourselves in relationships. What is that conditioning? How does it form our attitudes and behavior? How does it fundamentally create conflict in our lives? What is the nature and structure of that conflict as it resides in our thinking process? Reaching for these insights will bring inquiry into the roots of our disorder in a way that honors the place of intellectual capacity, therefore creating a world free of conflict.

When we are conditioned, we react in prejudiced ways which can hurt us as well as others. Prejudice is more than an incident in our lives. To change, we must alter whole patterns of our lives. In my country, our brotherhood is linked mainly to tribal identities. If a person does not belong to our tribe, we perceive him or her in a different way. We may shake hands or greet him, but in our hearts, we carry different opinions about him. These opinions make us treat him in a different way. This situation pains me. It is so complex that the only way I feel better is by sharing it with others. Our attitude is a result of an accumulation of unfavorable experiences, living and interacting with each other with prejudice. In this country, we are grappling with acceptance.

It is important that we welcome people as they are—as human beings and not as members of a different tribe. People everywhere most desire our complete acceptance, for it frees them to change into the kind of people they are capable of becoming. When we clean up our side of relationships by being more open-minded, their reactions tend to be more constructive.

There are a lot of people screaming in our society at a lot of other people, telling them to change. Meanwhile, we ignore the fact that we ourselves are refusing to give up our old ways for new. So I am doing this with the children in our Peace School. I tell young people that there will be tremendous rewards for them when they live this different life. Most are already experiencing such gratification that they want more. Then I tell them how to test these new methods and they notice the rewards. Once these are reached, they are deeply impressed.

Young people are fantastic; they are not locked up, like many of us adults, in a casing that can't be opened. Changing appeals to them because they have the capacity to admit that there is a better way of living. When adults are approached about trying something new, most will say this is what they have been doing all their lives, and see no reason to change.

It reminds of me of my boss at the Center for Law and Human Rights, where I worked as an editor for the *Human Rights Review*, a weekly paper that reported human rights abuses in the country. Benedict Sannoh, a fine human rights lawyer, used a laptop computer to type his documents. When I told him I wanted to upgrade his software, he vehemently refused.

"This is the only software I know how to operate and it does my work just as I want."

"But," I tell him, "if you have an upgraded version of the word processing program, it will enhance your skills even more and make your work easier."

"My work," he says, "is already easier."

One day he comes to my office, watches me use the upgraded version, and gazes in admiration.

"It is a nice program," he says, and leaves, but never considers changing his word processing software or learning new skills for it.

There are people who may nod in agreement and smile at new ideas that can enhance their interactions with the world around them, but not be ready to go out and change their lives.

At the beginning of a class, a girl raises her hand and says, "Why do you keep telling us that we can make our lives better and happier? I am happy with my life just the way it is."

At this, Mariam's hand shoots up. She says to this girl, "If you are so happy with your life, why are you always bugging Janet?"

Sometimes our thoughts and feelings are tied up in such tight knots, that we cannot see where they begin and where they end. Unless we become *aware* that we are caught in a knot in our brain, we can stay bound up forever.

This is how I see it every day. The people who claim that they are happy are those with the greatest human relations problems. To be happy, I think each of us needs to go in search of our unique, magnificent selves. When we find that splendor, we will have the tremendous reward of acceptance from others, which in turn will free them to then go in search of themselves. Finally, we will no longer have to fight, or run away. We can just be.

Sincerely yours,
Marvin

Lesson 7
Elements of Knot-Like Thinking

When I ask my children in the Peace School how they imagine Liberia will be in ten years, many of them are positive.

"There will be lights all over the streets like the way we see in the movies," little Janet tells me.

"There will be schools for all, hospitals for the children and new roads," another child responds.

Just when I am feeling defeated, I see these young children whose lives I have touched, looking up to me, seeing me as a role model and wanting to be like me. I think about all those who believe in me and who believe the world can still be a better place. That's when a passion lights up inside me and all seems worthwhile again.

— Marvin Gadeh Davis

Dear Dr. T and Jean…

September 2006 is a boisterous and curious month. This is the last month before the presidential and legislative elections of 2006, with 22 political parties registered, an unbelievable number for such a small country like Liberia. But this goes to show how polarized and deeply divided the country has become.

Parties have sprung forth during the electoral period just as rebel factions have emerged during the war. The National Patriotic Front started the civil war against the government of Samuel Doe, dividing the country into three blocs—those on the side of the rebels, those who support the government, and those who simply say that war is not the right way out of the Liberian political predicament.

In a matter of months, the National Patriotic Front of Liberia (NPFL) hatched another faction called the Independent National Patriotic Front of Liberia (INPFL). That group also took a large chunk of the Liberian people with it, supporting Mr. Prince Johnson, the commander, for the discipline he instilled in his soldiers. There was a story going around that he carried a small silver pistol that he shot on impulse. Many called him the no-nonsense general.

Then came the United Liberation Movement of Liberia (ULIMO), the rebel group formed outside Liberia, comprised mainly of Mandingo and some of the Krahn former government soldiers who had fled the war to neighboring Sierra Leone. A portion of the ULIMO was also Liberian, mainly Krahn and Mandingo sympathizers. In a matter of months, the group split along tribal lines into ULIMO-J (the Krahn faction led by Roosevelt Johnson, one of Doe's kinsmen), and ULIMO-K (the Mandingo faction headed by Alahagi Kromah). Then the number of factions increased. The Central Revolutionary Council (CRC) broke away from the National Patriotic Front of Liberia (NPFL). There were many others, including the Liberia Peace Council (LPC), led by George Boley, another of Doe's kinsmen, and the Lofa Defense Force (LDF).

When political parties were organized for the July 1997 elections, the population split along tribal, factional, or political lines. Obviously Mr. Taylor, the man with the biggest faction, won the 1997 elections. Many Liberians thought those elections would bring them peace, stability and national reconciliation. Instead, it brought them more wars. Eight years ago, they were on the same road. Now many look back in anger over the past twelve years. And what do they have to show for democracy? Heartbreak, scars, poverty and death. Nevertheless, many look forward with hope during this election season.

From a thousand pulpits and lecterns come words of hope. Ubiquitously, orators are encouraging Liberians to go out and vote for the party of their choice. Prayers are spoken for peace and security during this time. Election fever simmers across the country.

By the middle of September, Buchanan, as the second largest city in Liberia, has run up to the boiling point. Political parties are sprinting in and out of town like flies buzzing a lavatory. And the people are enjoying every bit of the frenzy.

When a political party is expected, its members gather in the morning under the welcome sign mid-way along Tubman Street, encouraged by drumming and dancing which continues for several hours until the presidential candidate and his entourage arrive from the capital and approach them. Finally, the parade begins, runs down the brief length of Tubman Street, and ends at party headquarters.

Many of the political parties don't have headquarters outside Monrovia. Only a few have offices in the leeward counties. In this case, the candidate ends up at the home of the local party chairman, or on Tubman Street, where he makes a speech embroidered with promises to rebuild a new country. A few dollars are thrown around; a few lucky people catch a couple. Those closest to the candidate get the lion's share. Before dark, the crowd disappears. The same scene repeats itself over and over again.

Because the parties are many, the same people keep waiting for the different ones. They watch the same cultural troupe, the same band marching to the same tune, but for different political parties. The voters know that after this, they may never see the candidates or hear about their parties again. Some presidential candidates will leave the country right after the results are announced. So the voters grasp at anything a party offers during the campaign: T-shirts, stickers, food and liquor. It is difficult to know who is for whom and who stands for what. The people waiting for the Unity Party today are the same ones who will be on Tubman Street dancing for the Liberia Unification Party tomorrow, wearing the party T-shirt of the day.

After this hullabaloo, life returns to what it was. People wake up the next morning not knowing what they will eat. Men walk up and down the streets hoping they will get a contract that can land them a few Liberian dollars to put bread on the table for their families. Young people huddle along the streets of Buchanan with arms folded, hoping that the election will produce a good president. School children again walk up and down Tubman Street in the rain, soaked to the skin without a raincoat. The town grows sleepy once more, as if it had not been on fire the night before.

It is a curious business in a curious month. September's biggest difficulty is finding a good president, which means finding the best person available for the job. This is difficult, probably impossible in Liberia. We have had a history of many bad presidents. It is particularly difficult for Liberians, because no one can tell what's going to happen to a president until he or she reaches this level of responsibility. The people have to pick from the 22 candidates on the basis of each one's history and expressed viewpoints regarding current situations. Then all they can do is hope.

Liberians have been doing this for ages. When Samuel Doe came to power, a lot of people were in high spirits, especially those Liberians who believed that the native man could do better than the Congo man. And a few years after, when the war had turned all their hopes to ashes, Mr. Taylor promised that he would rebuild what he had destroyed. He, too, left the country in ashes. In a situation such as Liberia's, where social and economic life has reached an all-time viciousness, the level of fear continues to rise at an alarming rate.

Fear is dehumanizing. It alienates people from each other and separates them from individually recognizing their own best traits. Fear of losing out, of making a wrong choice, of facing the unknown—all of these fears have been dominant and overbearing in the lives of the people. With the wind of the election blowing across the country, fear is now a deep-seated enemy that lives inside us all. It has divided the nation. The people want a leader who will take the country from its present state and bring the relief they deserve.

Liberians know that treachery lurks in the hearts of politicians. The person talking about democracy and freedom today could be the one training the secret police to kill and harass the citizenry tomorrow. After the elections, a friend next door could be a police informer or secret agent. The people know this.

There are those who will not believe in anything or anyone again. There are those who believe that nothing will change. Mary Johnson, a single woman with two daughters, one of whom attends the Peace School, expresses her apathy:

"It is like new wine in an old bottle. I have seen all this before. After all this talk, we will be going back to the same situation again. It is going to be a battle between us and them."

I was visiting the home of Ma Tetee, a renowned Bassa senior citizen of Buchanan, as her granddaughter had told me at Peace School that she had been suffering from malaria.

During our talk, several members of the women's wing of another political party came to visit, requesting her support. Here is how Ma Tetee responded to their solicitation.

"You are young and have a lot of energy, but soon you will grow old and tired, and you will sit down here like me with a long, sad face, staring into oblivion. We are living in two worlds in this country. The educated—or let us say the politicians—live in one world, while we, the poor ordinary people, live in another. They see our world only when elections are about to happen. After they get what they want, they will not see us again. When they look at our world, it will be six years later.

"My life is with my daughters, selling," she continues. "It is only when I leave my house to go to sell that I feel I am alive. Our hopes and expectations have no reality in the world of the politicians. We are all tools; our utility lies in the votes they beg for now. As soon as they get their fat jobs, all they do is fatten their bellies, leaving us in our chains of invisibility.

"Right now they are using you to speak to us, to get votes. Then, when they get whatever they want, they will throw you away like a rag."

Sister Jenny, one of Ma Tetee's friends, steps in. She says, "We have tried to enable our children to be somebody, so we send them to school—to government schools, where they promised to give the children of the poor free education. And you know what, young lady? Our children sit in classrooms where there are no chairs, no books and no educational materials, with inadequate, underpaid teachers. So what kind of education do you think our kids end up having? They get an education that can't ever make them competitive with other children in any sphere of life. So our children step right into our shoes, unable to improve their lives, unable to improve on what we have given them, which actually is nothing. And what is it that we bequeath our children? Only tears, pain, failure, hurt and frustration. What can a person do with these? Nothing, except live and work at a demeaning job. We are living here because we are strong, resilient people, people who have the capacity to absorb the blows we are dealt. We can suffer grief and desperation and still come up smiling. I am sure it amazes them when they come back to see us begging, and know that we are still alive."

"I know you are telling yourself things will be fine," Ma Tetee continues, "but nothing will change. It is only the people who push us around who change, but conditions and attitudes remain the same."

On my way home, reflecting on time spent with Ma Tetee, I think of a poem and how it pertains to our present crisis:

Liberians had hoped
To pick life's pleasant gains
They have found as all men find
Life's values stale and hoary
And now they walk
With bowed heads
Like drenched men from the rains…

— *Raphael Armattoe, 1913–1953*

When I ask my children in the Peace School how they imagine Liberia will be in ten years, many of them are positive. "There will be lights all over the streets like the way we see in the movies," little Janet tells me.

"There will be schools for all, hospitals for the children and new roads," another child responds.

I think and feel as these children do, and dream like them, too. What I am doing here in Buchanan is a drop in the ocean. Sometimes I feel I am wasting my time, the same way Ma Tetee feels when she speaks to the younger women who have trod the campaign trail to her house.

Just when I am feeling defeated, I see these young children whose lives I have touched, looking up to me, seeing me as a role model and wanting to be like me. I think about all those who believe in me and who believe the world can still be a better place. That's when a passion lights up inside me and all seems worthwhile again.

At a staff meeting we agree to send the children home during the week of the October 15th elections, and return a week after the results are announced. Everyone is hoping there will be peace after the elections. Some people are scared that if the results are unacceptable, any one of the presidential candidates could bring about war. And some people believe they will succeed, because there are still thousands of young ex-combatants around, feeling useless, preparing for any kind of chaos. I want to see how much we can do with the children before we close.

It is a quiet but windy evening that feels like rain, a very unexpected September event here in Buchanan. As I sit in my office preparing my teaching notes for the Peace School, I hope that the rain will stay away so that the children can make it to school. The children and I are going to look at ways that our thinking becomes tangled.

The next day in the Peace School, we discuss the elements of knotted thinking and how these elements can make us prejudiced. We are talking about how to *recognize* these elements— how they work, and how we can learn to free ourselves from these knots. We need to learn this now more than ever.

I now understand the conflict we all call war. Your book, *Peace – The Enemy of Freedom*, is about how conflict and prejudice are rooted in our brains, in the way we think, feel and act. If only we can get our people to see and understand this. Internal conflict is projected outward and creates global conflict. We want our children to understand this and to stop looking outside themselves for the cause of conflict in their human relationships. We must all look within.

Over time, as our brain ties itself in tighter and tighter knots, it naturally plugs up, like a mechanical device that shorts out because its cables are shredded, so we are kept from seeing things as they really are. We have to cut up these knots, awaken from our sleep, and discover the falsehoods that may have been running our lives.

"Is it possible to believe something all your life and then later find out that it is not true?" I ask the children.

"Yes," says Ben. He is one of our pioneer students.

"You want to give me an example of how you used to believe something and later you found out it was not true?" I ask him.

"My father used to tell me," he begins, "that I would not be able to play good soccer because my legs are short. At first I believed this and even though many of my friends told me I could play well, subconsciously I doubted my own ability, because my father kept telling me that I was wasting my time trying to do something I did not have the physique for. So I abandoned playing soccer, but my heart ached every time I saw my friends playing.

"When I got into third grade," he continues, "we played a game with the fourth graders and the players were not good. My friends begged me to join them but I did not want to play. After they begged me persistently, I agreed to play since my father was not around. My class beat the fourth graders by two goals. I scored the goals. I was the hero of the day and I was carried shoulder-high to my house. Now I don't listen to my father when he compares my ability to play soccer with the size of my legs. Someday I am going to be a professional footballer like George Weah."

"How did you feel when you realized that you could play soccer even though your father had told you that you would not make it because of the size of your legs?" I ask Ben.

"I felt good. I was relieved that I had come to the knowledge that I could do something with my body even though my father did not believe me. And I was happy when other people who did not know me started motivating me."

"When you realize that you have believed something for a long time and then suddenly you find out that it is not true, you do feel relieved," I tell the children. "It is like untying a knot that has been tightly wrapped around your brain for a long time—and then suddenly the cable breaks. You feel that a heavy load has been lifted from your shoulders. You realize that sometimes the repeated prejudice we learn from our friends, parents, teachers and other elders affects our mental wiring. Once we become aware of the false data in our mental computer that causes us to act unfairly, we are on our way to mental freedom and self-enlightenment.

The Strands of Knotted Thinking: Repetition

One element of knot-like thinking is *repetition*. It is hearing the same thing over and over again and saying it to others, whether it is true or not. Repetition often compels us to believe a statement is true simply because we have heard it so many times.

Stephen, the boys' prefect at the Peace School, explains repetition with a story. "When my brother came back from a refugee camp in Nigeria, he started telling my father all the time that Nigerians are not good people. When one Nigerian family tried to get an apartment from my father, he told them he was not renting it, which was not true. He had actually been looking for someone to pay the rent for the place so that he could pay our oldest sister's school fees at the nursing college. His refusal was based on the fact that my brother had said over and over that Nigerians are bad."

Nigeria has the largest population in Africa. While living and studying there for a year, I saw some bad Nigerians, but I was able to interact with more who were good. Is it a valid reason to pass judgment on an entire nation because of a few bad experiences in a refugee camp? Because this man's son tied knots in his father's brain, he turned away money he badly needed to support his daughter.

My little daughter, who is a student at the Peace School, likes to watch the premier league play soccer on TV. Her favorite advertisement is about a footballer who drinks Coca-Cola and suddenly runs to the soccer ball and scores a goal. The advertisement connects drinking Coca-Cola with scoring goals in soccer. Although she often drinks Coke, she is not able to score a goal, and, in fact, doesn't play soccer well. Companies spend billions of dollars on radio or TV to condition us to buy a product. And many people will buy a product just because it is advertised. Companies know that repetition works and that it influences people's decisions.

The Strands of Knotted Thinking: Comparison

Another component of knotted thinking I discuss with my students is *comparison*. Comparing one group of people with another leads us to see another group as "them" and our group as "us." Thinking this way leads to judging or ranking the various people we know as "better" or "worse," as "superior" or "inferior." And there is a natural tendency to place ourselves at the positive top of the list. Comparisons cause people to adhere only to their own group and to separate from any other. Here is how one of my pupils describes how comparison occurs in her family.

"We are only two children," says Sara. "My little brother is in third grade and very good at arithmetic. When I watch him do sums, I just can't believe it. For me, arithmetic is a problem. Every day my father compares me with my little brother. 'I don't understand what is the matter with you, Sara,' he says. 'You are so dull that you can't even add two-digit numbers, and you say you are in sixth grade.' Sometimes he says I am stupid and that I have my mother's genes. Because of this, I like to be by myself. I used to really love my brother but my father makes me hate him every day, especially when we are about to complete our test or the day we are supposed to receive our test papers or when our father is invited to the school to see our grades. Sometimes I wish I never had a brother, and because my father compares him with me every day, I think of my brother as belonging to a different family. I used to love my brother, but now every time my father sets me against him academically, I hate him. My prayer is that I will not fail. Otherwise, I will surely die."

Comparisons of individuals or groups cause separation, which automatically stimulates conflict.

The Strands of Knotted Thinking: Projection

Another aspect of knotted thinking is *projection*. This is the act of taking an image in our minds and throwing it onto another person, in the same way a projector throws an image of a movie onto a screen. For example, if we assume that we dislike Kpelle people because we believe they are stupid, they must dislike us in return. If they hate us, they are our enemy. So when we encounter a Kpelle person, we project our mutual dislike onto each other. We think to ourselves: "A Kpelle person? My enemy!"

Fourteen-year-old Thomas Johnson, whose friends in the Peace School affectionately call him Ronaldinho after the Brazilian footballer who is considered among the world's best, shared this projection story.

"Before the war, my father worked for a long time for a Lebanese man. He told me several times that the man was very mean, and underpaid him even though he worked in difficult situations. Before the rebels reached Buchanan, the Lebanese merchant left for somewhere abroad, without paying his workers. This really hurt my father and he is unable to hide his anger and hatred toward this man whenever he tells this story. He always tells me that Lebanese are not good people— that they are bad and mean.

"I am in the same class with a Lebanese boy," Thomas continues. "He is a very amicable boy, but whenever I see that boy, my father's story races across my mind and I tell myself, 'That boy is Lebanese. He is a bad boy. He must be mean like all Lebanese. He is my enemy.' And besides saying this to myself, I have made several boys in the class hate this boy."

I decide to share my personal experience of projection because I want Thomas and all his other friends to understand that projection is a human trait.

"When I moved to Gambia," I tell my students, "I moved into a community where many foreigners resided. I got a one-room apartment in a building I shared with two Gambian families. When I moved there, I made a serious effort to be friendly with the Gambians, but every effort I made was thwarted. The children were afraid of me when their parents were around, but would have a few exchanges with me when their families were out.

"One Friday," I continue, "I was not well and stayed home. The other occupants had gone to the mosque for Friday prayers. I was alone with only one of the children who had stayed home—I assumed because he was sick. Then a lady came to make inquiries about what plans the United Nations High Commission for Refugees (UNHCR) had for Liberian refugees. I was then Secretary General of the Association of Liberians in Gambia. The little boy overheard me speaking Liberian pidgin and, after the woman left, asked if I was a Liberian.

"Yes, I am a Liberian. Why do you ask?"

"Everybody thinks you are a Nigerian," he revealed.

In Gambia, the majority of the "alien" population is Nigerian, so most of the time, Gambians assume all foreigners to be Nigerian. And because they were the majority, Nigerians were also in the majority when it came to crime and other social problems in the foreign community.

"Is this why you don't want me to be your friend?" I asked.

"My parents are afraid of Nigerians," he responded.

"You mean they hate Nigerians?"

"I think so."

"But why do they hate Nigerians?"

"My father says that Nigerians are always in trouble with Gambian laws. They must be bad people. My father is a police officer and he says many of them are in jail. My father does not like them, so he thinks because of this, Nigerians must hate Gambians too. That is why when we see a foreigner, we think that you are Nigerian and believe that you are our enemy. Because we hate Nigerians, they must hate us too. My parents tell me to stay clear of Nigerians."

Later, the two families got to know that I was a Liberian and we started to be friends.

When the women cooked, they gave me food and the children came to watch TV in my house. And whenever the women saw me washing clothes, they would take the clothes and wash them for me. (By the way, it is not a good thing for a man to cook or wash his clothes in the Mandinka culture in Gambia when there are women around.)

When we engage in the act of projecting our thoughts onto others, it is important to be aware that the image is not real. It is not a fact. It is a judgment. And most likely, it is based on fear.

The Strands of Knotted Thinking: Identification

Another aspect of knotted thinking is conforming to the ways and values of a group for security and support—*identifying* with that group.

I was raised as a Catholic but I don't identify with that traditional system of belief, nor do I belong to any fraternity in the church. When one of my friends asked me why not, I told him it was not important. I said that I was raised a Catholic and that this was enough. When I asked why he was in a fraternity, he said: "It is good to be part of an organization in the church. You never know what will happen to you."

Many people join organizations to gain what they think is a sense of security. People identify themselves with organizations, nations, beliefs, assumptions, ethnic groups and political parties because they feel comfortable knowing that they are with others who think as they do. By belonging to a group, they feel protected from others who oppose them.

This is a natural survival instinct. Our ancestors lived like this. Whether living in a small tribe or a large, modern-day group, people tend to stick together for safety, to hold together as a tribe and fight against other tribes that are in opposition to what they stand for. Old tribal members used to think like all other members of their group, and become conditioned to think, act, and look like their fellow members. It made them feel safe.

We still do this today. When we identify ourselves with a group, we often define our-selves by our common experiences. As a result, we unconsciously shuffle our own person-ality aside and imitate the group. This helps us feel accepted and provides us with feelings of security and belonging. If we do not belong to a particular group or encounter a differ-ent group, it triggers our physical survival mechanism—"fight or flight". This interlocking of psychological identity with physical survival reinforces our fear and sets off the triggers which are at the core of all human conflict. The conditioning of the old brain in its hard-wired reaction to ensure physical survival and the new brain representing the symbolic need for psychological identity keeps the tribal divisions alive. Ironically, that which is in-trinsically whole—the human race—continues to create more and more conflict due to the brain's divisive nature of conditioned thinking.

A prime example is the political fever swirling across Liberia in this month of September. Although members of different tribes do live here, Bassas, being in the majority, claim Buchanan their home. Politics has polarized them. By joining a political party, the people want to belong, want a sense of security. So they dress the same way, sing the same songs and even share the same political view. They would do anything to ostracize another group of Bassa people belonging to a different political party. I know of families who stopped speaking to each other when the campaign started.

Angelina, a little girl in our Peace School, one day told me how, for weeks, the campaign has kept her from visiting the home of her best friend Aretha.

"My father supports George Weah, the football legend," she tells me, "and Aretha's parents support Ellen Johnson Sirleaf, the Harvard economist. Angelina's father says of Aretha's family, "Those people feel they are book people. Let them stay on their side with their books. I don't know what books have got to do with being president."

Aretha's parents say about Angelina's parents: "We can't believe people want to make president someone who did not finish high school. What is the relationship between poli-tics and football? People are still stupid in this country."

When we are unconsciously conditioned to put on a particular facade because we be-long to a particular social group, it is as if we are acting out an identity in a drama without thinking, looking at life through darkened glasses.

The Strands of Knotted Thinking: Obedience

Another type of knotted thinking refers to believing and obeying without questioning those in power. When we accept information that experts say is true and right, without finding out for ourselves, we are surrendering to *authority*. Some authorities or specialists have our best interests at heart, while others do not. We must choose carefully which au-thorities to rely on.

A doctor who specializes in heart transplants is obviously an authority in that field and we rely on that doctor for information. There are many kinds of authorities we need to rely on in this world where we never seem to have enough time to learn and know everything. Still, there are sources of information from certain authorities that are likely to be *unreli-able* only because it is in their interest to lie. These authorities claim to know what's best for us and want to condition us to believe what they say. We must be on guard and remember to question. Are they motivated by self-interest? Are they trying to sell us something? Are they trying to influence us with antiquated, conventional patterns of thinking so that we will be conditioned to think only their way? It behooves us always to be aware.

There is a natural need in human beings to put trust in our leaders, especially political leaders. But there are times when leaders are not what they seem. In rare instances, they may be better than they initially appeared, but too often they are worse. They carry around a certain kind of power, even on insignificant levels, and a certain strength that can blind us. We must always remember that no matter how charming a leader is, he or she is a human being, predisposed as we all are, to the same lapses of memory, inconsistencies, contradictions, mistakes and ignorance.

From an early age, we are conditioned to accept authority. An inner authority—some kind of inner voice—tells us what to think, what to say, and how to live according to certain values that may be based on race, culture, nationality or origin. There are also outer authorities, such as leaders, role models and sports legends who play on our inner authority, appealing to the ideas and feelings we have been programmed to believe will bring us security and happiness.

It does not make any sense to believe what someone tells us without finding out for ourselves whether it is really true. It is difficult to check into the authenticity of everything we hear, so we must be selective, check into the facts when we are really curious or when it is for our own safety. It is not healthy to automatically believe what our friends or authorities tell us. Detectives and scientists check the facts; so should we.

Strands of Knotted Thinking: Reinforcements

Another kind of knotted thinking utilizes rewards or punishments to modify—and then *reinforce*—behavior. People often reward children for behaving in accordance with what's deemed right, and scold or deprive them of certain luxuries for behaving contrary to their code.

People who are aware of the ideas and feelings we have been programmed to believe, may know which buttons to push to prompt us to think and act in their preferred ways. We must therefore always be cautious when people offer us information without proof.

I share my experience with my students at the Peace School. My father was an uneducated man who had a hard job earning a living. He believed so much in education that I grew up in a pressure cooker of expectations about my education. When I got good grades, I was sure of getting money for recess. When my grades were low, I would be deprived of certain amenities I enjoyed as his only boy in school. At the end of the school year, I would perform recitations, poems or take a lead role in a play. My father would beam with joy and at home would give me something extra for a job done well.

Many parents similarly give their children rewards and punishments for certain achievements and behaviors that please *them*, rather than considering what is appropriate or natural for the children.

Tom Williams, one of our children in the Peace School, puts it this way. "If I pass all my period tests, my father increases my allowance for lunch. When I fail in certain subjects, I have to wake up early in the morning to find my way to school. He won't drive me.

Sometimes I study my notes to do well in school because I want to please my father. I get nothing special out of it these days when I get good grades. It is for my father."

"My mother is a nurse and she wants me to become a nurse," says Mariama Jones. "She wants me to do well in science. Last year I failed biology and my mother did not buy anything for me for Christmas. My little brother, whom she wants to be an engineer because he is good at mathematics, had it all. These days when I sit in the exam hall, I only see the face of my mother, especially if I am taking a biology test."

Thirteen-year-old Ophelia Brown, one of our newest students, chimes in. "My problem is not with my school. I am doing well but I live only with my mother whom my father left to marry another woman who finished high school," she says. "My mother does not want me to be treated the way my father treated her, so she emphasizes that I must get a good education. I am doing well, but my mother does not like me to be friendly with the children next door. Their parents are from Ghana but the children were born in Buchanan. The main reason is that the boys in that home are always bringing girls to their house, and their parents don't say anything to discourage them. This is what my mother told me another time she met me on their porch. 'Don't forget that I gave you the life you are having. I am going to take it away from you the next time I see you sitting on that porch.'"

Reinforcing behavior through either rewards or punishments in homes that are suppressive, harsh, dictatorial and critical lays a fertile ground to grow weeds of knotted thinking and prejudice. When such parental rules are gospel, children are put on guard. As parents have the power to give or withhold their love at will, children watch acutely for signs of approval or disapproval. As a result of reinforcing this knotted thinking, children lose what they need most—support for who they truly are.

In such situations children learn that power and authority dominate human relationships—not trust and acceptance. Youngsters realize a hierarchy in society, one devoid of equality. This feeling deepens until our sons and daughters mistrust their every move. They must not do this or do that; they must not disobey; they must never say 'No'; they must never disagree; they must not play with a particular child. They must fight every bad thing inside them that their parents dislike.

Such a situation leads a child to fear imagined evil impulses in others. Children who are punished, shamed, discouraged and looked down on, naturally develop basic ideas of inequality and distrust. Required to repress their own impulses, they easily project them on to others, thus developing suspicion, fear, and a breakdown in human relationships. And we wonder why we have conflict and war?

Strands of Knotted Thinking: Unexamined Beliefs

Another element of knotted thinking is *belief*, something we accept to be true without examining it for ourselves. My grandmother was a great storyteller. She knew how to fill stories with intrigue and endless machinations. She knew how to fill my young mind with images and hold my heart in my mouth through the power of her narration.

She came to visit my father on the plantations in December and told us stories in the moonlight. In those days, our school had a long holiday from December to February. As a young boy, I had never had anything to worry about, and my grandmother talked on and on, until she left again to go and get ready for the farming season.

One day she told me that the moon and the sun were the same. In fact, she said the moon was just a replacement of the sun at night. As a child, when I saw the moon, I could easily believe that they were the same. I held on to this belief for a very long time. To me, my grandmother knew everything, and there was no way to doubt or challenge her credibility. Once a grandmother says something, there is no use asking parents. My grandmother had my parents before my parents had me, so she was the greatest authority.

As I grew up, I tried to find out if it was true that the sun and the moon were the same size and that the moon was a replacement for the sun at night. It is true that the sun and the moon look about the same size. I finally learned that because the sun is millions of miles farther away, they look the same, although the moon is actually much smaller than the earth, and the sun many times larger.

Let us be reminded that what may seem common sense can sometimes lead us off track. Some of our incorrect beliefs are not harmful; others may be. We must be careful with declarations we hear and the authority we give to those who say them. Even after we have made up our minds, it is always good to leave room for the possibility of new evidence. This is crucial for awareness, understanding and change.

Prejudice, as you well know, develops in our minds through any or all of these strands. Incorrect ideas cause us to judge others, especially strangers, and to project onto them our mind's image of who we think they are. Our ideas conform to those of our group, or result from obedience to authorities whose opinions and rules we fail to question. Our group leaders and other authorities constantly reinforce our prejudices through punishments and rewards, to keep us thinking and acting the way they believe we should.

We are all born into a world full of prejudice and conditioned thinking. The environment, community and culture we live in continue to program us on a daily basis. The situation created by conditioned thinking and prejudice is not any specific person or tribe's predicament. It is *the* concern for all of humanity. If we are acting in a prejudiced or conditioned way and become aware of it, we can actively make changes in our lives. Conditioning is not education; it is rote, programmed learning. Only when we receive intelligent guidance and then apply this newfound knowledge to arrive at *informed* decisions can we consider ourselves educated. We must learn to know the difference.

Regards,
Marvin

Lesson 8

Concepts That Numb The Brain

"We have learned in our Peace School how programmed images can form when we are under the hypnotic spell of knot-like thinking. We are now aware that we are perpetuating conflict when we repeat, compare, project, identify with and/or reinforce conditioned thinking by listening to authorities who may not be passing along accurate information. Enlightened by our new education, we have discovered that if we perpetuate the hatred passed to us by our ancestors, it is our own invention and responsibility. We cannot blame anyone else for it."

— *Marvin Garbeh Davis*

Dear Dr. T and Jean…

The Common Ground office is usually closed on week-ends, but I often go to the office until midday Saturday to complete unfinished business from the previous week. Because the office is very close to the main street, many of my students stop by to speak to me when they see the main door open or the office vehicle parked outside. I have a standing order with Security to allow any children from the Peace School to see me if they want to.

On one of these Saturdays, Cindy and Wodokueh stop by to speak to me on their way from the market. Cindy lives with her grandmother, who makes her cook on Saturdays. As Wodokueh had gone to visit her this Saturday, they went to the market together and decided to see me before going home.

While we are talking, I hear a knock on the door. I see Martin standing in the doorway.

"Come in, Martin," I call.

He walks inside and takes a seat on one of the chairs facing my desk. The two girls beg to take leave. Cindy is in a hurry to cook so that she and Wodokueh can go to kick-ball practice.

Martin and I exchange handshakes and before long the two girls are running jauntily down the hallway.

"So what's up, Martin?" I ask. I have adopted the way the children greet each other here, and I am reaping enormous benefits. The children can easily relate to me when I talk to them at their level in casual speech.

"Cool, I am fine," he says after a slight pause.

I can tell the boy will easily grow up to be tall. He has his mother's dark, good looks, but his somewhat serious face gives him a dignified look, making him appear older than thirteen.

"What about your parents?" I ask.

"My mother has gone to sell, but you know that my father is dead." There is a short silence and an air of tension hangs over the room. I break the silence.

"I am really sorry, Martin, but I didn't know. What happened?"

"My mother says he was killed by rebels in Nimba. I was only two. She says the men who killed my father were Gio."

"How does she know for sure that they were Gio people?" I ask. He fumbles with his fingers, lifting his head briefly to look in my eyes.

"My mother says she knows the man and she could show him to me any time of the day. She has told me several times that she will never forgive them."

"I know to lose your father is a bad thing, but have you seen it in your heart to forgive the people who killed your father?"

"Why do you want me to forgive them?" he asks me, incredulous. "My father did not do anything to them. If I grow up, I am going to pay back. Gio people are not good."

For a brief moment I am tempted to tell Martin that many innocent people died in the civil war. But my mouth is unable to open, so I hold the thought back.

"If you were able to avenge your father's death, would that bring him back?" I ask.

"No, but then I will be satisfied, and my mother will be happy that the killers of her husband have gone where they sent her husband," Martin says, with irritation in his voice.

Spontaneously deciding to share a parallel war wound, I move my chair from behind the barrier of the desk, and sit close. During the brief shuffle, our eyes make silent, pained contact.

"I tell you, Martin, my father was also killed during the war. Years ago, I used to feel like you. I, too, wanted to find the killers and avenge my father's death. But now I realize that avenging my father's death would start a new war—a war that my children's children will fight only because I made a decision to avenge my father's death by killing someone else's father."

"This is what my mother wants," he protests. "She tells me this every day. And when I finish school, I am going to make her wish come true. I want to be educated first and have some money, and then I can start to look for my father's killers," he says with youthful naïveté.

"No, Martin, you are going to school to be educated so that you can help your family and country. You don't want your children to fight another war. You want to live in peace. Avenging a loved one's death is not a way to peace."

"I want to live in peace," he smiles thinly, "but do you think it is right to let those Gio people get away with all the bad things they did?"

"You see, Martin, the past is always with us, always trying to claim a part of our lives in the present. Putting the past behind you will help you live as a new person in an old world, confronting and dealing with challenges of the present. You must learn to forget about your father's killers. It is difficult to do, but if you gather courage and start thinking in terms of forgiveness, your life will be a lot easier. Get an education, and help do things that will make your world peaceful, so that your children will not have to live in conflict and kill innocent people to avenge the people who will avenge you for avenging your father. You have the power to change the world. You are young. You are the future. You are life."

"Thank you, Mr. Davis," Martin says as he rises and prepares to leave. I reach into my pocket and give him 20 Liberian dollars so that he can get a taxi. There is no way to tell whether this boy will change his mind and forgive those responsible for his father's death.

"Thanks for coming, Martin. Please come and talk with me anytime you wish." I walk him to the front door and watch as he crosses to the other side of the main street to find a taxi. Back in my office, I reflect on the encounter with this teenage boy. I wonder how many young children are there like him in this country, growing up with the desire to avenge the death of a loved one? How many more of our children are getting prepared to fight a battle they do not understand? How many more parents in our country are raising their children under the shadow of war, to continue the war? How many of our children are being programmed to engage in a future conflict? How many more are being raised in a training ground across the length and breadth of this country, in an environment full of prejudice and judgment?

Do we remember our ancestors and how they lived their lives? Do we recall how they fought, ran away and were conditioned to have certain thoughts they believed would help them survive? They bonded as a group because they were afraid that if they didn't, they would die.

Tribal groups helped their members survive physically by guaranteeing them food, clothing and shelter. Each tribe was required to identify with a group by following the group's customs and traditions. Members had to attach themselves mentally and emotionally to the group and loyally follow tribal rules. This made the tribes more powerful and better able to take care of their members.

Once physical and psychological needs were met, the tribes felt safe. But over time, individual tribes grew, and tribal territories overlapped each other. Boundaries became difficult to hold on to. Since each tribe needed the same essentials, each began to see every other tribe as a threat. Since psychological survival of the tribes was tied to members' physical needs, members believed that their customs and traditions were also threatened. The resultant conflict led to war, not only over territories and physical needs, but also over whose beliefs should dominate, and whose customs and traditions should govern to ensure everyone's survival.

When I think of how we are living today, I wonder if the human race has developed at all since the days of our ancestors. Yes, we have been able to develop remarkable tools and technology that give us the ability to create more food, clothing and shelter. While there are still people who don't have a place to live or enough food to eat, we know far more about creating physical elements of survival than we ever have.

However, *psychological* conflict continues. Science offers no way to resolve the different ideas people have about how life should be. It's inaccurate to think that wisdom has accumulated solely with the advent of science. Though more scientifically informed, today we face the same basic problems as our ancestors. The major twist is that the stakes are dramatically higher. Now, because we have used science to create a technology that can kill more people more quickly, but we have done very little to over-ride our gross ignorance and prejudice, we have unnecessarily caused the deaths of millions of people,

Prejudice is certainly at the heart of many social dilemmas: racial tensions, nuclear proliferation, poverty, and hunger. Our simple inability to see prejudice prevents us from clearly understanding what is at hand, and thus how to act with sound reasoning. This lack of common sense spills out of our high offices on to our community streets.

It seems that our old brains, the ones our ancestors have passed on to us, continue to lead us into endless struggles. Despite the fact that there have been attempts to make us more peaceful, our conditioned brains continue to drive us toward distrust, hatred and violence.

Today, we still live in small groups, much like tribes. It may not be like those of our forefathers, but we live in tribe-like organizations. We live in families and belong to clubs, organizations, and houses of worship. We support different soccer teams and opposing political parties. All of these groups help to establish our identity, our sense of who we are, although we may not rely on them for our safety in the same way as in the past.

As the world becomes a smaller place, we must all depend on each other for survival. Neither the old tribes nor these modern groups help us feel safe. Instead, they divide and even prevent us from contributing to the welfare of one another as one group.

Human history is filled with conflict. For thousands of years, we have attempted to solve violence with more violence. This savagery is not only a Liberian problem, but a *global* one. When we will stop this plague of brutality?

If we picture a sixteen-year-old boy taking an AK-47 rifle and shooting another human being, we might be compelled to ask, "How can a human being—especially one so young— treat another human being in such a way?" But is it any different from the news stories in our local papers and on our radio or TV stations? Have we really changed at all?

If we only had two brains—one for emotion and the other for reasoning. The reasoning brain could switch off the emotional brain when an individual is faced with a problem that requires the application of dispassionate logic. Unfortunately, the components of the brain are intricately intertwined, so that even the most reasonable among us can be driven to fury and depression by a seemingly infinite variety of factors.

How can we have peace when people continue to take sides? Can there be agreement or a single pursuit of peace when tribe-like groups still seek security by insisting upon maintaining established beliefs, traditions and rituals?

We may think that congregating in interest groups will bring unity, but if we think globally instead of nationally, we might realize that separate interest groups with different beliefs will never create a whole. Human beings divided against themselves can never be united. We can never agree when people root for their group against another, or when each group claims its ideas and beliefs are the best. How many different races are there? There is only one. The human race.

My students and I have learned many new things in the Peace School. We have learned that there is a difference between an opinion and a fact. There is a difference between getting information first-hand and assuming. There is a difference between understanding and judging. We have learned that our brain, operating in a mechanical way, is programmed to create images, many of which aren't real. We have discovered that fear can create incorrect images that get stuck in our brains, and that conditioning helps us hold on to these images—sometimes forever, if we don't wake up. We have learned that prejudice is a reaction, and that in order to act from the truth, rather than to react on the basis of others' opinions, we must think for ourselves.

Before Janet came to the Peace School, she could not stand her stepmother. "I used to see her as a devil, only because she is my stepmother. And in my mind, stepmothers were bad. I never saw any good at all in anything my stepmother did for me. Even when she cooked and I ate after school, I never said thank you. After all, it was my father who bought the food."

When her friend Mabel told her about the Peace School, Janet decided to join immediately, not because she had a passion for the after-school program, but as a way of evading the presence of her stepmother.

"Things have changed since I came to the Peace School. I now understand that my stepmother is a human being and I have not been appreciating her as a person. All the things that I did to her came from my mind. The image of a stepmother as a bad person was in my mind and I used it against my stepmother. When I made a decision to treat her as a person and act like her own daughter, things started to improve between us."

Today Janet enjoys a good relationship with her stepmother. When I last visited her home, her stepmother said, "Thank you for the Peace School. It really changed my daughter. Her change in attitude has also affected me. I really do love Janet now."

We have also learned in our Peace School how programmed images can form when we are under the hypnotic spell of knot-like thinking. We are now aware that we are perpetuating conflict when we repeat, compare, project, identify with and/or reinforce conditioned thinking by listening to authorities who may not be passing along accurate information. Enlightened by our new education, we have discovered that if we perpetuate the hatred passed on to us by our ancestors, it is our own invention and responsibility. We cannot blame anyone else for it.

All the actions we take begin in the brain, which is the center of tumultuous activity—especially when we are in conflict. The brain is the source of our thoughts, feelings, and actions. The brain stores all kinds of information and can retrieve millions of bits of knowledge to help us live.

Just as the most expensive computer can make mistakes, so can the brain, the reason usually being that the user feeds it incorrect information. Sometimes it takes a while to discover that the information we have is incorrect. Sometimes we get so accustomed to such incorrect information that we find it difficult to change.

On an ongoing basis, Marion's mother tells her that when she grows up, she must never marry a Bassa man. Her reason: Bassa men are lazy and are hooked on having a good time. Marion grows up and, of course, meets a Bassa man who is very nice and honest to her. He tries to show her in all ways that he really loves her, but Marion is suspicious that if she returns the Bassa man's love, she may die of hunger on her matrimonial bed while her husband is away having a great time.

Can we see a correlation between Marion's experiences as a child and her relationship with this Bassa man? Do we think that the teachings of her mother in her early years may have conditioned Marion to behave in a certain way as an adult? Can we see that Marion's conditioning to be wary of Bassa men could lead to a major problem in her life?

Jerry is a fellow whose father told him persistently as a boy that if he did not rough somebody up now and then, he would wind up being bullied by someone else. Jerry grows up and becomes President of Liberia. He builds a reputation for bullying, making sure to demonstrate his power, so that his people will not gain control over him. In his dealing with other countries, Jerry continues these aggressive tactics.

Can we se how Jerry's conditioning in his early life greatly affects his later life? Can we see how his personal conditioning winds up affecting people nationally and globally? It is this broad perspective we must show our children.

If we condition our young people to think that Bassa people are lazy, Kpelle people are stupid, Gio people are violent, and Mandingoes are selfish, how long will it take to correct this information? Maybe forever. The images these labels hold are very strong. How much careful attention and awareness will it take to change their thinking and the way they will see the world?

It is important, therefore, to become conscious of our thoughts about others as well as our thoughts about ourselves—how we bully ourselves in the same way that others bully us. Though they don't intend to, our brains sometimes create conflict. The information we feed them may be incomplete, or the way we sort out the information may be incorrect.

My students and I review circumstances that numb our brains.

Self-consciousness. This is how we see ourselves, often based on our own embarrassment as we imagine others' criticism of us.

People have said to us, "You are too shy," "You are too fat," or "too thin." Our teachers may have accused us of being slow, lazy or talkative. Our parents might have said we are too weak or too quiet. These opinions form pictures in our minds about who we think you are. We develop a value system: are we good, or are we bad? When this information is pro-grammed into our memories, it significantly affects the way we look at ourselves. As a result of this conditioning, at a gathering where we feel self-conscious because we're a stranger or because we feel our clothes are out of place, we realize how acutely aware and concerned we are of how others see us. But we are really doing this to ourselves. We are prejudiced against ourselves because we were bullied into believing we were inferior in some way.

Mai explains self-consciousness to me this way. "My father says I am too fat. He says it is not good for a woman to be fat like that. This affects me to the point that if I am ap-proaching a group of people and they start to look at me, I start to feel bad. I even misstep sometimes. I can see how their eyes pierce my body. It embarrasses me. When I get home I start to worry about my size. I ask myself, 'Should I eat less, sleep less and exercise to get small?'"

John is short and he is self-conscious about it. Mai is self-conscious about being over-weight. They tease each other about these things. When John and Mai confront each other, they learn nothing new about themselves. All they do is call each other names. They see their differences and forget their similarities.

Janjay spent some time on the Ivory Coast with his mother during the inter-factional fighting in 1996. He complains about how she used to feel being a stranger in that country.

"You don't understand the language the people speak, and when you say something in English, they see you as a fool."

When I ask Janjay if he had been conditioned in any way before he went to the Ivory Coast, he says, "My mother kept telling me, when we were sure that we would go to the Ivory Coast, that Ivorians are rough and impolite. They don't like foreigners, especially from English-speaking countries."

I ask him, "If you had the chance to go back to that country, what would you change in your attitude?"

"I would try to make friends," he says. "We stayed on the Ivory Coast for a year, but I never made any friends. I only played with Liberian children my age. These children and I were taught in the same way. If I had made friends, I would have learned French and better understood Ivorians."

Prejudgment. This brain-numbing effect occurs when we come to an incorrect conclusion because of limited information. For example, if our family has conditioned us to believe that Krahns are mean and love only people from their tribe, and we are conditioned to believe this without examining it, then we are *prejudging* Krahns. This kind of attitude can be very harmful, because every time we see Krahns, we assume they're mean. We create immediate conflict in our minds.

Every time we use previous knowledge to label new information without first confirming our findings, we are prejudging—which is prejudice. Because the tendency of the brain is to compute new information based on old, it will struggle to find a new label for data that it is different or novel. It may choose a category that matches most closely to other files already stored in its database. If we become aware of this process, we can examine a label and in so doing, it corrects itself. Or, at the very least, we can question it.

"Have you ever met someone you disliked instantly?" I ask the children. "Perhaps the person reminded you of someone you had a conflict with in the past, or the person comes from a place where you lived before and you had a bad experience with people there. Our memory can cause us to react in this way. When this happens, it is important to catch your brain in the act—and correct it. Your *awareness* leads you to think. If you think, you will realize that you have no reason to prejudge this person because of your past experience."

When the brain prejudges someone, it *stereotypes*, which means it categorizes that person in a certain way, putting their image into a convenient slot. This is a dangerous way of thinking, because it does not allow us to address a specific behavior, a unique problem or a particular individual. Here are two of many possible examples:

"Mariam complains a lot. Why are Liberian women so emotional?"

"My son never shows any emotion. Is he a real man?"

These conclusions demonstrate the short leap from observing to labeling that creates prejudiced, stereotypical beliefs. When we are prejudiced, we create separation between ourselves and another person. Thus, prejudging creates conflict.

I tell the students, "If you catch yourself in the act of prejudging, it is a sign that you are becoming *aware*. You are beginning to *see* how you have been conditioned. This is a wonderful step, because it means new learning is going on. Once you look at prejudice and see it, it ends. At that point, it removes conflict from your lives."

Repression. When we have painful thoughts and feelings, we want to forget or bury them. So we hold them back, hiding them from ourselves, pretending they never occurred, attempting really hard to extinguish the memories. In this great effort, we create more conflict, because repressed thoughts don't go away. They only hide deep inside us, bubbling beneath the surface.

I tell the children, "Repressed feelings and thoughts accumulated from the past affect how we behave in the present. These feelings often come from self-judging and negative views we have about ourselves. This happens because people we trust have made us feel bad for feeling certain emotions, thinking certain thoughts, or acting in a particular way. In hiding those feelings, we only make our problems worse, because they build up the conflict inside us.

"For this reason, it is good to express painful feelings to someone we trust, in order to reach an understanding of how and why the brain repressed the pain, and how this caused our conflict. Just being able to *see* this, as it happens, creates awareness, which prevents the brain from continuing to create more unnecessary conflict."

I ask my students, "Have you ever heard of a brain maze?" They all shake their heads, looking curious..

"Well, when we prejudge, stereotype or repress, we create feelings and thoughts that are not true. By piling up feelings and thoughts that are not accurate, we stray farther and farther from the truth. We wind up with a brain maze that ties our thoughts into a huge knot. Here is an illustration:

'He is short.'

'We are tall, so he hates us.'

'Because he hates us, we hate him.'

'We hate him, so he is our enemy.'

'I am afraid of my enemies.'

'I feel I must defend myself against him, and fight him.'

"Can you see how one thought leads to another—and then another—and then another?

"Can you see how our brain's conditioning can cause conflict inside us? The more we allow this conflict to grow, the more we are likely to project conflict onto other people. And if a lot of people in the world project their conflict onto others, we are faced with a global conflict.

This is how every war starts. Isn't it exciting to realize that we actually have the power to stop a war, before it starts—just by becoming aware of our thoughts and actions, and changing the way we communicate?"

I will stay in touch and am looking forward to speaking to you next week,
Marvin

Lesson 9

Generalizations Are Misleading

"The children at the Peace School have begun to notice the differences between opinions and reality, between assumptions and firsthand information, between prejudging and fact-finding. We have learned how mechanical our brains are, and we have seen how they are programmed to create images, many of which are not true. We have also seen how our brains can form these images when we are under the hypnotic spell of conditioned thinking. Our children are aware of how repetition, obedience to authority, and reinforcement work to create false images in our brains. They have grasped how we tend to view the world incorrectly when we identify strongly with various groups, stereotyping others and projecting our biased images on them. It's a lot to learn, but our children are learning it."

— *Marvin Garbeh Davis*

Dear Dr. T and Jean…

Liberia fought a war for more than a decade. More than 200,000 people died. Some statistics put the figure as high as 300,000. While the real figures will never be known, the number of casualties is nevertheless disquieting. The Liberian civil war remains one of the bloodiest, especially considering the evil perpetrated against innocent civilians.

The war is over and the nation is gradually turning to democracy. Leaders are calling on Liberians to reunite and live in peace, because they believe it is only in peace that we can rebuild our country. But despite these calls, there are opposing factions everywhere we turn in this nation. People here hardly agree on anything these days.

But how can there be agreement when there are always sides? How can there be agreement when Liberians live out their lives in tribe-like groups, believing and acting according to traditions and customs, unwilling to change? Wouldn't it be possible to end conflict and violence if no one were to identify with either side? Or are we too conditioned and programmed to see this simple solution?

The young people are learning to be aware of a lot of things on our journey of discovery. In this new sphere of human endeavor, we have learned about prejudice, how we are all intolerant, and some possible ways to deal with it. We are learning about the effects of prejudice—inside us, outside us, around us, and how to recognize when it exists. The young people at the Common Ground Society Peace School and I are determined to learn rather than to protect ourselves from the truth.

Let me share with you what we have learned, thanks to your curriculum, *Why Is Everybody Always Picking on Us?* The children at the Peace School have begun to notice the differences between opinions and reality, between assumptions and firsthand information, between prejudging and fact-finding. We have learned how mechanical our brains are, and we have seen how they are programmed to create images, many of which are not true. We have also seen how our brains can form these images when we are under the hypnotic spell of conditioned thinking. Our children are aware of how repetition, obedience to authority, and reinforcement work to create false images in our brains. They have grasped how we tend to view the world incorrectly when we identify strongly with various groups, stereotyping others and projecting our biased images on them. It's a lot to learn, but our children are learning it, and more:

+ We have seen how fear creates negative images that get stuck in our brains.
+ We have learned how conditioning causes us to hold on to these images, perhaps forever, unless we find a way to wake up.
+ We have also discovered in the Peace School, to our surprise, that any ancestral hatred we continue to feel is our own invention.
+ We have learned that prejudice is an automatic reaction.
+ We know that it is possible to become *aware* that we are reacting.
+ Once we bring that awareness up, we can *act* rather than react.
+ To do so, we have learned that we must think for ourselves.

Today the children and I are learning about generalizations. We want to understand how generalizations are at the root of human conflict. We want to learn what happens inside us, all around us, when we generalize about a person or members of a group, which is so widespread in Liberia today.

There is a common saying in Liberia: "Never wash your dirty clothes in public." It has a lot to do with fear. At the Peace School, we are not afraid; we want to discover, we want to know the truth and not fear it, so we are marching on to discover what the effects of generalizations are, and how these effects develop from prejudiced thinking.

To start our lesson, I ask my students to think of at least ten words that disrespect, dehumanize or bring other people down. I ask them about words they know or words commonly used to put down other ethnic groups.

"These are words that produce such strong reactions in you that they cause you to feel hatred and prejudice," I tell the students. I create a summary of this list on the board, incorporating every word my 20 students have written on their papers.

+ Red
+ Stupid
+ Lazy
+ Selfish
+ Mean
+ Violent
+ Rude
+ Bad
+ Greedy
+ Kwi (book people)
+ Eating dogs
+ Drinking

Now I ask the children, "Take a moment—stop in your tracks—to consider the fear and hate that these words carry in your mind." Then I ask for a volunteer.

James Johnson, a Bassa boy, says that when he uses the word "red," members of the Kpelle tribe come to mind. "Kpelle people love to wear red," he concludes, laughing teasingly.

"I also think of Kpelle people when I use the word 'stupid,'" says Janet, another Bassa girl. "You know Kpelle people are stupid."

Samuel bursts in, "Bassa people are lazy. All they like is to enjoy themselves, so when I use the word *lazy*, I am thinking about Bassa people." Samuel is a Kpelle boy.

"When I use the word *mean*, I am thinking about Mandingo people. Mandingo are so mean, they can only share with Mandingo people," says Joyce, a Vai girl.

"Gio people are *violent* people. They cannot have an argument without fighting," Mariam interjects. She belongs to the Mandingo tribe.

"When I use the word *bad*, I am thinking about Krahn. Krahn people like killing," Thomas says with a frown on his face. I later realize that Thomas lived with his mother in southeastern Liberia when the civil war started.

"Gio people are *greedy*. They want to have everything for themselves. They act like Mandingo people," says Marion.

"Congo people think they are the only *kwi* (those who know the book) people on earth. They can tell you about civilization every day, as if they started civilization," says Theo, who used to live with his people in Brewerville, a small Congo settlement outside Monrovia.

"Gissi people love *eating dogs*. This is their biggest meat," explains Thomas, who lived on the Liberian agricultural plantations before coming to live with his mother in Buchanan.

"Bassa men like *drinking*," says Martin who belongs to the Kpelle ethnic group.

When we utter any one of these statements to ourselves, we tend to accept them, especially in our own circle. But when we hear them read out loud one after another, it becomes clear to us that they all stem from conditioned thinking. Conditioned thoughts erupt into feelings such as hate, triggering pictures of falsely-perceived enemies.

It is so easy to get caught up in this web of prejudice. In our everyday conversations, hurtful words are used all the time. The people who use them are either unaware of the pain they cause, or fully aware and use them on purpose. In any case, they cause conflict.

In class we conclude that some people think it is fun to use hurtful words— whether to degrade another person or to express conditioned thoughts. But if we are ever tempted, it is good to put ourselves in someone else's shoes and ask how we would feel if we were the ones victimized by such words and names.

We play the Association Game from your curriculum, Dr. Terrence and Jean. It helps people understand how words and names pop into our heads unawarely, thus testing the students' ability to observe how prejudice builds. We learn the kinds of associations we make, how deeply ingrained they are, and how we make them every day without thinking.

I want to share with you a segment of this game from one of our sessions. On the board, I write a group of words, which we go over one by one, and the children write the first word that comes to their minds without thinking.

The First Word:

Soldier
Police
Blackman
White man
Friend
Enemy
Girl
Boy
Foreigner

Here are the results of this exercise:

The First Word	The Associated Word or Phrase
Soldier	Bad
Police	Corrupt
Black man	Uneducated, uncivilized
White man	Educated, civilized, knows everything
Enemy	Wicked
Girl	Lazy
Boy	Strong
Foreigner	Different

The object of this activity is for the children to uncover their conditioned thoughts and feelings, so they can become more aware of thoughts that muddy their brains.

Words can easily become attitudes. Using harmful words is one way we let our prejudices show. Another way is thinking in lazy, sleepy, tired ways and making generalizations about people without taking the time to discover who they really are.

When we generalize, we act on past experiences to make an assumption about a person, place or thing, Generalizations are reactions that result in prejudiced thinking. The students and I review some examples.

A *stereotype* is the first example. I make sure they understand that it is a standardized mental picture that represents an oversimplified opinion, attitude or judgment held by members of one group about members of another group. This broad, general view of the world is based on formulating a single opinion of a group, rather than looking at each member individually. We call it lazy thinking, for in the short term, it seems to be an easier route.

In another Association Game, I ask the children to search the databases of their brains for stereotypical images. As soon as an image buds, I ask them to take a mental picture of it and write it in each space provided. I have intentionally left blank spaces between the first few words and the children's responses, to make it clear how my children in the Peace School describe the following groups:

Americans are	IMPORTANT
Black people are	not intelligent, clever
Kpelle people are	stupid
Bassa people are	lazy
Mandingo people are	shrewd and business-minded
Gio people are	rough

Once they have written their own responses, I ask, "Have you stopped to question your reactions? Are you going to assume that that they are correct and that you plan to act on them?" They stop to consider their responses.

We move on to *bigotry*. I explain that this word is based on the word "bigot," which refers to someone who is strongly partial to his or her own group, belief system, race or politics, and is intolerant of those who are different. A bigot has a fixed mind-set, an immovable way of thinking that divides members of his group from members of another group. Bigots see their group as superior to any other group, which separates them from others. Dividing the human race into differing factions is a strong sign of prejudice, and it's an act that creates conflict and separation. Isn't our goal to bring people together rather than separate them?

In July of 2005, Common Ground participated in a three-way project with the Atrium Society of the USA and the Bangladesh Battalion 6, to start the Peace School at the Bassa High School auditorium. We recruited 60 children for the six-month project. One day I suggested to the children from the Peace School located at our main office, that we have a joint class with the children at the Bassa High School campus.

"They should come here to us. There is no need to go there to them," said Vonziah, one of our pioneer students.

"Why not, Vonziah?" I ask.

"Our class started this Peace School thing. They should walk to us."

Because they are the pioneer students of the program and know a lot more about this topic than those at Bassa High School, many of the students feel they are special and unique. Even at the hall, the students from the Common Ground Society office Peace School want to sit only with their classmates. When it is time to eat, they want to eat only with members of their own group. This is an example of the superiority part of bigotry, showing how we normally separate our own group from other groups to strengthen our own bonds by stressing that we should not join in doing anything together with *them*. Doing so helps us buy into the false feeling of thinking that we're "better than" *them*.

The students begin to grow aware of their thoughts on this matter, and it is rewarding to see their insight.

Next, we discuss discrimination, the act of seeing the difference between one thing or person and another, and how to make choices based on those differences. We do this every day in our lives. We choose rice over *fufu*, a white shirt over a blue shirt, African movies over American movies. There is nothing wrong or bad about choosing one thing over another. We have to make choices in our lives every day as rational human beings.

But what if we discriminate on the basis of opinions that have no truth? What if we make choices based on wrong stereotypes we carry in our brains? This kind of discrimination creates conflict. When we have an image in our brains of a certain group as "'stupid," "lazy" or "uncivilized," and then decide not to make friends, or we call them bad names because they belong in that group, this is discrimination. This is reacting to an individual based on a stereotype we have been conditioned to believe. The resulting conflict inside us promotes hostility and conflict outside us.

The Morris family has two children, a boy and a girl. In 2005, the mother of the family asked me to enroll her daughter, Marpue, in our Peace School because she did not have money to send the girl to an academic school. She thought we were teaching the children to read and write. When I asked why she wanted Marpue to come to the Peace School, she said that her husband was not working, so they could not send their two children to school. They decided for the boy to go and the girl to remain. When I asked why they decided to sacrifice the girl, she said, "We don't have money, and you know boys can do better in school than girls."

The first part of her answer was valid, but the second part was discriminatory because of the stereotype Marpue's mother and father carry in their brains about daughters. Many families discriminate: it is common in Liberia for parents to send their boys to school and leave their girls home.

Scapegoating is a fascinating form of generalization. When a mistake is made or a problem happens, our brain sometimes searches for someone to blame, someone to find fault with, someone who isn't us. Some scapegoating is the result of treating people only as a group they belong to, a group about which we have a conditioned opinion, without regard for the individuals in that group.

We try every year at Common Ground to have some kind of activity for the children on Independence Day. They normally agree to play a game of soccer and kickball. This year we decide to invite a team from the Moore Town community. During the discussion, Tom, who doesn't live far from that community, has a strong opinion.

"We should not send for those children from Moore Town," he says angrily.

"Why, Tom?" I ask.

"The children from Moore Town love to make *palaver*" (trouble)," he replies.

"Do you have any evidence for what you are saying, Tom?" I ask.

"Last year," Tom begins, "we from the Bassa community played a game with a team from Moore Town. The game ended in a fight."

"Who were those fighting?"

"Two boys from the area attacked one boy who came from our community to watch the game."

"Were these two boys playing on the team?"

"No, but they lived in the community."

In the conversation, I gather that Tom's wish to exclude the community is based on a conditioned thought about children from Moore Town. He thinks that they are trouble-makers just because he watched two Moore Town boys fighting during a game. As a result, he anticipates other fights when the Common Ground football team invites the children from Moore Town to play. So he does not want to have a game, or any contact, with children from that community. He does not care which part of Moore Town they come from. He blames *all* the children from Moore Town for that one incident. This is an automatic reaction with no basis. It is a gross generalization.

In the end, we played the game with a team—but a different team—from the Moore Town community. We won. And there was no fight. Our opponents were invited to dinner at our office, and there was no incident.

Just as prejudice provides a target for scapegoating, scapegoating feeds prejudice. It allows us to push a problem away from ourselves by placing it—out there—on another person or group. This leads us to believe that the solution to the problem is out there too. We forget to ask ourselves whether the roots of prejudice are outside us, with other people, or deep inside our own thoughts.

The conditioned mind is a dangerous mind. I ask my students, "Can you see how all these forms of prejudice—stereotyping, bigotry, discrimination and scapegoating— are dangerous perspectives that live inside our minds?" They are fixed images programmed into our brains by our ancestors—those from long ago, as well as those from a few minutes ago.

We are born in a world where many prejudgments already exist. Without questioning them, our parents, teachers, and friends teach us to think in the "old" way, not because they are bad people, but because they were also taught these things by their parents and they, too, did not question them. All of us have inherited a huge database full of incorrect data. By relying on this old disc, we make improper decisions, choices and judgments all the time. It is as if our shadows are constantly following us.

At the root of our prejudices are the brain's automatic reactions which produce hate, anger, distrust, rivalry and antagonism. We have within our power as human beings, the ability to stop this programmed way of thinking, which can lead to new discoveries in our lives and within our human relationships.

Here is how the children and I are learning to stop thinking in a programmed way in the Peace School. When we see prejudice happening, we immediately engage in a STOP/THINK moment. This STOP/THINK moment allows us to pause and examine the prejudice. During that moment when we stop and think, a new awareness engulfs us and we begin to see clearly. Because of this awareness, we are able to stop prejudice—immediately—in its tracks. Although this process requires many words, it happens in a moment.

Oliver Mason is the shortest boy at the Peace School. The mention of the word *short* used to trigger a "get ready to fight" response in Oliver; he did not give a hoot about who said it. When he came to the Peace School, this problem was enormous. Even when the word was mentioned without a hint of a correlation to Oliver, he still grew angry with the person using the word.

One day he complained about Janet, his classmate who called him *short*. He nearly started a fight, so I called him into the office. Oliver and I went through a STOP/THINK moment. It was intended to help him see the word in a new light, and gain a fresh awareness so that the mention of the word would not make him want to fight.

"What makes you so vexed when you hear the word *short?*" I ask him.

"It is not the word alone; it is the way people use it and what they are telling me alone, that many other persons don't hear when they speak."

I realize Oliver is talking about the hidden meaning people attach to being short in Liberia. Children in the peace school have said that when a child tells his friend he is short, it refers to more than his physical stature. It implies that he is eating his mother's food for nothing, that he is not able to stand up for himself, that he is too old, or a myriad of other, associated shortcomings. Because Oliver is short, he is overly sensitive to the covert remarks made about short people.

"You want to tell me what *you* hear when the word is used?" I ask.

"Some people mean that I can't defend myself because I am short," said Oliver. "Others think that I will never grow tall. At school the children mean that I eat too much without growing. I want them to stop it and sometimes when I stand up to them, they get scared."

"Has it ever occurred to you to stop and think when people call you *short*?"

"There is no need to stop and think. I already know what they mean. It is right in my head."

"By reacting this way," I say to Oliver, "you promote trouble and confusion between you and the people who use this word that sets you off. I want you to start all over again in a fresh way. Maybe this can stop you from getting into trouble with others. It may help you in making new friends as well as keeping your old ones. Are you interested, Oliver?"

"Yes," he said. "I want to hear it."

"The next time you hear someone call you *short*, or you hear the word *short*, stop. Just stop. Think for a moment."

"Why?"

"When you hear the word *short*, your brain interprets this word to mean greedy, stunted, and lazy, and so the thoughts associated with these words in your mind create anxiety and fear—and you get ready to fight. But if you stop and think, you can take a moment to ask yourself if the meaning you have attributed to this word is really how these people are using it. No one means to hurt you, make fun of you, or pick a fight with you. Are you willing to try this?"

Oliver is not fighting anyone these days because of the word *short*. What he does now is stop and think in the moment whenever he hears the word. As a result, instead of a conditioned reaction, he takes thoughtful action. In our class we say that when we hear something that irritates us, or makes us want to fight, hate, or envy someone, the thing to do is to STOP and THINK. In that brief moment, conflict stops. As a result, we are very likely to come up with a new, fresh way of responding, because we have a new awareness that makes us act intelligently.

Thinking and acting out of prejudice can be cruel and destructive. When people practice another form of generalized thinking called *tribalism*, they favor their own tribal members with special treatment. Outsiders may be accepted or denied based only on which tribe they belong to. Problems caused by tribalism were at the heart of the Liberian civil war. Depending on their identified tribe, some were merely denied opportunities, while others were raped, maimed or otherwise treated inhumanely. Still others were killed. All Liberians remember when Doe threatened to wipe Nimba County of the map of Liberia, so badly did he want to reduce the inhabitants of that county. All of us can recall so much heartbreak around Liberia during the war, not the least of which were the Lutheran Church Massacre, the Cow Field Massacre and the Harbel Massacre.[1]

---

1   The 1980 coup which began Samuel K. Doe's dictatorship had its roots in cultural differences between Liberia's Krahn and Dan/Mano ethnic groups. The coup also ousted an Americo-Liberian minority. In 1983, Doe's former comrade, Thomas Quiwonkpa, fled to the United States. Quiwonkpa's supporters, mainly decommissioned security personnel, took refuge in neighboring Cote d'Ivoire, where they began training to

These are only some of the dangers of prejudice. As we can see, prejudice has the potential to lead beyond the most deadly outcomes imaginable, to the annihilation of millions of people. I ask the children, "Does it amaze you to know the incredible damage and far-reaching effects of prejudice?"

Toward Christmas of 2005, the Kpelle father of a Peace School student came to see me concerning a problem he had with a Bassa student's father. The Bassa man owed the Kpelle man $2,000 Liberian. He had promised to pay the Kpelle man back, but hadn't done so. Angry, the Kpelle man decided to take him to court.

I invited both men into my office. The Kpelle man explained that although he wanted to give his Bassa brother some time to enable him to pay his debt, he thought if he did so, the Bassa man would interpret his sympathy as stupidity. Because of his conditioned beliefs, the Kpelle man assumed that the Bassa man preferred to enjoy himself during the Christmas season rather than reimburse him. In short, he was ready to go to any lengths to prove to this Bassa man that Kpelle people are not the stupid people that Bassa people imagine.

The people who taught us to think in this way are not bad people. They were taught to think by *their* families and friends, but these old, generational ways that have glued themselves to us cause relentless pain, over and over again. As we discover that we are knowl-

---

overthrow the Doe regime. When the Gios and Manos of Nimba County ran into political conflict with the Krahns, individuals in the U.S. who did not belong to these tribes quickly took over the conflict.

Thus, under pressure from the U.S. and other creditors, after four years of military rule, Doe's government issued a new constitution on July 26, 1984, allowing the return of political parties he had outlawed, marking the beginning of a multi-party election campaign. The presidential election of October 15, 1985, featured five different political parties, with televised debates involving all five candidates. Although the election commission claimed that President Doe received 51 percent of the vote, many observers charged that Doe had stolen the election.

Their accusations included widespread fraud, rigging, corruption and prevention and/or delay of registration of other political parties and popular leaders so they could not enter the campaign. Thus, the period after the elections saw increased human rights abuses, corruption and ethnic tensions. Some attributed this civil conflict to the Liberian people's reaction to the rigging of the election. Some called for the United States to intervene in Liberia to remove President Doe after he was elected.

On November 12, 1985, former Liberian Army Commanding General Thomas Quiwonkpa returned to lead the invasion of his own county from neighboring Sierra Leone. He almost succeeded in toppling Doe's government, but members of the Krahn-dominated Armed Forces of Liberia repelled his attack and executed him in Monrovia. The soldiers who claimed on television that they had captured and killed him, paraded his body parts around the city in a grisly ritual that Liberians will remember for years.

As a result, Doe's government then launched a bloody purge against the Gio and Mano ethnic groups in Quiwonkpa's Nimba Country. Babies and young children were targeted and killed indiscriminately. There were reports that Doe even threatened to wipe Nimba County off the map of Liberia, so badly did he want to reduce the inhabitants of that county. Simple prejudice during this civil war in Liberia led to three massacres: the Lutheran Church Massacre of more than 600 people who had gone to seek refuge in the town of Sinkor, the Cow Field Massacre of 48 people, mostly children, and the Harbel Massacre of hundreds more. Through wanton shootings, bludgeoning and mutilations of helpless refugees at Harbel, Doe's men murdered at least 547 and injured at least 755, including 103 infants.

Former President Taylor got huge support from Nimba in 1989 because the Gios and Manos believed that then-President Doe killed many of their people. By supporting Taylor, they believed their tribe would become stronger and no one would treat them the way Doe did. They wanted to show people that they were capable of doing anything. Doe's soldiers had treated many badly only because they came from Nimba County. To take revenge, the Gio and Mano soldiers began to kill the Mandingoes, whom they believed had supported Doe. The Mandingoes fought back. Ultimately, they all attacked each other, killing thousands. Innocent people from every side suffered—all because of tribalism. It mattered not whether their leader was Doe or Taylor: because of ongoing prejudice between 1990 and 1994, another 150,000 Liberians died.

edgeable enough to think intelligently and act accordingly, we are also learning that we alone are responsible for our actions.

The election results are announced today, the 15th of October 2006. No one party is able to get the 50% needed to win the presidential race. So the two political parties— the Congress for Democracy led by football legend George Weah which pulled the highest votes, followed by the Unity Party headed by Ellen Johnson Sirleaf, the Harvard economist—will have a run-off in two weeks. The campaign resumes.

People will begin to return to where they were before the politicians came along to announce they would change our lives, sharing their big dreams to rebuild Liberia. A great many Liberians have been searching for some new meaning in their personal lives during the past few years. In Liberia today, no social emotion is more widespread than the conviction of personal powerlessness. Ordinary people are shriveled, fragmented, weighed down, beleaguered and imprisoned. Having lived in emptiness for so long, they feel less than human. The capacity to feel, see, hear and touch is shrouded in veils of obscurity.

Thus, no one seems to be growing toward a goal anymore; a sense of purpose and meaning does not exist for the majority. Everything stagnates and everyone's pent-up potential turns into melancholy, despair and eventually self-destruction. The signs are everywhere and that is why many people have been pinning their hopes on this election.

Even the children are excited about the election. They are looking forward to a new Liberia. This is how I tell them to look at the future: "Only within you lies the reality you are looking for. No one can give you anything you don't already have within yourself. No one but your own soul can throw open to you a colored gallery. All that you can be inspired to receive from someone is the opportunity, the impulse to see the world intelligently. People may help you make your dream world visible, but you are the one who has to walk the path and cover the distance to get there."

I will give you details as things progress,
Marvin

Marvin, Mardell Joy and Emily

*Students Winnie Wilson and Linda Tokpah
studying at the peace school*

Peace School Children

AhutinJuah Town

Celebrating Peace in Buchanan, Liberia

Students Fatu Lassana and Blojay Weede
are studying the curriculum
Why Is Everybody Always Picking On Us?
Understanding the Roots of Prejudice

Students of the Peace School with Mr. Davis

Girl pumping water

Lesson 10

Prejudice at Its Worst

"I tell my students that we need to be aware of prejudice as it starts growing inside ourselves, before it bursts into conflict outside. Our awareness of prejudice allows us to pause to examine it for any scrap of truth. We need to stop and think. In the resulting moment of enlightenment, we can be free. This freedom stops prejudice from spreading into hatred, war, genocide and all the devastating consequences that prejudice unchecked can create."

— Marvin Garbeh Davis

Dear Dr. T and Jean,

This particular lesson is the most difficult for the young people, as well as for me, since we have been recent victims of war. But I think that we need to go into this so the children can settle into a broader world view. They need to see that their personal difficulties are a human condition created by prejudice, and not just an isolated incident that happened to them and their families here in Liberia. Even though prejudice is a global issue because it produces *all* human conflict, the roots of prejudice grow in each one of us due to our conditioned thoughts.

I tell my students that we need to be aware of prejudice, as it starts growing inside ourselves, before it bursts into conflict outside. Our awareness of prejudice allows us to pause to examine it for any scrap of truth. We need to stop and think. In the resulting moment of enlightenment, we can be free. This freedom stops prejudice from spreading into hatred, war, genocide and all the devastating consequences that prejudice unchecked can create.

We begin our talk from your curriculum, Dr. T, on the many cruel and destructive forms of prejudice. As we read, I explain that even though these tragedies are difficult to talk about, we need to be informed and allow our awareness to help us. It will enable us to take a "Stop! Think!" moment, to consider what could possibly cause anyone to inflict such harm on other people. Although learning about these forms of prejudices can never right the terrible wrongs they have caused, our awareness of them can help us *prevent* future wrongs from happening in our own lives, and help us *prevent* another civil war here in Liberia. If the people involved in past wrongs had only better understood prejudice, those deeds would never have happened.

I ask the children, "How do you define racism?"

"When you talk about racism," Martin says, "you are talking about the difference between white people and black people."

"Racism is the difference between Liberian people and people from different countries," Cindy adds.

"For me," Christopher points out, "racism is about how my family is different from other people's families."

I accept all their answers, but I delve into the issue of racism a little further. The study of race was originally meant to define people in a useful way—to classify us by who our ancestors were and who we are. To do this, scientists studied physical characteristics—the color of hair or eyes, the size and shape of nose or mouth, the bone structure—the features that make people from one race appear different from people of another. The word "race" in this case is used only for objective descriptions, without prejudice or conflict. The word "racism," however, uses this information in a negative way.

Your curriculum asks: "How did race turn into racism?" Racism is the form of prejudice that judges others based on a stereotyped image. Racism occurs when one group of people believe that they are superior to another group of people. Believing they are better than others allows the self- proclaimed "superior" group to make fun of, or hurt, the "inferior" group. Of all forms of prejudice that exist, racism is one of the most horrible. Nevertheless, it has existed for centuries and is still alive today. In the extreme, this kind of prejudice can create the negative feelings that cause great conflict.

The children and I then move to one of the most devastating forms of prejudice—genocide. When I ask my students about genocide, not one of them seems to have heard the word. I discover that many adults around here don't know the meaning of the word either.

Your curriculum says that the word comes from the Greek word *geno*, meaning "related to" and the Latin word *cida* meaning "killing." Genocide is the crime of deliberately and systematically wiping out a race, culture, or religious group. Targeted members become victims simply because they belong to the group. Reduced to numerical statistics, individuals are completely dehumanized.

The crime of genocide involves many acts committed with intent to destroy—in whole or in part—any designated group. The term "in whole or in part" means that there is no limit to the number of people against whom these acts may be committed. Examples include:

- Killing members of a targeted group
- Causing serious bodily or mental harm to members of the group
- Deliberately inflicting physically destructive conditions of life on the group
- Imposing measures intended to prevent births within the group
- Forcibly transferring children of the group to another group

There are a number of points to note about these acts. I explain to the children that the perpetrator may not only be a state government or its military, but an international organization, a terrorist group or a guerilla organization. The word "destroy" is critical. These acts of coerced removal are carried out with intent to eliminate a deep-rooted group from a territory. To destroy a group's culture, genocidal acts may involve forcing their children to learn different languages and customs.

Genocide is generally considered one of the worst moral crimes committed against any people it controls—by a government or any ruling authority, including that of a guerilla group, a quasi state, a terrorist organization, or an occupying authority. Popular thinking often declares that such horrific practices occurred many years ago and very far away. However, the history of the world shows that never were so many millions of people deliberately killed through genocide as during the 20th century, and mostly by so-called civilized governments.

When I tell the children that more than 340 million people have been victims of genocide in the 20th century alone, many of them are stunned. I make specific reference to the Nazi killing of more than six million Jews from all over Europe.

Martin asks: "What did the Jews do to the Nazi people that made them so angry to have killed them like that?"

Before I can answer, Pius jumps in: "What did innocent civilians do to have been killed by rebels during our war?"

I tell my students that no justification is strong enough to take a person's life. Nor is there any basis for hating another group to the point of wanting to wipe them from the face of the earth. "If you young people can understand this now, the better it will be for our country, and for the world." The people killed in genocide are not casualties of war. They are most often killed by so-called *civilized* governments. People always have a way of exonerating themselves in such situations. Even those who commit genocide have their own motives which they believe are justifiable.

In order to prepare this lesson for my students, I needed to do a lot of research, Dr. T., and study what your curriculum was saying, so I could be as clear as possible in presenting these facts to them. To start, the children and I discuss some of the possible motives for genocide.

There has been considerable research on why a perpetrator would want to destroy a group or, if not destroy the group as such, murder people because of their group membership. Causes are often complex and intertwined, but one can usually extract at least one major motive.

One such motive is to destroy a group that is perceived as a threat to the ruling power. Such, for example, is what happened in the 1970 parliamentary elections in Pakistan. West

Pakistan's military seized East Pakistan, conquered as many Hindus as possible, and murdered more than a million Bengali leaders, intellectuals and professionals.

A second motive involves deeply felt emotions that motivate the destruction of people who are envied, resented or despised. The genocide of Jews throughout history, and in particular during the Holocaust in Germany, was fundamentally an act of religious and ethnic hatred mixed with envy and resentment over their apparent disproportionately high economic and professional achievements.

A third motive for genocide is the pursuit of an ideological transformation of society. In communist societies, for example, genocide targeted landlords, kulaks, nationalist "right wingers" and counterrevolutionaries, who were murdered for resisting transformation or being perceived to be enemies of the ideology.

A fourth motive is so-called purification, or the attempt to eliminate from society what are perceived as alien beliefs, cultures, practices and ethnic groups. Examples are the systematic attempts of China's Mao Tse-tung and the Soviet Union's Joseph Stalin to eliminate disbelievers from their communist societies, and similar attempts by Christians who killed non-believers during the Crusades in the Middle Ages.

Another motive is economic gain, where rapacious colonial powers of such individuals as Belgium's King Leopold (who personally owned the Congo Free State), are the cause of mass murders of tens of millions in the colonies who got in the way, resisted the rape of the colony's wealth, or were worked to death.

Regardless of the motive, the decision is made to attack and destroy those in the out-group. It may be justified as a righteous campaign to exterminate "vermin", to cleanse the society of "filth," to recover "ancient greatness", to save the nation's race, or to "revenge past wrongs."

In its final stage, perpetrators deny that genocide has taken place. The destroyer hides the relevant official evidence, burns bodies, leaves unmarked graves, or invents a reasonable rationale for the killing, such as:

"They were rebels."

"They were killed during the civil war."

"They helped our enemies."

The perpetrators may even harass those who claim that genocide occurred. The most far-reaching official denial today is by the Turkish government regarding the genocidal murder of more than a million Armenians during World War I. According to the Turks, the Armenians died as a result of an invasion by Russia, when the Young Turkish government attempted to deport hostile Armenians to a different part of the country for their own protection.

One of the unfathomable things about the act of genocide is that all normal constraints against killing are set aside in the name of a so-called "higher aim." For Adolph Hitler, the higher aim was "racial purity" of the German people. I ask the children, "Is this a 'higher' aim?" How can murder, the lowest form of human behavior, be twisted so much that it convinces thousands of minds to believe that it is the 'highest'? How can a desire for 'racial purity' be acceptable justification for causing millions of people to be wiped from the face of the earth? How can any human being see this as a higher aim?" Only if those minds have been tied tightly enough by the knots of conditioned thinking, that en masse, they are hypnotized to react when told to take aim, and shoot.

For Stalin in the Soviet Union and Mao Tse-tung in China, the "higher aim" was economic. Millions were killed in order to "build socialism." While it is difficult to even admit that this kind of human behavior has taken place in modern times, our hope is that by looking at these examples, our knowledge and understanding of their causes can help prevent them from happening again.

The children and I also discuss the topic of "ethnic cleansing" that appears in your curriculum. Ethnic cleansing is an insultingly polite term for genocide. People try to hide its terrible meaning by using a euphemism. One of the worst forms of prejudice, ethnic cleansing is a well-defined policy of a particular group to systematically eliminate another group from a given territory on the basis of religious, ethnic, or national origin. Such a policy involves violence and is very often connected with military operations. It is achieved by all possible means, from discrimination to extermination, and entails violations of human rights.

The purpose of ethnic cleansing is to remove the conditions for potential and actual opposition of any kind, by physically removing any potentially or actually hostile ethnic communities. Although it has been motivated by a doctrine that claims that an ethnic group is literally "unclean" (as in the case of the Jews of medieval Europe), more often it has been a brutal way of ensuring that total control can be asserted over an area. Ethnic cleansing is often also accompanied by efforts to eradicate all physical traces of the expelled ethnic group, by destroying their cultural artifacts, religious sites and physical records.

From early 1992 until late 1995, the Bosnian campaign, involving three historically bitter rival groups in the former Yugoslavia, led to the systematic genocide of thousands of ethnic Albanian (Muslim) civilians. After the break-up of Yugoslavia, the Orthodox Christian Serbs and Catholic Croats, in their quest to annex Bosnia and Herzegovina, committed mass murder, rape, destruction, detention, and deportation against the Muslims in their massive ethnic cleansing.

"Silent ethnic cleansing" is a term coined in the mid-1990s by observers of the Yugoslav war. Western media generally focused on atrocities perpetrated by the Serbs. Observers dubbed these atrocities "silent" on the grounds that the media wasn't giving equal-time coverage to all sides. Who should possibly stay silent and what could possibly be cleansing about anyone's death?

Closer to home, the 2004 mass raping and killing campaign in Sudan have become widely known. Janjaweed militias (non-Arab shepherds with the support of the Sudanese government and troops) organized a campaign to rid themselves of 80 black African groups from the Darfur region of Western Sudan. Thousands of people were murdered, and human rights groups say there was a systematic campaign of rape, intended to humiliate and punish non-Arab groups. What causes people to act in this way?

The next issue in your curriculum is slavery. *Slavery* is a system wherein one person can actually own another, demanding labor and other services. Historically, slavery has been used to secure forced labor from slaves with no right of refusal, no right to leave and no reimbursement other than food, accommodation and clothing. A specific form of slavery, known as chattel slavery, is absolute legal ownership of persons, including the legal right to buy and sell them.

Although there is no longer any state that legally recognizes, or will enforce, a claim by a person to a right of property over another, the abolition of slavery does not mean that it has ceased to exist. According to verifiable reports, there are millions of people throughout the world, mainly children, in conditions of virtual slavery, as well as in various forms of servitude, which are in many respects similar to slavery. Child slavery was on the rise in 2003. There are countless other forms of servitude such as pawnage, bonded labor and servile concubinage, which are not slavery in the narrow legal sense. Critics claim that people are stretching the definition and practice of slavery.

Although officially banned, slavery is still practiced widely. African United Nations peace workers have acknowledged the existence of slavery in Sudan, where its markets continue to sell humans. An advocacy group linked with Anti Slavery International states that, worldwide, there are 27 million people in virtual slavery today. In Mali, the price of slaves has been reduced to a low of US$40 for young adult male laborers and US$1,000 in Thailand for HIV-free young females suitable for use in brothels (where they frequently contract HIV). This represents the price paid to sellers, who are sometimes the parents of these children. Today's rates represent the lowest price that has ever been paid for a slave in raw labor terms. The price of a comparable male slave in 1850 America would have been about US$1,000 in the currency of the time, which represents US$38,000 in today's dollars. Therefore, slaves, at least of that category, now cost only one thousandth (0.1%) of their price 150 years ago. Such are the economics of contemporary slavery.

In some parts of the world, slavery is practiced in subtle, less noticeable ways. An abusive husband may treat his wife inhumanely because he feels he owns her. An oppressive boss may feel he has the right to degrade his employees because he is paying their salaries. Parents may violate the rights of their children because of a misdirected desire for power and control. Many people believe that slavery emerged simply as an economic necessity of convenience. Is it possible that slavery developed as justification for people to do what they want to people they disrespect and dislike?

Some of these instances represent the worst prejudices in human history. Because it defies common sense to go to such extremes to eliminate other human beings, it is difficult for us to understand why such injustices occur. The more the students and I think about this together, the more we find it astonishing that people can treat each other in such cruel and inhumane ways.

I ask the young people, "What could cause a group of people to deliberately organize the destruction of another group of people? Who is it easier to hate, and want to kill: individuals or groups? Which seems less personal for you? What do you think about these so-called higher aims of genocide? Can you really find any good reason or any justifiable cause?"

Marion says, "I can hate somebody but not to the point that I would like to kill them."

"When people make me angry, I hate them," Trokon says. "It happens to me often, but it does not lead me to fight, or want the other person to die."

"There is no reason to kill another person," Cindy declares. "We all have hurt someone one time or another. If everybody tries to kill somebody, then who will remain on this earth?"

"Life is very important. No one should hurt other people. To me, killing someone is just wrong," Pius states.

Ben adds, "There can be no good reason for killing someone. Just ask all those who killed people during the war. They will not explain anything good except nonsense."

I cannot help but wonder if these children would continue to think and act in this way if there were another civil war and people they know were killed.

I tell the students about the history of man's inhumanity to man and that we have always had minorities. In ancient Greece and Rome, the bulk of work was done by slaves drawn from the most common type of minority: other ethnic groups. Other targeted minorities were defined by their religions or occupations.

During the Middle Ages, craft and trade "guilds" passed their skills from one generation to the next and kept outsiders from getting in. Kings, queens, nobles and even religious leaders held great power. Each of these influential authorities held within them the same potential: to be divisive or to be supportive, depending on the controlling influence of that human's prejudicial conditioning. Those who grew the food and made the goods everyone needed were at the bottom of society.

India is a country in which some people believe in previous existences. They believe that how we live today depends on how we lived in an earlier life. India is also a country with a caste system. A caste is a hereditary group whose members intermarry only with each other. Each has its own occupations, its own rules relating to kinship, its particular brand of tribal traditions, its particular idiosyncratic customs and even its own, specific diet. Castes are graded in a social hierarchy in which each person expects respect from inferior groups and gives respect to superior groups. According to their generally accepted beliefs, the caste into which one is born depends on one's *karma*—one's accumulated "good" and "bad" deeds in a previous existence. The way to achieve higher status in future incarnations is to accept one's station in life and live accordingly.

There are many castes, but the lowest are the Shudras, who today constitute most of India's artisans and laborers. Below the Shudras are castes with no designations—regarded as "Untouchables" because of their association with "unclean" occupations. Some scavenge and some clean public toilets with their bare hands. These groups have always been subject to considerable prejudice. The great Indian leader Mohandas K. Gandhi tried to ensure that they were treated humanely and bestowed on them the name Harijan, or children of God, by which they are now popularly known.

Even though the Indian constitution now outlaws "untouchability" and provides each state with special benefits for these people, the Untouchables still exist and continue to do the work of their ancestors. Although having one's life dictated by hereditary differences seems obviously unjust, most Hindus regard the caste system as a fair and sensible system. They believe it because that's what they've been conditioned to believe, and because this prejudice has been passed from one generation to another.

I ask the students, "Have you every heard of the term 'pecking order'? It's a way of life natural to the animal kingdom in which the stronger creature survives by dominating the weaker. The stronger traits are genetically passed on, to ensure the survival of the species. In the same way, if one of our tribal ancestors were sick, injured, or too old to work, he or she might have been sent away to ensure the safety and comfort of the tribe. Sometimes the weak member was simply sent away to die—a cruel act, but one the tribe deemed necessary for its survival. Survival for our ancestors meant that everyone had to be fit and able to do his or her job. This is called 'survival of the fittest'.

"Human beings have carried this thinking into modern times, even though the world is vastly different than it was thousands of years ago. Even though they live in security and safety, many people continue to look at the world in terms of a pecking order. They act like members of primitive tribes still trying to prove who is most correct, strongest and best. But today, this way of thinking is more likely to cause trouble than to achieve safety. Today, we say we want to live together in peace, but strongly identifying with a 'tribe' only delivers us the opposite. Today, fighting to be the most powerful group works against our security. It creates conflict between people and keeps us from acting as a single species.

"Today, majority groups deal with minorities in usually one of two ways. Minorities must either become part of the mainstream culture, or be persecuted by it. In the process of becoming part of the culture, values and ways of thinking are exchanged and shared between a minority and the majority. Persecution and oppression based on ideological thinking, on the other hand, have separated people and led to segregation, slavery, and genocide. As we can see, prejudice can lead to the deadliest outcomes imaginable, including the annihilation of millions and millions of people.

"Identifying ourselves with a particular group can lead us to carry out some of the worst forms of prejudice that we have talked about. If you identify yourself strongly with your church, do you think you might want to fight members of other churches if there was a conflict? What about a political party, a football team, your tribe or country? People who have committed some of these acts did so because they aligned themselves with a particular group and wanted to ensure that the group survived at all costs."

Thinking of your words, Dr. T, I wrap up by saying, "We need to see that we have been conditioned for millennia. We have been taught to believe that in order to be physically secure, to have food, clothing and housing, we need to identify psychologically with our particular group. Therefore, one's group identity is linked to survival, no matter what, both mentally and physically especially through the old brain's fight or flight mechanism. Today, all of this creates division; it fragments the human race and hence creates conflict.

"What is the most amazing fact of all? It is that all of this starts in our own brain and is continually being projected as our 'reality'—so we are constantly recreating and sustaining the conflict by the way we think!"

Today I am happy that this particular class is over, for all the terrible suffering caused by prejudice is difficult to entertain in one's mind and hold in one's heart. Still, I believe that when the children know what prejudice is, when they can talk about it intelligently and recognize it in action—they will be able to *prevent* it, and such a result will be more than worthwhile.

Take care,
Marvin

Lesson 11
The Problem with Perfection

"I am teaching young people to understand the causes of the problems that have left our country one of the poorest and least developed in the world. Many of them are enduring the consequences of the war, but don't understand the causes. By teaching the causes of violence—even if it is teaching only a small group of young Liberians—it is my hope that they will be able to resolve their differences without fighting, now that they have seen the results of war and violence."

— *Marvin Garbeh Davis*

Dear Dr. T. and Jean…

I heard one mother tell her daughter the other day, "If you don't respect me, you will never get any blessing from us in your entire life." The little girl ran away shivering. She was scared. How could she live her life without being blessed by her parents?

Many of us are brought up to be "good"— meaning that we accept and do what we are told by adults. Learning to be intelligent is the ability to understand what is "right" and "good." We are not likely to be aware that this "learning to be good" is a continuous process in our lives. So we grow up following the ideals of the old, rigid definition and never evolve.

I lived only with my father from the time I was nine years old until I reached fifteen, when he remarried. My father was a tapper, working in a low-end agricultural job, and he wanted me to be successful, to be a good person in life. Being successful meant we had to be educated, to score good grades in school, never get into trouble or disappoint school authorities. Then we could get good jobs, marry, raise children and enjoy the good life.

Typical of many parents, someone like my father considered school to be the training ground for young people. It was worse for children from single-parent homes. In many instances, parents just surrendered that responsibility to the school. If the school knew how to provide education for children, then it must also know what was right for the children. Thus, the discipline, training and making of a good child rested with the school.

When I was in fifth grade, all the students feared Mr. Sampson, more commonly called "Teacher Pepper." If one of us did something "'wrong" at home, the parents would come to the school and pass the job of disciplining to Teacher Pepper. Everyone knew Teacher Pepper. I overheard one mother telling her friend to take her troublesome son to Teacher Pepper, because if she did, her son would change.

One day, a girl falsely told Teacher Pepper that I had littered papers over the classroom floor. When he told me to pick them up, I told him that I wasn't going to, because she had lied. Teacher Pepper never took "No" for an answer, and he took this one personally. In front of the whole class, he whipped me. I cried and cried until my friends laughed and then felt sorry for me. For two days I could barely sit down. When I went home and related the story to my father, he told me that if I continued misbehaving at school, he would come to school and pass me to Teacher Pepper himself.

"How can you be a good person if you defy your teacher?" he questioned me. He did not care to listen to my side of the story or even want to look at the marks on my buttocks.

So I continued going to school, afraid to ask the teacher anything, even if I had a question. Many students went to school like that, afraid to question, to gain ideas from teachers. To many parents, that is being good; that is the route to success.

There were many times when I was unhappy. Why couldn't my father see or listen to my side of a problem before defending the school authorities? Why did he believe the school all the time, as if the school authorities were angels? Why couldn't he try to imagine how I felt about this brute? Why couldn't he at least listen to me after my ongoing nightmares of Teacher Pepper frowning at me like a monster and then choking me?

Yet I wanted to be good, to be somebody. If my grades were good, then it meant I was listening and not arguing. I was being a good boy. If the grades were bad, then I was making trouble at school again and needed some whipping from Teacher Pepper.

To assuage my soreness and dislike for school authorities, my father would say to me, "All educated people have a story. Education is not easy; you suffer, then you enjoy. You see how I am suffering now. It is because I did not go to school. I don't want you to be like me."

I believed my father. I was brought up to believe all he said, and that I had to suffer to be educated. Thus I took it all from Teacher Pepper for three years until, for some unknown reason, he was dismissed from the school system. But he had lots of replacements. Some of them whipped even harder.

According to my father, if I suffered, I would be educated. If I was educated, then I would not live like a tapper, and I would not sleep in the rat hole my brother and I shared with our father. I was scared of so many things. I was scared that we ate only once during the day and once at night. I was scared of how my dad woke up in the middle of night to get ready for work. I was scared about never having enough to eat and scared of hearing my father always complaining about money. I did not want to be like my dad, so I listened and followed the ideas of adults without questioning them. If that was the way to be good, to be somebody, then I had to follow that path. I thought adults knew what was right and good for me, so I bowed down to them.

Many of us have parents and/or other elders who instill thoughts and feelings into us. When this happens, we rarely question what's told to us. In our Liberian society, it is disrespectful or rude for young people to challenge or question things said to us by our elders. The child who questions what he or she is told by adults is not likely to be blessed by them.

In short, I was conditioned to believe that my parents and elders knew what was right and good for me. I did not listen to my own inner voice. So I reached a point where I could not tell the difference between what was good or bad, right or wrong. I became robotic, uncertain of any move unless I was told to move. I needed confirmation from others to feel safe enough to take each next step.

I truly believe my parents and elders meant well for me. How could I speak ill of a man who worked as a tapper, a job that allowed a man only a few years to live unless he was as strong as an ox? How could I blame elders in our community who looked out for all the children? But my parents and the elders around me did not realize that preaching good-ness all the time created conflict inside me. I felt conflicted between their judgment and an impossible ideal. If I did something they considered bad, they judged me for being less than perfect. If I did something they considered good, they praised me, holding me up against an image of perfection they had in their minds. Either way, I felt conflicted.

When my grades were good, my dad would say to me, "If you continue like this, one day you could become a superintendent on this plantation where you are now growing up as a tapper's son." Only an educated person could achieve this ideal: to be a superintendent—at that time, one of the best jobs on the plantation.

For me, perfection as an ideal was destructive. I tried to work hard every day to please other people. Even if I tried hard and felt that I had achieved something, there was no way of giving myself a pat on the shoulders until "others" confirmed or assured me that I had done something right or good. I felt like I was climbing a mountain with a rope tied around my waist, a rope controlled by people pulling me back down. Every step I made toward the top was countered by a step back to the bottom.

Because I could not live up to the expectations of my parents and elders, I felt their prejudice, and built mine. I saw a line between us—they were them, and I was me. While they had good intentions, their attempts to forcibly make me "good" ended up by making me feel more and more worthless.

We need to help our children understand what creates behavior—what makes us act in certain ways. We need to help them understand who they really are, and not condition them to act in ways that create conflict. This will prevent our children from experiencing insecurity, self-doubt and low self-esteem when they grow up. The intelligent way to bring about good behavior is not through judgment and comparison, but through intelligence and learning.

Most of us hurry our children too much; we make them grow up too fast too soon. We push our children to achieve, to succeed, to be somebody, to be the best, according to our own definition of success. We push them in their early years toward many kinds of achievements and expose them to experiences that tax their capacity to adapt. Pushed and pushed, but never honored for who they really are, they grow up with a fear of failure. Forced to excel too quickly, they often feel hatred for, turn against, withdraw from, or lose interest in the very subjects of their elders' desires. The danger here is that they skip spaces in their childhood, or their growth ladder, which they never have the opportunity to inhabit again. We make them walk without crawling. In the end, they are likely to build resentment, and rebel in later life.

Nothing is wrong with ensuring that our children succeed, but offering them sensible, affectionate nurturing is most supportive. Many of my colleagues who are teachers think I make too big an issue of this point, but I think the whole school system is intensely focused on the philosophy that "if they do *this*, they will get *that*." There is so little in the school system that asks us to accept students just the way they are. There is only acceptance of those things that agree with some particular teacher's idea of what should happen in any given moment.

One student said to me, "You know, I am never trusted in my house. And I never do anything right. The only thing my parents tell me is that I am stupid." When we grow up in an environment like this, how can we find our real selves?

When we hear parents say that they love their children, they are talking about conditional love. "I will love you if you get good grades. I will love you if you wear a certain type of hairstyle, if you stop wearing baggy pants, if you stop walking about after school, if your friends are the right kind of people."

Their love is not based on "I love you because you are my child" or "I love you because this is the way you are." When parents' love is conditional, there is no way that their children will ever measure up to their expectations. As a result, children simply feel unworthy.

Constantly bowing to our past, our parents and our home training ensure that these actions persist into our adult lives, in turn determining how we see and interact in the world. This trained conditioning warps our behavior. We fashion our lives according to the desires of our parents and elders. We work so hard to please them that we leave no room to please ourselves. This gives rise to conformity. Because we are always trying to please others, we try to live up to their standards. Assuming their thinking must be better than ours, we are blind to the fact that their conceptual view of the ideal world is only a stereotype. It is our job to use intelligence to avoid passing on information to our children that has no verifiable scientific basis.

When individuals or groups establish ideals, it creates conflict within the human race as a whole. Yet striving to be perfect, to be right, still goes on all over the world. The idea that "I" or "my group" represents the right, pure, perfect way, that *we* are the ones who know and *they* are the ones who must follow, always leads to violence and suffering.

There is another side to this. The more we are locked up in other people's expectations of our lives, the more we look down on ourselves. This not only keeps us from being ourselves, but separates us from all the people around us. We feel increasingly inferior, the more exalted we hold that sense of what should or should not be. Unless we turn away from this tremendous alienation from ourselves and from everyone around us, we will lose ourselves irretrievably. We will never discover our innate abilities. We all have them. We just have to pull off the blanket that is smothering them.

Our children grow up believing that beauty is connected only to mini skirts and baggy trousers, hairstyle and lipstick. We don't teach them that they are beautiful because they are uniquely created. Instead, they learn that beauty arises in people who fear their God and act according to the teachings of their book's guidelines. We tell our children that only these devoted followers will be rewarded. Some texts have been so twisted that their believers see their God walking behind them with an axe, ready to cut them down.

We cannot remain prisoners of the past. We need to awaken intelligence so that together, in the present, we can reshape the future.

In our Peace School, I ask Janet, "What do you think about your parents wanting you to be good?"

She answers, "It is hard to please my parents, maybe anyone. Because there is so much pressure on me to do well, I do not understand what I do. I don't do what I like, but instead I do what I hate. I don't do the good I want to do; instead, I do the bad that I do not want to do."

Janet's explanation points to human imperfection and the mental anguish young people undergo when they are pressured to be good.

Hammering our ideals into the heads of our children will not make them perfect, because we ourselves are not perfect. We only compound conflict and prevent our children from using their personal intelligence. Trying to be perfect creates conflict—because *no one* is perfect.

I was invited by a youth group to speak to them on how we can avoid violence during the campaign and again after the election results are announced. On my way to the program, I saw a woman who pointed to me and then asked a young man who was standing nearby, "Is this the man they are waiting for, to speak to the young people?"

The young man answered, "Yes."

"But why is he wearing jeans and a T-shirt with sneakers on?" she asked. "I thought they said that the man is educated." They were speaking in the Bassa language, which the woman assumed I did not understand. I did not let on that I did.

As I walked to the program I started to think about the woman. For her, being educated meant that one dressed in a certain way. Or if one is invited to speak to people, one has to dress formally. She did not believe I was educated, because she had been conditioned to believe that educated people have to be well dressed. This also meant that anyone casually dressed had to be uneducated.

During the war, Mr. Taylor told the young men in his army that the peacekeepers had come to take away their motherland and if they succeeded, the whole army would become the foreigners' prisoners. He was their leader, an authority who convinced these young people that he had their best interests at heart. When they believed him, many of these young men became just as prejudiced. Out of fear and pride for their country, they followed his instructions, obeyed his rules and fought. Those who dared to dance to a different tune got his wrath. However, many of the others who followed unquestioningly were left to rot in unknown valleys and jungles.

Although we now live in a modern world, whatever that means, we still carry within us our ancestral nature. I ask my students, "Do you remember learning about our ancestors who lived in tribes and groups because there was a sense of security and safety by living in numbers? An individual felt safe being in a group rather than being alone. That was the beginning of *identification*, the need to belong to a group and keep it together for self-preservation. Our ancestors then developed repeated practices and rituals, which were designed to keep the group together. To create a special identity, these practices became more established customs, which time turned into traditions that finally grew into a fully developed culture, which was then passed from generation to generation."

Today, even though the world is vastly different from thousands of years ago, many of us still live and act like those primitive tribes, still trying to prove that ours is the best and the strongest. And we are ready to go any lengths to prove this.

In Liberia we live in tribes, each having its own culture which has been maintained for years and is still passed on to the children. To ensure that its customs and traditions are kept intact, every tribe is bent on making sure that no one downplays its culture. People still look out for members of their own tribe. Sometimes qualified people are denied opportunities solely because of their tribal origins.

We all really want to live and survive in peace. Tribal identification winds up delivering the opposite. Fighting to be the most powerful works *against* our security. It creates conflict and keeps us from acting as a single tribe, a single nation, a single race—the human race.

We came into this world already conditioned and prejudiced. We were socialized never to question the programming of our birth culture. Hence, many of our beliefs today could stem from an old tribal inheritance that we have been conditioned to claim as our legacy.

I ask the students, "What does it means to be good?"

Janet answers, "To be good is to respect my parents and elders."

Thomas Johnson says, "Being good is to study hard and obey what the teacher says."

And Marion Dean adds, "Being good is going to Sunday school and treating other people as you would have them treat you."

I notice all the children nodding their heads, and say, "So, you agree that you have been brought up to be good, and you believe that being good is important in life." I see more earnest nods around the room. "Why?" I ask.

"If you are good, you can become a big man in your country," says James Williams.

"You can have a long life and many blessings if you are good," Thomas Johnson says.

"Everyone will say to your parents, 'You have a good child,'" says Cindy, "and this will make your parents proud of you."

While it is true that all the children agree that it is important to be good in life, they all have a problem with the way their parents and elders teach them to be good.

"It is good to tell your child to be good, but when my parents beat me because they want me to be good, it scares me," Marie Jackson declares.

"My parents don't beat me if I do something that is bad to them. My father only shouts and shouts at me all day. Sometimes his shouting is worse than his beating," Ben Dickson says.

Marie Johnson shares her ordeal with the class: "I live with my father and stepmother. My stepmother never bothers me if I do something she thinks is wrong. She waits for my father to come home. That is when all hell breaks loose. My father will yell, curse and slap me. When my stepmother asks me to do something now, I only want to do it right for my father. And when it is time for him to come home, I start to worry, hoping and praying that I have done the right thing. And sometimes when I am lucky and my father says I have done the right thing, instead of being happy I feel worthless. At such times, 'good' doesn't mean anything to me anymore."

Conditioning someone to be perfect is neither constructive nor helpful. Being told we should be perfect can create conflict inside us, sometimes causing us to doubt our self-worth. High standards are admirable, but if we are forced to live up to impossibly high standards, we experience conflict and pain. If our ideal of 'being good' is someone else's 'bad', then we again judge ourselves and create more conflict.

There is a huge difference between conditioning and educating, but when we are young and learning, it is difficult to see that difference. Early on, we need intelligent guidance to help us make appropriate decisions. This is education. But sometimes authorities believe they know better than we do, and want to condition us to accept their beliefs without question. Some will take advantage of our conditioning by telling us anything to make us fight and kill *their* enemies. Some nourish us in a healthy and constructive direction, while others poison us with selfish and destructive advice. We can't figure out who is telling the truth and who isn't, and this prevents us from getting the education we need.

It is important to understand the difference between being educated to use constructive and intelligent thinking, and being conditioned to believe destructive and ignorant thoughts. Understanding the difference between conditioning and education is what gives us real power.

We must question any organized belief system to find out for ourselves if it represents truth or falsehood, health or destruction. If we don't question the established ways of society, any authority can take advantage of us. We then act like robots, mechanical beings, programmed and controlled by others. If we don't understand prejudice at its roots and end it before it begins, we are destined to pass our prejudices on to our children, in the same way they were passed to us.

One of the greatest truths is the fact that life is difficult. Once we see this truth, we can gather the courage to transcend it. Once we truly understand and accept it, then life is no longer difficult. Once it is accepted, the fact that life is difficult no longer matters.

Liberians are a group of people who understand this truth. When we reflect on the desperate conditions of our lives over the past fifteen years, we can easily acknowledge that life is indeed difficult. But Liberians are a resilient people too. We understand that if we accept the fact that life is difficult, we can easily transcend the problems associated with our lives. After spending a night visiting with our family, a friend of mine from Senegal asked me how Liberians have been managing their lives without light.

"It is simple," I tell him. "For us, in our world, light does not exist. So why worry about something we don't have? To live without electricity no longer matters. We just want to get by one day at a time."

"Your people are a resilient lot," my friend concludes.

It is true; resilience is the stuff Liberians are made of. Even the children know it. They walk to school. Their fees are rarely paid on time. Some stay home for days waiting and hoping for their parents to get the money for school fees. Many wear worn-out uniforms and walk in bare feet. Many hardly eat one square meal daily. But one can never tell what goes on in the hearts of these young people just by looking at them. They always wear a smile on their faces.

During the last visit before I finally came home, I was scared. I doubted that I could live in Liberia. But when I looked around and saw how people, even in more desperate straits, got along with their lives without complaining, I learned a new lesson about life. I realized that problems are the cutting edge that distinguishes success from failure. Problems call forth our courage and our wisdom. If we want to encourage growth of the human spirit, we must enhance the human capacity to solve problems. Benjamin Franklin got it right when he said, "Those things that hurt, instruct."

I have been here for almost two years now. I am learning to understand the difficulties that people face every day. Instead of fearing the pain involved in those difficulties, I am confronting and solving problems every day. And in solving my problems, I help others confront their own frustration, grief and sadness when they feel powerless in difficult situations. Instead of moaning incessantly, noisily, about the enormity of my problems or burdens, or making others feel that my difficulties represent a unique kind of affliction, I am developing the discipline and the basic tools required to solve life's problems.

More importantly, I am teaching young people to understand the causes of the problems that have left our country one of the poorest and least developed in the world. Many of them are enduring the consequences of the war, but don't understand the causes. By teaching the causes of violence—even if it is teaching only a small group of young Liberians—it is my hope that they will be able to resolve their differences without fighting, now that they have seen the results of war and violence.

The real joy comes from making the most of our lives in any situation. It comes from a fervent desire to make our lives more worthwhile and to leave positive marks on the lives of the people we touch. Many of us cry for peace, to make the world a better place, but sometimes we expect others to take that lead. This is everybody's personal responsibility. The world is laid down to prepare a way for us to see how we can use our innate abilities to make it better. But to do this we must step forward, each one of us in our own, unique way.

I am learning to step across my part of the universe by developing a mature awareness of the biases and prejudices that are a residue of my personal upbringing. This awareness represents a new way of thinking:—silencing the familiar, and embracing the strange. This transition, like many in our lives, has been problematic and painful for me. But I am gradually working my way through it all, giving up old, cherished notions, abandoning deep-rooted ways of doing things, and looking at life in new ways.

Many people are unwilling or unable to suffer the pain of giving up the old, so they cling, often forever, to their old patterns of thinking and behaving, failing to negotiate any crisis or new development, and missing the opportunity to grow up and experience the joyful sense of rebirth that accompanies a successful transition into greater maturity. Giving up something that we deem part of us can be painful. It means negotiating a new balance. I am re-learning, re-negotiating the curves and corners of my life, giving up parts of my self that no longer serve me as a human being.

The only alternative is not to travel on life's journey at all. It may seem strange, but most people do choose this—they stop short, in order to avoid the pain of giving up parts of themselves. They shun the opportunity to relish the rebirths of their minds.

I know what it is to give up part of myself so that I can cross the threshold into a new life. I know it because I undergo that pain every day. But I am making that effort, and the rewards are many. I am learning to understand prejudice at its roots, and how to end it before it ever develops into a problem in my mind. In this way, I am destined to pass no prejudices on to my children, so they will pass none on to theirs—and that is exhilarating.

Sincerely yours,
Marvin

Lesson 12

Preventing Peace

"One important step in preventing conflict and creating peace is for us to avoid identifying with tribe-like groups or organizations. We must also avoid dwelling on painful memories of the past, and understand that the past is gone and that we have the intelligence to act differently in the present. If we teach our children to understand the effect of the past on their thinking now, and start a fresh life of their own, the past will never lay claim to their lives. When we prevent prejudice, we eliminate the very thing that prevents peace."

— *Marvin Garbeh Davis*

Dear Dr. T. and Jean…

A cloud of fear hangs over our nation. Liberians remember our civil war with horror, dreading that another might descend. As a result, they are doing all they can to ensure that war never breaks out here again.

We protect and isolate ourselves inwardly and outwardly. We have begun building defenses mentally, so that we will not be hurt in the future. We reflect on the past over and over, resolved never to repeat the tragedy. However, as we continue to cling to the old, familiar methods of security for our people, their culture and traditions, we are building more barriers to peace.

Some people believe we fought the war because we were not patriotic. Or not nationalistic. Others believe that the war was a curse on us, because we were not living as their God commanded.

They say that we need to change our ways; otherwise, their God will punish us again. These Liberians believe this is the way to bring about peace. But how can this bring peace when each group claims that its words are the best and only true ones to be followed? How can this bring peace when these groups are divided against each other?

There is a terrible irony here. We are conditioned to believe that this is a means for peace and salvation, yet due to the fact that conditioned thinking is divisive, any duty-bound belief system will conflict with other systems of belief and eventually create war. Every war is, at its roots, ideological. We are killing each other over ideals. Yet we continue doing the same thing over and over again—creating the ideal that is divisive, the ideal we think will protect us. When this creates conflict, we reiterate that we need to be peaceful. We fall back again on our divisive, tribal ideals of "peace"—and we are at it once more!

Politicians are saying that we need to teach our children to be more patriotic if we don't want another war. How can teaching patriotism bring peace to our country when we have hundreds of political parties and interest groups, all of which claim to know the best way forward for peace and national reconciliation? Which group's formula are we going to use in teaching patriotism to our children?

Our intellectual ideals speak eloquently about peace; yet our actions remain divisive, antagonistic and self-centered. How can we bring about peace when we teach our children that only *our* culture and traditions are valid, and that the culture and traditions of people different from us are not good? When we think like a group of squirrels locked in a hole, terrified that other tribes will attack us or have something against us, how can peace be possible?

People say "Love thy neighbor," but this implies a pre-existing fear of our neighbors. In Liberia, there is much preaching of "reconciliation" but this suggests an underlying meaning that *our* tribe must stick together so no *other* tribe can conquer us. How can a nation so deeply fragmented have peace when the breath of prejudice fills our skies?

Stephen, one of my students, gives me a fine illustration of how our actions prevent peace, even though our intentions are good:

"My mother and another woman were good friends, and due to their friendship, our two families became close. We used to eat in each other's homes. The children from our neighbor's house used to come to our house to watch TV, since they did not have one. My mother had a misunderstanding with this neighbor. It strained our relationship so much, that the elders in our community called the parties together and resolved the problem. My mother and her friend made so-called peace, but that peace does not look like peace to me. The woman told her children not to eat in our house or watch TV there anymore. When my mother noticed this, she told my two sisters and me not to go to our neighbor's house or eat with them either. Now we are very careful how we interact with that family. We are living together 'in peace', but we don't know our neighbors' needs and they don't know ours.

"Before my mother and her friend had their misunderstanding, I used to come home from school and eat with my friends if my mother had not prepared lunch. Now if lunch is ready after school we just sit there and wait for my mother to finish cooking. I am sure the children from the other family do the same. And we can't say anything about it. My father says there is no bad peace, that at least we are not at each other's throats. But this does not feel like a good peace to me."

Rose, another student in our Peace School who has a Ghanaian father and a Liberian mother, shares a similar story:

"One day I got into a fight with a friend," says Rose. "She got injured below her elbows. My mother said, if you want our family and those people to live in peace, then stay at your own house. If you stay in your place and they stay in their place, we will be in peace. I don't know. The girl used to be my best friend before the fight, but now we don't visit each other anymore. I have to walk a long distance to see my other friend. My mother says it's better, because she does not have to settle disputes anymore. 'We are in peace,' as my mother says, but we are afraid of each other. Everyone walks their own line. How can you be in peace with someone and be afraid of them, or not be able to speak to them?"

Instead of being conditioned to think in the strained model of peace that our ancestors have practiced, it is more appropriate to think about and understand what people do to *prevent* peace. Rose's mother has conditioned her to think and behave according to her own concept of "peaceful" ways. This obsesses her daughter so much that she stays at home, remains isolated and stews over how to avoid offending her friends. Every thought she thinks about being peaceful isolates her more and intensifies the conflict between them. When Rose acts in the way her mother perceives as being peaceful, she feels judged, and fragmented.

"I feel like someone is pulling me. It makes me angry and I sometimes feel bad about myself. And I kind of want to feel like doing something different from what my mother wants me to do, but I am afraid," Rose explains.

When we allow people we perceive as authorities to persuade us to behave in a way they believe is right or peaceful, we tend to make ourselves fit their description. Yet, each of us is an intelligent being with the ability to understand what prevents peace and what it takes to act in a nonviolent way. We do not need an authority to tell us how to be. We must look at all the evidence available and achieve an insight of our own about what it means to try to be peaceful.

The use of words such as "should" and "ought" create conflict. I ask the children what they think about the following sentences:

"You ought to have known better."

"You should have acted like a gentleman."

"You should have noticed that he was not a friend."

As we discuss the impact of such words, they realize how "should" and "ought" triggers us into acting from conditioning and rendering judgment on others. "You ought to have acted like a gentleman" implies that the person is not a gentleman. Though being a gentleman might be a good thing, we are saying that this person did not act in a certain manner that meets *our* standard definition of 'gentleman'. That is a judgment, not a fact. It is our opinion, not necessarily the truth.

One important step in preventing conflict and creating peace is for us to avoid passing judgments as truth. We must also avoid dwelling on painful memories of the past and understand that the past is gone and that we have the intelligence to act differently in the present. If we teach our children to understand the effect of the past on their thinking now and start a fresh life of their own, the past will never lay claim to their lives. When we prevent prejudice, we eliminate the very thing that prevents peace.

We need to see the difference between a fact and an opinion, between first-hand information and an assumption. When exploring the cause of a problem, it is wise to be thorough. Falling in love with the first answer that comes into our consciousness makes us naturally leap to conclusions, grasp at quick guesses, and lock ourselves in assumptions.

One day the students arrived at the Peace School not knowing I was already in my office. Those who were not already sitting in the classroom either lounged on the porch or ran around the building waiting to see me arrive. At 4:00 pm, the time to start class, all the students came in. Moments later, my car drove into the garage and I heard the students shouting, "Mr. Davis is here, Mr. Davis is here." To their surprise it was a mechanic who stepped out of the car. The car had been in the garage all day, so the mechanic had just driven it to the office. He asked for me and they told the man I was not in the office. Suddenly I walked into their midst and they were shocked.

They had based their conclusions on the fact that I had always driven the car myself to come to Peace School. They had also ignored the possibility that Common Ground might have a guest who was using the car. They never considered any other possibility, falsely concluding that because the car was gone, I was not yet in the office. This was a simple but excellent lesson for them about conditioned thinking.

When my students demonstrate old thinking, or appear closed to new information, I like to remind them that it is far better to *learn* about ourselves than to *protect* ourselves from new thoughts. By doing so, we can eliminate the thoughts and feelings that prevent peace.

Dr. T and Jean, do you recall my telling you before about Mai, who had heard some people say that I was a "heart man"? Because her father badly wanted to send his daughter to our Peace School, he made up his mind to come and see me at the office to find out the truth for himself.

"Is it true that you are a heart man?" he asked me.

"Sir," I told him, "you can register your daughter at this school and be assured that there will be no unseemly behavior here."

The man had acted courageously. Like a scientist, he believed that one had to make a decision based on facts and first-hand experience, which meant asking questions rather than jumping to conclusions. Though it would be difficult for a heart man to admit to such a crime, the man still believed it was a good thing to ask—to have another side to the story.

Instead of keeping his daughter away because of rumors, he decided to confront the thoughts in his mind. He saw all the images created in his mind caused by this rumor and decided to seek the truth himself. He cleared the way for peace, and today we are friends.

When prejudice inside us is seen as it is happening, it can stop at that very moment. By recognizing prejudice right away, there is an opportunity to change our thinking by eliminating the old divisions that prevent peace.

When we see no right and no wrong, but only a problem that needs resolution, peace is a possibility.

When we see no one as "better" or "worse," and notice similarities rather than differences, we are living in peace instead of trying to bring it about.

When we *act* based on what we really see rather than *react* based on a remembered fear, we feel less conflict and live more peacefully.

When we realize that we are the ones who keep hatred alive inside us, hatred stops in its tracks, and we live peacefully.

When we recognize elements of knot-like thinking in our brains and don't act on them, we live peacefully.

When we receive proper, intelligent guidance to help us make informed decisions, we obtain a real education, which helps us understand what prevents peace.

When all nations understand that fighting to be "the most powerful" creates conflict between people and keeps us from acting as a single race, all that prevents peace fades away.

I am sure that some of the thoughts I am expressing here are new to many people. Some insights may even collide with long-held convictions. But what's most important is that we can change the world if we think for ourselves.

We need to recognize that we create conflict by the ways we've been conditioned to think and act. One of the greatest goals in life is to bring about an understanding of, and respect for, all people in the world, beginning with ourselves.

Our ancestors lived in small tribe-like groups to feel safe and to survive. Today we live and interact with billions of people around the world, and every day, we increasingly depend on each other for survival. Individual tribes need to learn to recognize that established beliefs divide the human race into opposing factions. We must question any beliefs that are a threat to the survival of the human race.

The Chinese say, "A journey of a thousand miles begins with the first step." This means that each and every one of us must *take* the first step. We may not cover a thousand miles in a day, a week or a month. There will be times when we have to rest. But deep in our hearts, once we have taken that first step, we have started our journey to the discovery of a new and exciting life—free of prejudice.

In our class, we use the activity from your curriculum called "Be Peaceful." I want to share with you both, Dr. T and Jean, what this does for the children here in war-torn Liberia and how much it means to them and to me. For this activity, the students are divided into two groups—The Sensible Rule Group and The Conflict Rule Group. The children write on a flip chart some rules they believe are sensible and some rules they think create conflict. At the end of the exercise, I realize that most of the rules the children share in class are either rules they learned at school or in their homes. Let me share a few of them with you.

Conflict Rules

1. Small girls must not wear mini-skirts.
2. One must never challenge an older person.
3. Never argue with adults even when you know they are wrong.
4. You must be the first to speak when you meet an older person.
5. As a child you have few rights; you must wait until you're older to claim them.
6. It is not good for children to go to a video club.

Sensible Rules

1. To cross a road, you must look left and right before crossing.
2. It is good to think before you act.
3. You must not believe everything you hear unless you have evidence.
4. It is good to know that no one is better than anyone else.
5. We are all human beings.
6. It is not good to judge others; we all have faults.

After the rules are read, I encourage discussion about them. Not everyone agrees on the propriety of the entries.

Martin says, "Adults can be wrong sometimes. It is good for a child to challenge an adult if he feels that the adult is not right about an issue."

But Janet disagrees. She says, "In Liberia, it is not proper for a child to challenge an adult. It is our tradition to respect older people."

Marion scrunches up her eyes, tightens her mouth and raises her voice. "Tradition? Tradition! Tradition is what's going to kill us all. We must speak against the bad aspects of our tradition."

Wodokueh argues, "Not all children can watch videos at home. So there is nothing wrong with going to a video club if there is none in your home."

Thomas disagrees. "There is nothing wrong with a child going to a video club, but many video clubs show bad movies, and once a child is inside the club, he is not considered a child. He can see anything, and some of the videos are not good for children to see."

Today our children are under lots of pressure to follow rules.

"Don't do this."

"Don't do that."

"You must never question your elders."

"Be good."

While some of these rules make sense, there are many more that cause conflict. Instead of helping us survive, some rules serve only to separate. It is very helpful to see the difference between rules that are sensible and those that create conflict. My students are learning so much.

In our class today, we are looking at what *prevents* peace. I find that asking questions evokes in the young people their own intelligence, for I am not telling them what to think or do but rather "educating" them to think for themselves. I work to "draw out" of them their own responses. I ask them to avoid answering the questions immediately, but rather let the questions lead them to observe their states of mind, to let a question stimulate their self-awareness.

In this way I am showing them that it is not knowledge by itself that can lead to stopping the conflict created by prejudice. Rather, it is this awareness and insight into conditioned, prejudiced thinking at every moment that can free them from the conflict that prevents peace. I am showing them that knowledge has a place in understanding conflict, but by itself, it cannot end conflict. In fact, it can make the conflict worse if knowledge becomes the ideal, if it becomes "the way" to bring about peace.

Here are some of the questions I ask my students based on your curriculum's Lesson 12—*Preventing Peace:*

   ✦   What do you think causes prejudice—education or conditioning?

   ✦   Do you think it's more helpful to be conditioned to be "good," or to be educated about what "good" is, by understanding what prevents "goodness"?

   ✦   Do you think it's more helpful to be conditioned to think peacefully—or to understand what people do to prevent peace?

   ✦   When you act in ways that people around you call "trouble-making," "conflict-producing" or "bad," do you feel judged?

+ When you act in ways that people around you perceive as "proper," "peaceful," or "good," do you still feel judged? Why is that?

+ Is it because you've been *persuaded* to act according to what certain authorities believe is the "right" way?

+ When you are *forced* to be peaceful—or forced to do or be anything—what are some of the thoughts that run through your mind?

+ Do you feel pushed? Do you feel angry or bad about your "self"?

+ Do you instinctively want to push back?

+ When you become aware of what creates your behavior, and how we've all been conditioned to act in ways that cause conflict, are you less likely to feel bad about your "self"?

+ Why do you think so?

+ Do you think it might be because you have an opportunity to see for yourself— to think for yourself about what creates conflict and prevents peace?

+ Do you think that instead of being told what "peaceful" is, we can look at all the evidence and come to an insight of our own—what it means to *try* to be peaceful?

+ When we are judged by other people to be "troublemakers," do we tend to judge ourselves the same way?

+ When we are conditioned to believe that we don't know how to act in respectful, peaceful ways, do we tend to make ourselves fit that description?

+ Do you have the intelligence to understand what prevents peace—that is, what *causes* conflict? Are you *aware* of what it takes to act in nonviolent ways?

+ When you *see* what it means to be in conflict, have you already begun to understand why we don't act peacefully?

Sincerely yours,
Marvin

Lesson 13

The Anatomy of Respect

"The conditioned person lives statically, measuring his every move against the expectations of others. His life is just a repetition of the past, re-enacting memories. Respect is not a conditioned response. The intelligent person behaves respectfully from a natural sense of living in the present."

— *Marvin Garbeh Davis*

Dear Dr. T and Jean…

The other day, in a taxi, I overheard a woman express her frustration to a fellow passenger. "I don't understand why we are made to respect people so much in this country, especially those who are in power. We lift our leaders to such a height that they start to see themselves as superhuman beings, creatures that are sent from somewhere to rule others. And then when they hear a lone voice of dissent, that person is considered disrespectful to higher authority and is charged for gross insubordination or contempt."

Once home, I pondered what the woman had said. As children, we are conditioned to respect adults. We must not challenge our parents and never argue with elders. We must obey rules. This is how the Bassa people put it when they want their children to keep their feelings to themselves: "A child should only be concerned about what to eat and not what to talk about." That is, a child's duty is to find food, not to express his inner thoughts. There is a common saying, "Children should be seen and not heard."

So many children grow up respecting people by accepting their rules and regulations even if those rules are problematic. We are taught to listen and to follow, not to argue or to challenge.

It is no wonder many adults are confused and terrified when they see a child who is an exception—a child who wants to go after truth, a child who knows when to agree or disagree with an adult, a child who never assumes, but questions. We hear adults calling such a child "troublesome," or "disrespectful." This is a form of prejudice.

In our society, respect has always been equated with keeping silent, giving up our rights, accepting what authority asks, doing without questioning, and not challenging authorities whose self-interest appears to override the wishes of the people.

When we say someone is "disgruntled," or dub another "the politician," or "the opposition," in many instances, we mean that person is a lone voice expressing individual rights or challenging an authority for not doing the "right thing."

The other day, a parent who came to pick up her daughter after Peace School heard her daughter ask me when I expected my wife to come. The mother hurriedly pulled the girl towards her asking, "What right do you have to ask a big man like that about his wife, you little girl?"

I had to intervene and tell her that the children in the Peace School have the right to ask me any question, because there are no wrong questions in the Peace School. Some parents believe that the Peace School allows their children to be too forward in asking about anything that comes to their minds. To many, this is disrespectful.

The issue of children's rights is a new phenomenon in our society. There are parents who can't tolerate it. "This child rights business is making us unable to raise our children the way we want," one parent told me. What this parent was implying was that she wanted to raise her child in the old way, the same way her parents brought her up. The old way means "don't question adults or authorities, because doing so is disrespectful."

Many people here have a lopsided view of respect, which they define as "absolute submission to adults or authority". When we respect adults or those in authority, we are supposed to listen to them, even if they are talking nonsense. We must never argue, especially with an elder, since it is assumed that older people know better.

During our discussion of the anatomy of respect, the children make a list of actions required of them by society, families, and school authorities. If they deviate they are dubbed "rude" or "disrespectful." Here is a partial list:

+ As a child, never join an adult conversation.
+ Do not pass between two adults when they are talking; pass on the side.

- It is never good for young people of the opposite sex to hold hands in the presence of adults.
- Do not put your hands in your pockets when talking to your teacher. Wait until you are an adult before putting your hands in your pockets.
- Don't argue with adult people.
- Do not look directly into the eyes of any adult who talks to you.
- No woman should challenge a man.
- Do not call an adult by his or her first name.
- Do not tell someone who is older that he or she has said or done something wrong.

The issue of respect versus disrespect is important to my students, so we decide, as an experiment, to explore the subject. To do this, we are going to create a new, respectful human being in our class. The character in this activity lives in real life, and will live every day learning to be respectful. It is difficult because we agree not to attempt to make the person an ideal or perfect person. Being respectful is not meant to be an ideal. It is meant to be a way of life.

We are not judging this way of life, but creating one to study and observe for ourselves how it works. We want this person to be human, like you and me—not a perfect being, but someone who makes mistakes and can learn from them. We want this person to be interested in understanding how humans are conditioned, and, as a result, learn the best way to survive in the world today. *(For simplicity, I am going to use the neutral gender, as 'one' seems more inclusive than 'his' or 'her'.)*

To create this respectful human being, the children divide into five groups, each responsible for exploring one aspect of our new person's education:

- Words
- Thoughts and Feelings
- Education
- Conditioning and Actions
- Influences and Interests

Our main job is to build and educate this respectful human being. I give the children ten minutes to cluster in their groups and discuss their assignment.

I ask the children in the first group, "What kinds of words do you think this respectful person will need to demonstrate respect?"

They shout their phrases: "Please." "Thank you!" "Excuse me, please." These are words our respectful person will use.

I ask, "Do you think a respectful person needs to know the importance of asking questions, in order to learn? Do you think one would need to ask, "Who? How? What? Where? Why?" Would a respectful person who disagrees with another person, use the words, "You're wrong!" or would one be more inclined to say, "I mean no offense, but I respectfully disagree"?

We now turn to the second group of children who are looking at what would influence our respectful person's thoughts and feelings. I ask them:

- What kinds of thoughts would you teach this person, to ensure that one is a respectful human?

- Would you teach this person to question? Assume? Judge? Respect others' beliefs?

- Laugh at others?

- Would this person's self-image be confident? Would this one be a braggart? Loud?

- At ease?

- Would our respectful human enjoy work? Enjoy play?

- How would this person feel about sports? About music?

The children decide upon someone who is confident, but not overly so, someone at ease, but ready to challenge something that doesn't feel right, someone who accepts people as they are, but is always looking for ways to improve.

Despite these positive attributes, the children, conditioned by their upbringing, believe that respectful people must not put their hands in their pockets when speaking with adults. To be respectful one must not challenge authority. One must not question anything. Once one has an assumption, there is no need to find out the facts.

I continually remind the children that a respectful person does one's best never to assume anything—but always questions, in one's own mind, whether a certain thought or action feels right. The students are torn, because they have been taught that respectful children do not challenge authority, that respectful children fight for traditional beliefs and cannot bear to see their side lose.

We then move to the groups handling our new person's education, conditioning and actions. I ask them:

- How would this person be educated? Would one be taught only by one's school, or would one get help from one's family and friends?

- What concepts would one be educated to learn?

- Would a respectful human be conditioned at all? In what ways?

The children decide that our respectful human being would be taught by teachers at a school, with outside help from family, church counselors, youth leaders and friends within one's community. Some of the children say one would be conditioned to accept everything one hears from authorities, follow instructions, and never challenge one's elders. Others say one would be taught to respect traditions and culture. Some say one would be an active part of one's community because that is where one will feel one belongs. Others say that our respectful being will fight to make sure nobody takes away another's respect and pride. One will always fight back and will never be able to walk away from trouble. One will react based on what one has learned and already knows. When feeling fearful yet able to conquer an enemy, our respectful human will fight, but if feeling unable, our human would flee.

The children's conditioning and prejudices are showing themselves loudly and clearly. When we turn to the groups handling the respectful human's influences and interests, I ask:

+ Do you think this person would have role models? Is it good to have a role model?

+ Would this person get helpful advice from family and friends, or just old rules to follow?

+ How would this person respond to biased television reports? Would one be disappointed? Enraged? Unmoved?

+ What kinds of interests would our new human have? Would one enjoy books?

+ Television? Music? Visiting friends?

Again, the children reflect the old-brain conditioning they have inherited from their elders.

"Our respectful person will have role models because always being compared with others who authorities think are successful means they were respected," says one child.

"Every time our respectful human thinks about doing something, that person wants to be like everyone else—those ideal people parents and teachers talk about and compare their children with, every time they do something they see as wrong."

"If our respectful person reads anything in the newspaper or hears any news report," says another child, "one readily believes it, if it is something one wants to hear, but gets angry if the story does not seem pleasant."

"When our respectful person reads anything bad about somebody, there's never any question about whether or not the report is truthful. It's quickly believed," another child responds.

The children come to the conclusion that our new, respectful human being loves television programs that are biased, that if the story is malicious and affects the character and reputation of someone the viewer does not like, this person is unmoved and uncaring. The respectful human spends free time watching cartoons, visiting friends and going to concerts.

At the end of this activity, I am feeling a sense of despair, because I see that the children have created the kind of respectful person they have been taught to believe is the only kind. As I ask questions about the exercise itself, however, I begin to discover a change in their thinking.

"Did you enjoy creating your part of our respectful human?"

"It was fun at the beginning, but I became bored as we added different attributes to our respectful being," Thomas declares.

"Did you find it difficult, easy or problematic? And, why?" I ask.

"It was difficult because we had to make the character," Cindy explains. "We had to give that person traits we wanted, not what the character wanted. We wanted to create a respectful person, and so we had to make up the way we think respectful people ought to be. It is not easy, because making someone this way is not natural."

"This person is not free of prejudice," Ben says. "Because we had to make our individual accept everything people said, it is unlikely that our respectful human will ever try to find out the real facts. If our character hears that white people are cleverer than black people, for instance, our person will believe it, and judge all black people as stupid and white people as clever, without having any facts to prove that conclusion."

"There is a lot of learning this person has yet to do. Our respectful human has to remember new ways of living that will improve cooperation with others," Pius explains.

We have been trying to create a respectful person based on what we have been taught is respectful. We have been giving special traits to our respectful human and have discovered, in the end, that we have created someone with more than the usual share of human faults. The children see this, and I am relieved.

This is the way we end up when we want our children to behave in an ideal way. We are responsible for our children having to face the same problems we have had. Instead of allowing them to decide what is respectful or good for them, we *tell* them what is respectful and good. Hence, they end up with just as many troubles relating to the world as we have had.

It remains obvious that young people need guidance and boundaries, but the question is how one brings this about. Parents must enforce rules for proper behavior. There are many intelligent ways to help children discover values—such as respect for sane and healthy living. Parents need to refrain from conditioning their children to learn values that set them up against an "ideal."

If a child is conditioned to act ideally—contradicting one's innate soul—that child will live like a programmed robot, at the whim and caprice of others. If encouraged to act intelligently, however, that child will grow up alive, awake, mentally alert, and respond to each moment as it comes.

The conditioned person lives statically, measuring every move against the expectations of others. Life is just a repetition of the past, re-enacting memories. Respect is not a conditioned response. The intelligent person behaves respectfully from a natural sense of living in the present.

It is only when we act from intelligence that we realize we are alive. To be alive is to act in the moment, based on inner feelings and not on others' expectations. Trying to measure up to another person's ideal image is a judgment against our selves in favor of one ideal. Surely there must be another way we can educate young people to be "good," respectful human beings without imposing ideals based on judgments or destructive prejudice. Helping young people to lead healthy, sane and respectful lives comes about when they understand what is *not* healthy, *not* sane *and not* respectful. With this understanding, they develop personal insight.

When we can trust them with this insight, they will develop the intelligence to understand what constitutes proper behavior—without our having to drill them on "moral" behavior, or an imposed "goodness." It is this confident intelligence that will guide young people to make right decisions, not only for themselves but also with regard to everyone else in their lives. This is real respect, based on human understanding and on caring for one another.

I think this exercise of creating a truly respectful person must be done at the Peace School again—but with an attempt to build a person who does not carry the weight of old beliefs.

I ask the children a few more questions:

"Would you want to be this person? Why?"

"Is this person a human you would want to spend time with?"

"Do you think we should do this exercise again and create another respectful human being?"

"Do you think the new one we create might turn out differently from the one we created today?"

I end this lesson by summarizing our main concluding points: "Respect happens when you consider another person important enough to give your attention. It is an act that puts another person before you. Respect cannot come about through prejudice. It comes from a longing for understanding and a love for intelligence."

Regards,
Marvin

Lesson 14

The Art of Insight

"To really discover the source of prejudice, we need to see and experience it, as it is occurring in the brain. This is what is known as *insight*—which means, "seeing into." It is entirely possible to become aware of prejudice as it happens, and this true observation gives us the opportunity to end it."

— *Marvin Garbeh Davis*

Dear Dr. T. and Jean…

My students and I have been discussing prejudice for some time now. I want to be sure they know exactly what prejudice is.

As you suggest in your curriculum, I say to my class, "I want you to *show* me prejudice. How do you know when you are seeing prejudice? Can you show it to me?"

The students look puzzled. They know what prejudice is but having to show it to me confuses them. There is a moment of silence, and then Janet breaks it.

"Prejudice is when you don't want to be friendly with another person because he comes from a different community."

Thomas Johnson takes a turn. "Prejudice is to look down on someone because he comes from a different tribe."

"You are both correct, Janet and Thomas," I respond. "But what you both have given me are words. I want one of you to *show* me prejudice."

Just then, Christopher Vonziah stands up and walks over to where Thomas Johnson is sitting. Thomas seems to be holding something in his hand under the table. Christopher puts his hand under the table and brings out a red cap, lifts it up and shows it to the class.

I am now the one who is confused. What does a red cap have to do with prejudice? I do not betray my bewilderment. Pretending that I do not recognize it, I ask the students, "What is in Christopher's hand?"

"A red cap," the children answer in chorus.

"So why is Christopher showing us a red cap when we are talking about prejudice? What is the connection between this cap and prejudice?" I ask Mai, but Wodokueh interrupts.

"Don't you know that Thomas is Kpelle?"

"Yes, and so what?" I ask.

"Kpelle people love red, Mr. Davis." Christopher is showing the cap because Janjay has been mocking Thomas since he arrived at the Peace School with the red cap on his head. That is why he took off the cap and decided to hold it in his hand, to hide it from all the other students."

I take the cap from Christopher and ask him to sit down. I give the cap back to Thomas and I ask the children to give themselves a round of applause.

All of us now know what prejudice is and can recognize it when it is taking place. We can all easily explain prejudice, but it is sometimes difficult to show it. People easily remember verbal examples, but my students were able to visually demonstrate their prejudice. With this example, we were able to experience the effects of prejudice. We were able to see how it is easy to separate ourselves from one another, which creates conflict. Thomas has been embarrassed for wearing a red cap, which Janjay thinks he is wearing because he is Kpelle and Kpelle people love red. Because of this, Thomas feels separated from Janjay, thus hiding his cap under the table instead of displaying it on his head.

This may be a simple example, but it is where prejudice starts, the very prejudice that most definitely leads to war when these students become adults—fighting over tribal symbols such as red hats, red flags, or other items that stand for one's tribal identity.

Words have a place in the explanation of prejudice. This is the first step toward understanding prejudice. Explanation helps us understand a problem, but it cannot solve the problem. We need to move beyond.

Christopher showed us prejudice and we saw it in the moment. We even saw its effects.

"Is it a good thing to be able to recognize prejudice the moment it happens?" I ask them.

Ben shoots his hand in the air. "It is good to see prejudice happening, because when you see it, you can stop it."

I prod him. "How have you been able to stop prejudice, Ben?"

"We just stopped prejudice now. Because of this, Thomas is able to wear his cap without fear, which he could not do moments ago. Janjay also realized that he acted out of prejudice. Both of them can now go home in peace."

Aminata steps forward. "Because we just stopped prejudice, the rest of us will not be part of teasing Thomas about his red cap. We also realized it is very wrong to say things about other people unfairly just because they come from different tribes. If this had not happened, many children would have joined Janjay in making a mockery of Thomas, and many children would have joined in on the way home. This was prejudice in the making. It is bad, and I have decided that I am not going to be part of it."

"We can decide to be part of prejudice, or choose to question it," says Stephan Kalimu. "The way to make this decision is when you recognize it, right when it is happening."

In the incident in our class, the children were able to see how prejudice separates people, thereby creating conflict. *Explanations* cannot end prejudice. We can end it only when we are actually aware of it as it occurs, while we are *experiencing* it.

Most people think they understand prejudice because they have a memorized description of the words that define it. They believe that they have the solutions for prejudice. We cannot solve prejudice by thought alone. Prejudice is not a "problem" to be solved, but a reality to be recognized in action.

To really discover the source of prejudice, we need to see and experience it, as it is occurring in the brain. This is what is known as *insight*—which means, "seeing into." It is entirely possible to become aware of prejudice as it happens, and this true observation gives us the opportunity to end it.

It is natural for human beings to offer their educated ideas and opinions to others. When people learn something they believe is important, they want to pass it on to others. Someone may try to convince us that a particular conflict is going on because of the action taken by one group. Many will gossip about diverse theories of how the entire conflict started and then render judgments about it. I have heard different people try to convince me of their version of the causes of the Liberian war. Some even lay the cause of war at the feet of one person.

I tell my students what I have learned from your books—that we need to develop a heightened sense of awareness that helps us detect prejudice. In the Peace School, we have a project called ARM, which helps us look at three levels to deal with conflict arising from prejudice:

A = Avoidance (first level)
R = Resolution (second level)
M = Management (third level)

Level 1 – Avoidance. The first level occurs at the root of the feeling. The moment we witness prejudice about to occur, we catch it in the act and avoid it. This is stopping prejudice before it starts. It means that we are each aware of our state of mind in the moment, able to see whether we are acting out of prejudiced thinking or not.

For instance, suppose someone calls us a bad name. Our natural reaction might be to call that person a bad name in return. But instead—to stop the conflict before it starts—we take a "STOP/THINK!" moment. Then we walk away, or we make a joke about it, or say something like "Why did you call me that name? Are you vexed about something?" This gives us time to stop and think.

After introducing Level One, I turn to my students as though I can read their minds. "I know you might be saying to yourself, 'Why should I sit there as if I am mute, and allow someone to call me a bad name without paying that person back?' That is quite understandable. But here is the point. You can choose to stop prejudice in its tracks by *not* participating in the act. You stop a conflict both in your mind and in the communication between you and your attacker.

"This is a new way of thinking, and hence acting, that confers amazing power on all who can master it! This new way of thinking can be compared to being in a car that is about to hit a wall. By stepping on the brake in time, a potentially nasty accident is avoided.

"Let's imagine your communication to be a 'wall of conflict.' By recognizing that you are acting out of prejudice, you step on your own brake and keep yourself from hitting the wall—thus preventing the crash into conflict. This is a simple thought, but it packs a great deal of power."

Level 2 – Resolution. The second level happens when prejudice has already become an issue and is clearly already causing conflict. In order to end the prejudice that is causing the conflict at this level, we must resolve it. It is too late to avoid or prevent it, but we can still find a way to end it.

I say to the children, "Let's assume again that someone calls you a bad name and you are unable to walk away, joke about it, or stop yourself. So you call the person a bad name in return. The conflict begins." The children nod their heads, realizing that at this stage, it is too late to avoid the conflict.

"Although this happened before you realize that you made a mistake in calling that person a bad name, you also understand—even after the fact—that you still have the power, right in this instant, to stop the conflict from intensifying." The children's mouths drop open, their eyes intensify, really focusing.

"When the other person at this point calls you another name, says something bad to you, or walks up to you threateningly, you can attempt to stop it by talking it out. You can say, 'This name-calling is not working for me. I think there is a better way out of this. We can talk about it.' This is a powerful form of mental self-defense." The students take a breath, smile, lean back in their chairs.

"Resolving conflict can be fun, because it can make you feel that you are doing something intelligent. Also, it's your brain that does the work instead of your body."

Ben Killen of our Peace School puts it this way: "If you use your head, your body never suffers."

Level 3 – Management. The third level takes place when a conflict created by prejudice is inevitable. It has reached a point where it's too late to avoid it or resolve it. All we can do is manage it—do our best to keep things under control.

For example: two children have called each other bad names, and have begun to fight. One person's nose is bleeding and the other's glasses are broken. It now seems impossible to stop until somebody is knocked out.

Either child can still hold up a hand and say, "Enough. This is going too far!" Better still, one can walk away, call for help, or choose to fight just long enough to allow an escape route. It's important to notice they still have choices. When we don't make the appropriate choices, or don't even know that we have choices, a conflict gets out of hand.

This is the kind of uncontrolled conflict we see when racial, cultural or national groups go to war over their beliefs, as in Sudan, Iraq, the Ivory Coast, Nigeria, Liberia and Sierra Leone. In these countries, hatred and bigotry have carried people to levels of conflict that seem unbelievable. Just one gunshot, fired at Bhuttuo near the Liberia-Ivory Coast border, sucked us impetuously into a civil war that lasted for more than fourteen years, killing more than 250,000 of our people.

It is important to realize that such acts happen everywhere. They have happened around the world for centuries and continue to happen now. It does not matter what part of the planet we come from. All human beings are capable of joining in the uncontrollable conflicts that prejudice causes.

I ask my students, "Why do we wait until it is too late—until we have to *manage* a conflict? Wouldn't it be easier to *resolve* it before it gets out of hand? Or better yet, wouldn't it be easiest to *avoid* it?"

Whether prejudice has led us to problems at the first, second or third levels, the most important thing we can do is to take responsibility and understand its root cause. We must say to ourselves, "I have somehow been a part of creating this situation. Now I must be a part of understanding and ending it."

Recently in class, a boy asked me to excuse him so he could go to the parlor for a drink of water. He met the secretary, who dipped water from the bucket into a glass and gave it to him. While he was drinking, the glass slipped from his hand and smashed on to the floor. When the office security people confronted him, he said that the glass slipped from his hand because the secretary filled the glass with water. In other words, had the secretary not filled the glass, it would not have slipped from his hand.

After school, the boy told me he was afraid to admit that he had mistakenly broken the glass. His reason was his fear that he would be beaten or asked to pay for the glass. His father would beat the hell out of him. He wanted to apologize, so I suggested that he first accept full responsibility. By convincing his inner self that he was the one who had accidentally done something wrong, he would be making genuine amends.

"Always face up to the truth," I told him, "no matter the consequences. Whenever you do something wrong, you need to tell the truth and take responsibility."

This is an episode with a child, but many adults behave in the same way. They are unable to accept responsibility for their actions. Every day, I ask myself: "Am I one of them?"

I tell my students that we cannot solve life's challenges unless we take responsibility for our actions. We cannot resolve a conflict by saying "It's not my problem," or by hoping that someone else will solve it for us. So many seek to avoid pain by saying to themselves, "This situation was caused by other people or by social circumstances beyond my control. Therefore, it is up to them, or up to society and the government to resolve it for me."

By casting away our responsibility, we may momentarily feel comfortable with ourselves, but in that moment, we cease to resolve the challenges of living. We stop growing as human beings and become society's dead weight. All we contribute to ourselves and society is pain.

When there is a conflict, it is productive for each of us to have an honest inner talk with ourselves. "Since I may have taken part in creating the conflict situation, let me think of some way I might be helpful in resolving it." We can resolve a conflict situation only when we say, "This is my responsibility and it's up to me to resolve it."

If we can *manage* it now, perhaps we can resolve a conflict the next time by changing our response. Better yet, if we can *resolve* it now, perhaps we can avoid the next one altogether by changing our response. The very best scenario is to *educate* ourselves about the cause of conflict so that there won't be any next time, because we will have cut it off at its root level—stopping it before it ever starts.

To stop conflict at the first stage, by avoiding it, shows *insight*. This is the ability to recognize conflict, real or potential, as it is arising from prejudice, and to be aware of that prejudice right as it is happening. Then it can stop immediately. Since insight allows us to stop conflict at the first stage, attaining it always is our highest goal.

Stopping conflict at the second stage by resolving it shows *hindsight*. True, there was prejudice, which caused a conflict. Yes, what the other person did was a reaction to that prejudice. Still, ending conflict at the second stage, through hindsight, showed an understanding that it was prejudice that created the conflict.

Stopping conflict at the third stage, by managing it, is *late sight*, because we are too far-gone to stop or undo what created it. The only choice left is to clean up the mess, repair the damage and get on with our lives.

What about the next time? Will we be able to stop conflict at its root the next time we are confronted with it? As with any activity in life, practice enhances our skills. As we practice these new skills and get better at examining our thoughts, our ability to stop conflict that arises through prejudice will improve quickly.

You sent us a poster from your curriculum, *Why Is Everybody Always Picking on Us?* I pasted it on a wall in our Peace School, because it outlines the twelve steps that help resolve any kind of bullying or other conflict nonviolently. I constantly discuss and review the key points with my students:

Twelve Ways to Walk Away with Confidence

1. *Make friends with the bully.*
During one discussion to review this point, the children suggested that they share some of their lunch with the bully. In rural areas in Liberia, this works easily because only a few children can afford lunch. Sharing lunch can turn bullies into friends, as they hope the treats will continue. And he or she will probably offer VIP protection!

2. *Use humor or a sensible joke.*
We talk about how some bullies will still attack if the joke is not a clever one. Our goal is to turn a threatening situation into a humorous one.

3. *Walk away.*
I advise my students, "Don't get into it; just walk away. It takes a big person to walk away from a fight. People may think you are lazy, but which is better: going home with or without a bloody nose? Winning means making a choice based on your convictions and being able to stick to it, despite the noise of conflict all around you in the market."

4. *Agree with the bully.*
I say to my students, "Let insults go without fighting back. If, for example, the bully says, 'Get away, you short thing!'—just say, 'It's true. I am exactly the same height as my father.'"

5. *Use cleverness.*
I counsel the class, "Suppose the bully is waiting for you outside the school gate. You might be tempted to sink into despair about how this happens every day, but that's the bully's conditioning of you, and it's old thinking. Don't worry about tomorrow; it will solve its own problems. Today, you can just tell the bully you are waiting for your big brother, and the fact that you are waiting for an older person might make the bully leave you alone. Tomorrow, you may decide to go home through the market, strategizing that the bully will not want to attack you in an area where there are lots of people. Because

you're thinking freshly every moment, the next day you could take a short cut, a less popular route to get around the school fence."

6. *Refuse to fight.*
I discuss useful proverbs with my students, such as, "The real winner of a fight is the one who avoids it," and "it takes a big man to run away from a fight."

7. *Ignore the threat.*
"This is risky," I point out, "but if you ignore the threat, the bully may think that you can defend yourself. The bully might think that although you are not the talkative type, that you are strong, and believe in action."

8. *Use Authority.*
I promote this guideline by saying, "Walk home with a teacher or your big brother. You can call an adult to your rescue if the bully tries to attack you."

9. *Reason with the Bully.*
I remind the students: "Use the most powerful tool you have—your brain. If you use it well, your body will not suffer."

10. *Scream/Yell.*
I explain, "If you shout powerfully, the bully might run away. You might attract the attention of other people. The bully may get confused when you shout in a powerful way. Bullies prefer to attack easier, quiet targets."

11. *Stand up to the bully.*
I encourage the students to hold on to their sense of justice. "Stand up for yourself. Tell the bully, 'I don't want to fight, because I don't believe it is the right thing to do—it's not because I'm afraid.' Just say a firm 'No' to the bully."

12. *Take a martial arts stance.*
"When all else fails," I say to my students, "pose in a martial arts stance. The bully will realize that you are not a sitting duck. Most bullies are scared and lack confidence. Martial arts are all about confidence. That's why you never see a martial artist fighting in the market. If a person poses in a martial arts fighting position, the situation has reached a serious point. But if you practice the other eleven of these twelve ways to walk away with confidence, you will most likely never get to this point."

One of the most valuable tools in searching for understanding is inquiry. When we question, we can find out for ourselves whether something is true or false. To know the truth, we must gather and observe facts, and from these facts deduce or create insights. Insight is being able to see clearly what's happening as it occurs. It is first-hand experience. We don't need to memorize information about prejudice. Instead, we need to develop the ability to recognize and understand such a situation so we can end it. The next time we are faced with conflict, we can accept responsibility rather than blame others.

I know the difficulty we have in accepting responsibility for our behavior. It lies in the desire to avoid the pain of the consequences of that behavior. If we are to be healed, we must learn that our life is a series of personal decisions and choices. If we can accept this, then we can become free human beings.

By questioning, we become more fair-minded, more objective. We can look at a problem, see it for what it is, and accept responsibility for taking part in its avoidance, resolution or management.

One evening I decided to spend some free time with my seven-year-old daughter. She had been away with her mother for about six months. This moment was intended to help make up for some of our lost time due to our separation over the past half-year, and to build a closer and happier relationship.

For days she had been urging me to play a game of soccer with her. The game is "man on man," meaning that both team members share the same set of goal posts. Each player can kick to score and at the same time defend the same goal area. She agrees and we start the game.

However, she soon asks, "Can I use the bathroom?" After that, we play a bit more, and she asks "Can I get a cold drink?" Less than ten minutes into the game, my daughter, drooping, asks, "Can I take a bath?"

"Let's play," I say to her. "I thought we agreed that the first person to win ten goals would mean the stopping point." So we play for another ten minutes, during which time she slows down more and more. Finally she says, "I'm tired. I just want this game to end. Can't we leave now?"

I am vexed. "You have been coaxing me all week to play a game of soccer. Now you are running away without completing one game. If you knew you would not finish a match, you should not have asked me in the first place," I reply angrily.

So we play for another five minutes and while trying to kick the ball, she falls. She hurts her elbow which starts to bleed. I rush to examine it and take her inside to clean it with alcohol. She cries and cries, and after bathing, she goes straight to bed without studying.

That evening, I sit alone in the room, looking at my daughter sleeping like a log. I call to her softly, but of course she does not answer me. A twinge of guilt envelops me. I had started the evening in hopes of making up for the separation between us, but our time together ended in further division and injury. My desire to finish our game had become so important that I forgot the reason for playing—to build a relationship with my girl, not to win.

This was my old self—the self who kept wanting to win at everything. If I wanted to prove myself, I had to win. After that incident, I told myself that I had to change, because my need to win, my competitiveness and the seriousness with which I took everything, had worked against me. If I continued this behavior, it would alienate all the people I care for. If I did not transform my behavior, I knew my actions would cause many more evenings of unnecessary accidents and bitterness with people I love.

As a father, I have recognized that my attitude got in my way of becoming a new person. To be the kind of father I want to be, I need to give up some part of myself so that I can move on. For that internal change and awareness to take place in my life, there would have to be new growth that would take away a substantial part of my old self. This is the inevitable cost of transforming life: giving up the old self for a new self. This is what it means to accept responsibility and make amends with new attitudes.

This is my new struggle. This should be the struggle for the human race, if we really want to live together in peace. This is the challenge the children at the Peace School are now facing. They want to live a life that blossoms into enlightenment—and peace.

Take care,
Marvin

Lesson 15

Prejudice Is an Automatic Reaction

"I explain to the children that when we are babies, we cannot identify our relatives or our tribe. As we grow up, we are taught that we belong to a particular family and tribe, we learn to speak our dialect and we begin to see differences. We go to a particular church, attend a certain school, cheer for a specific soccer team, and wear an exclusive color at political rallies. Our family, tribe, church, and school all impress upon us that this is the only proper way to conduct our lives. In other words, we are groomed automatically to be prejudiced."

— *Marvin Garbeh Davis*

Dear Dr. T. and Jean…

It is a beautiful October afternoon here in Buchanan. The rains are gone and the sunshine is becoming more constant. Many people tell me they hate the rainy season because it interrupts the movement of hustlers, especially now that employment stands at zero here in Buchanan. A lot of people prefer the dry season because they can get out and shop. Even if they don't buy anything, the fact that they are out there looking helps the hustler hold on to his faith that something might come his way. That opportunity drowns in the rainy season.

As with everything in life, there are costs for the dry season. Dust smears the walls of homes near Tubman Street and turns corrugated roofs brown. Inside the bedrooms of roadside houses, the dust sticks on ceilings, clings to curtains, swathes dressers and infiltrates cupboards. One of my students who lives very close to the main street told me that her mother has now packed all her church-going clothes and occasional suits in a valise right under her bed. She is not going to start hanging them up again until the rainy season starts.

While walking the streets, we're coated, too. By the time we reach our destinations, our noses are full of dust and our hair has turned a mix of black and brown. But in Buchanan, dust is a small worry. People just move on, trying to get ahead.

Now that elections have come and gone, October brings a feeling of relaxation among the people. We now have a new president in the country, so the fussing, cursing and divisions within communities are receding. People are getting on with their lives again, placing their fate in the hands of the politicians. Our children are back with us in the Peace School. I am happy to have them back, and we are all happy that nothing extraordinary happened in Buchanan to significantly change the way of life here.

Today is our first class after the elections. The children sit in an arc around our conference table while I sit at the head. We continue to talk about prejudice, specifically about how it is an automatic reaction.

We start today's lesson with a story from one of your books, Dr. T., about a young man called Kaspar Hauser, who was kept in a dark cellar where he was chained in a harness that was attached to a stone floor. Kaspar lived in this dark cellar for the first eighteen years of his life. His only distraction was a toy wooden horse. For all those eighteen years, the only word Kaspar knew was "horse." He lived and slept in darkness, until an old man in a dark hat and robe came into the cellar and took him to a local town. There he left him, with a note in his hand asking that someone take care of him.

"This is a true story that took place in the 1800s," I tell my students. "The people who lived in this small town in Germany did not know what to do with Kaspar, so they locked him up in one of their jail cells until a professor found him, took him home and cared for him for the rest of his life.

"Kaspar would often fall into a deep sleep, from which he could not be awakened. People thought that he was retarded and felt sorry for him, but there was nothing wrong with him. He was completely normal, except for the fact that he had never seen anything outside the dark stone cellar where he had lived his life for eighteen years.

"As cruel as this life was, Kaspar proved to be a model of how prejudice works, for he was completely unprejudiced. He had no preconceptions or ideas about anything. His mind was clean, blank. When he saw a candle and tried to pinch the flames with his fingers, he suddenly experienced shock and pain for the first time in his life.

Kaspar had no experiences except darkness. He had not seen birds, trees, the sky, flowers, did not know the difference between seasons. He was like a newborn in a man's body.

I lifted my head from the book for a moment and checked on the children. Immersed in the story, they couldn't wait to hear Kaspar's fate.

But I digress a moment, Dr. T and Jean, to tell you that in Liberia, parents tell their children all sorts of folktales The essence of these stories is to educate children about the consequences of their actions. For instance, one very popular folk tale series is about a spider. If the spider dies of greed, parents tell their children that greediness can cause death. This is how Liberians teach their children to build a sense of right and wrong.

The story about Kaspar is not the kind that one will hear parents telling their children under the moonlight or around the fire hearth in Liberia. At the end of Kaspar's story, the first reaction I notice from the children is one of disbelief. Many find it difficult to imagine someone living in a dark cellar for eighteen years. I pause for a moment and let the children dialogue.

"Did Kaspar really live at all?" Martin asks.

"Yes, he really lived," I answer.

"I feel real sorry for him then," Marion interjects.

"How did he eat?" Janet inquires. But before I can answer, Pius stands up.

"He was not hungry because he never saw any food. If you don't have something and don't see it with other people, you might not want it," Pius concludes.

The class suddenly churns with debate.

"Kaspar was stupid."

"I feel sorry for him."

"No human being could live like that for eighteen years."

"The story does not sound normal."

"It is not the kind of thing human beings would do."

I interrupt them. "Do you think Kaspar felt threatened when the old man walked into the cellar and unchained him? Why, or why not?"

Wodokueh raises her hand. "Kaspar was afraid when he saw the old man, because this was his first time seeing another human being like himself."

"Do you think Kaspar had any feelings of fear?" I ask. "If so what would he be afraid of?"

"I don't think so," Cindy volunteers. "There was nothing to be afraid of. Kaspar did not live with anyone; he was not in a village or a town. He had no brothers or sisters. He never went to school. He was not afraid because he had not seen anything all his life."

At this moment I bring home the story's key significance—Kaspar's lack of prejudice. While it is true that Kaspar was a normal person, he did not have any prejudices, no preconceptions about anything or anyone. His mind was clean as a slate; he was a baby in a man's body. He did not know the difference between a black and a white person, a Kpelle or a Bassa person, a thin or a fat person. Kaspar had never been taught to feel better than other people or to call people names. Kaspar is proof that we are not born with prejudice inside us.

I explain to the children that when we are babies, we cannot identify our relatives or our tribe. As we grow up, we are taught that we belong to a particular family and tribe, we learn to speak our dialect and we begin to see differences. We go to a particular church, attend a certain school, cheer for a specific soccer team, and we wear an exclusive color at political rallies. Our family, tribe, church and school all impress upon us that this is the only proper way to conduct our lives. In other words, we are groomed automatically to become prejudiced.

I want the children to know that we are not born with prejudice. It is something we learn and, unfortunately, it seems natural. Without any preconceived ideas and images of self or others, prejudice cannot exist. Prejudice takes root in the human brain according to how the brain is trained to think and feel. "So," I say to the children, "if you want to break free of prejudice, look at the world through Kaspar's eyes."

"How can we see the world through his eyes?" little Janet questions me.

"We can do this by having a clean mind when we see something. For example, Janet, the next time you see a fat girl walking along the road, instead of laughing at her because she is fat, see her as a human being. Get to know her. If you feel she is different, make her your friend, and you might see that she has a beautiful heart. As soon as you see this fresh side of her, you will start to accept her more readily as a human being rather than as someone you make fun of, just for being different."

Thomas raises his hand and adds his experience to my explanation. "I went to see my brother after school one day on his school campus so that I could get the key for our house, because I was not well and could not stay in school. Because our home is far away, I decided to stay in my uniform. It was recess time when I got to my brother's campus. As I approached the campus, everyone's eyes were on me. I could barely walk when I reached the main building where most of the students were sitting in groups eating their lunch or just talking. I heard one boy say, 'What is this boy from Seventh Day Adventist School doing here on our school campus?'

"I felt threatened and told myself I had made a mistake to come to my brother's campus wearing my school uniform, particularly at a time when everyone was sitting outside looking at me. Fortunately for me, my brother appeared and called me. I felt that I had been rescued from a bully who was about to whip me. My brother walked with me until I reached the school gate and gave me the key to our house. The children in my brother's school knew I was a human being like them, but they were only looking at my uniform, which made me different from them on the outside."

Thomas is a quiet, soft-spoken child. I pictured some of the students taunting him only because he came from a different school. I felt touched as I tried to imagine how he must have felt and what kinds of thoughts must have run through his mind. "That was a bad experience, Thomas, but it also made you understand how automatic our reactions can be.

"For instance, we can all imagine being introduced to a stranger from Nimba County. We shake hands, but in that moment, we start to think about the tribe he belongs to. We assume that because he comes from that tribe he might be 'this or that.' Based on our preconceptions, we treat him in a particular way."

"But why is it that people behave like this?" Martin asks. "Sometimes you know that what you are doing is bad, but you can't stop doing it to other people."

"This is because of our conditioning, Martin," I tell him, as if I were consoling a troubled child. "When we are really young, Martin, we are taught to separate, to love and to respect only our own. We learn to identify with our own kind and to see difference as a point of enmity between ourselves and others. In short, we just get used to this kind of attitude—so much that we find it hard to change."

"Is there a way to change this attitude?" he asks me.

"There *is* a way, and that is why you are here. You are a new generation that must carry the torch that unites all people. You are the people to start this new wave of change in our country," I tell the children. "It is not going to come easy, because as I said, we are used to it. Our brains are programmed to react in this way. So learning new ways makes us feel unsafe.

"It is like asking an old man who has for years been typing with his two index fingers to now learn how to type with all ten fingers. It will be difficult. The man will not feel safe walking in new terrain. His two fingers have served him well over the years, so why should he start using ten? He even believes that his two fingers can type faster than using ten fingers. No matter how you explain the advantages, the man will find it difficult to accept the new idea.

"That is what happens to us—our brains go back to the old ways we are accustomed to. But if this man decides to enroll in a typing program that will change his style, he could type 56 words per minute in a matter of weeks!"

You know what I am doing here, Dr. T. and Jean? I am telling my students that they are young and that they have the power to change their world now.

"If you apply new learning to your life," I explain to them, "and embrace a new way of thinking, then you can truly start the change we are all talking about in our country and the world. You are the future, the brightest hope that can emerge from the ashes of our civil war."

It looks like I am making a speech now. My voice begins to crescendo and a new stillness envelops the classroom. I want the children to understand this. I want them to know that it is in their power to change the world if they make that choice now. But the upsurge in my voice recedes and I continue with the lesson.

At this point, I give the children three excellent ways to respond to a situation.

"First," I explain, "*Become aware of new information you need.*

"Any action you take that is not based on awareness is really a *reaction*. I want you to understand that when you react to a stranger or someone different from you, your reaction is mechanical unless you make yourself aware of what is happening. Awareness gives us information we did not have before, and this awareness affects the way we think about a particular situation.

"Awareness," I add, "stops us from giving in to our automatic reaction—the old way we react when we see a foreigner, for instance, or someone from a different tribe, school or church. Awareness creates a moment that makes us realize that the old way does not work. Awareness creates a moment of 'STOP/THINK!' In this moment, we allow new thinking to happen. When this new thinking occurs, we act (rather than react) in a new way.

"Second. *Concentrate on what you need to do differently with this new information.*

"Once we are aware, we stop the reaction in its tracks, and we are ready to act instead of react. In this 'STOP/THINK!' moment, we can ask ourselves questions such as:

'Is this a conditioned action?'

'Is my mind open to new information?'

'Is my inner X-ray machine working?'

'Is this constructive or destructive?'

"Third. *Focus on the new way until you understand it.*

"We are conditioned as a result of time and repetition. So to make a new response part of our lives, we need to take the time to practice, focusing regularly on our new way of thinking and behaving. If we understand how conditioning works both inside and outside us, we can learn new behavior, just by keeping our minds open to new possibilities.

"We must always be brave enough to stop mid-action, if our behavior could prove destructive to ourselves or someone else.

"Can any of you demonstrate your understanding of these new ways of thinking and behaving, by giving a practical example?"

John comes forward. "When I see a foreigner, my first reaction is to think he is different, not a part of my people. So the first thing that comes to my mind is to be afraid of him because he is different."

I ask my students what kind of new information John would need to become aware—to be able to respond correctly when he sees a foreigner.

Cindy says, "John does not have to treat a person in a bad or suspicious way because the person is a foreigner. Foreigners are human beings too."

I am touched by this response. I tell the students that by becoming aware of this new information, John will be able to think about the situation with a new perspective, and act in a new way.

Continuing to explore the example, I pose another question to John. "How will you respond with your new awareness?"

"I decide to make friends with the foreigner. I shake hands with him and find out something about him, his country, his family and his people."

You see, Dr. T. and Jean, John has stopped to think. His new awareness stops his reaction in its tracks. In that "STOP/THINK!" moment, John has decided to befriend a stranger instead of treating him with suspicion.

But there is more to this. I stress that we all need to create a new awareness by suspending each old thought. At first, it will take time to see and recognize all our old habits. Once we have practiced, it will take no time at all if we are constantly aware in each moment, looking at each thought as it arises. With practice, in every new encounter and situation, if we recognize the old way and avoid acting from it, we will be able to change our habits and open our minds to new possibilities, to new ways of thinking and acting.

Finally I emphasize to my students that people are not born with prejudice. The strange life of Kaspar Hauser proves that someone who is prejudiced must have learned those prejudices. Although we are all born innocent, we come into a world already infected with the prejudice virus, so it is a matter of time before we catch it ourselves. And while it is true that we are all subjected to the effects of prejudice, we can free ourselves from conditioned thinking and action—simply by being aware.

We reach the end of another lesson. It has been a wonderful session. The children are beginning to leave for their homes again. I walk out of the classroom and stand in front of the porch to watch them go. Those whose homes are not very far away walk in groups. Those who come from far away—communities toward the Atlantic Ocean—stand on the side of the road that faces the office and wait for a taxi. I count three boys and one girl. They live as far away as the Monrovia Junction community. It is a long way from Common Ground.

I return to the classroom to pack my curricula and books and remove the flip chart from the hall to my office. Martin is standing there, by my books.

"Aren't you going home?" I ask.

"I will go home, but I wanted to help you pack your things today," he answers, a smile stealing across his face.

"That's nice of you. Thank you, Martin."

In the past, some of the students have helped me packed the room before leaving. They do it voluntarily and spontaneously. My regular guy is Thomas, but today it's Martin's first time. Usually he is one of the students who hurriedly leaves when classes are over. I understand, because he lives in the Dirt Hole community, the only participant from that community in this class.

I lower the flip chart while Martin packs the books and curricula, which we both take into my office. Next he brings the board markers while I neatly arrange the chairs around the table in the hall. Back in my office, I thank Martin and we walk toward the door.

Martin says shyly, "There is something I want to ask you, Mr. Davis."

"Go ahead," I answer, putting my hand around his shoulder.

"Do you believe there will be no more fighting in our country?"

"What do you think, Martin?" Instead of answering his question directly, I ask him another. As much as possible, I always try to help my students reason their way toward an answer, rather than simply spoon-feeding them one. Of course, this works well only in the context of a certain kind of question. If, for instance, one of my students asks me "Who was the first President of Liberia?" it is extremely unlikely that I can assist him to reason his way toward the correct answer, particularly if he is too young to have heard about J.J. Roberts. But there have been many instances where I have applied the questioning technique. I enjoy encouraging the children to use their mental powers, and take pleasure in seeing their intellectual awareness grow.

Martin thinks a minute before responding. "I don't know. Sometimes I think there will always be peace, but sometimes I think we could fight another war again in this country."

"What makes you think there could be another war, Martin?"

"I am not sure, I just sometimes feel so."

At this point, I realize the struggle Martin feels between his emotions and his intellect, and decide that empathy would probably feel more encouraging than additional questions. "I understand how you feel, Martin. We all feel that way sometimes. But we must work for peace if we want to live in peace. One way of doing this is by changing our attitude toward each other. We need to respect differences and to consider all Liberians as part of the human race. We must understand that this country belongs to *all* of us. If we do this Martin, then we can keep the peace we are having right now. Peace begins with us, you and me, and the way we live in our communities and families."

I am not sure how Martin feels about my comments. He was born in a village in Bong County, where people fled when rebels attacked their hometown in District 3. His mother would have bled to death, had it not been for one of the rebel commanders who drove her to a nearby town where Medicines San Frontier operated a clinic. His mother told me that Martin is a real gift from God. She can't believe he is alive today. For more than six years, he suffered different types of ailments—measles, malnutrition, malaria—so she did not believe he would live.

Dark clouds have started to encircle the skies of Buchanan. It is getting late, so I decide to give Martin a ride home. Buchanan in its post-war state is still a great city by our standards, as it is Liberia's second largest city with more than 20,000 people, and some call it our second capital. Though not spectacularly destroyed like Ganta City whose center was left in rubble, outside the heart of Buchanan, there are acres of residential area in dust and debris, such as the Oriental Timber Company area and the former LAMCO mining company. However, as I drive down the main street, it looks almost untouched.

Martin lives with his parents in a flat on top of an apartment building on an undistinguished street in the Dirt Hole community. Before the war, it might have been home to a Lebanese merchant, a local government official, or one of the staff members of LAMCO. Now dozens of families overcrowd the building.

As I bring my car to a stop in front of it, a little boy approaches us. Barely taller than the car, he is dressed in short trousers and a Manchester United soccer jersey bearing the name of Ryan Giggs on its back. His hair is unkempt, half eaten by ringworms. His bare feet are covered in mud, his body unwashed. I scrutinize him with attempted firmness, but the boy's expression has an impudent charm. He reaches to open my door and before I know it, he stretches his hand toward me for a shake.

Martin's parents come down to meet me. From the top of the building, I can see several people bending over their balconies to catch a glimpse of the person who has driven into their yard. I have met Martin's mother before but not his father, Mr. Johnson. As we shake hands, he smiles as if to emphasize that he has heard my name many times in their conversations at home. He offers me a seat beside him and offers me something to drink. I ask for water. As we talk, Martin's mother splits firewood.

Liberians refer to the era before the war as "normal days". "In normal days," Mr. Johnson begins, "I was a waiter in the LAMCO mess hall. Then during the war, I worked as an unwilling cook for one of the generals. They were the worst moments of my life."

As he reminisces, I see clearly the contradiction between his life at LAMCO and now. "The rents were low, the food cheap, the drinks cheap and there were lots of tips from all the Europeans who visited the mess hall. Since then, everything has been a nightmare, returning home from the refugee camp in Sierra Leone and coming home to nothing but shame and disgrace." He lights a cigarette, noting with distaste the nicotine stain on his fingers.

"They [the government and the United Nations Refugee Agency] asked us to come home and see where we are," he tells me. "Instead of going back to the mess hall, I am a security guard at the cinema. This is a job that is so insecure. There is not a month that passes by without the dismissal or the termination of someone's contract. I could go any moment."

"Things will be better again," I try to assure him. "We just need peace and maybe the country will rise again,"

"It is not going to rise for people like us." Mr. Johnson says. "Maybe for you people who are younger and educated, maybe for Martin and his sisters. I want for my boy to be educated so that he doesn't live the way we are living now, like rats and roaches in a pig hole with people whose paths would have never crossed yours in a lifetime. Thank God for some of you book people who are teaching them about peace. If all the book people had thought like you then, we would not be here now. But if our children understand the value of peace, then they might not have to live the way we are living now. Right now, my brother, I am just waiting for my time. This is no life. This is another kind of death; you are alive and can't do anything for yourself. So what is the use of living?"

I thank Mr. Johnson and his wife as I take my leave. Mr. Johnson asks me to drop Martin off on the main road to get them some candles for the night. On our way, I start to think about my discussion with Martin. It reminds me that all of life represents a risk. Of all the thousands of risks we take in a lifetime, the greatest is the risk of growing up.

Growing up is the act of stepping from childhood into adulthood. Actually it is more of a fearful leap than a step, and it is a leap that many people never really take. Though they may outwardly appear to be adults, even successful adults, perhaps the majority of grownups remain children psychologically until their death, never truly able to transcend the borders of childhood to maturity.

I think about the young people I am working with every day here. Will the moments we have shared together at the Peace School help them make that journey from childhood to adulthood? Will they be able to make that responsible transition, even if it means being out of step with all that seems right? Will they be able to accept the consequences of their decisions? There is no way I can know the answers to these questions, but I find consolation in the fact that I am presently making my own contribution, planting the seeds and allowing that sovereign hand of fate to make the seeds blossom.

As I drop Martin off at the junction, I watch him cross over and walk into a shop. Looking at him through the rearview mirror, several thoughts run through my mind:

There goes somebody's boy
Another gem in the human meadow
His future now being plotted by his parents
Just like a road map
"You will go to college," I hear them tell him,
"And earn a degree
Then go to medical school and

Be the doctor I never became,"
But in his heart
He wants no part of his parents' plot
He wants to chart his own course
To soar gracefully over
Hills and valleys
In a big blue balloon
And drift lazily across the Liberian skies
From Mount Nimba to Wologisi
From Cape Mesurado to Cape Palmas
North, South, East and West
Wherever the hand of providence will direct his life
Even if it means being called crazy
Take the leap into the unknown
With his destiny in his own hands
With an incredible bravery divorce himself
From the whims and caprices of everyone
And be the soul he was made to be.

Once back home, sleep catches up with me again, and summons me to bed. With my mosquito net neatly tucked around the borders of my bed, I climb under my sheet. Outside in the night, I hear a man singing, accompanied by an instrument I imagine is a native concertina. It is a sad, haunting song. I am sure the man sings in Bassa, but it is difficult to decipher the words from my room. The singer sounds forlorn and hopeless, singing songs of love and departure, muffled and heartbreaking, an attitude that fits the surroundings, but then he suddenly gains strength at the end, as if in conquest. Gradually the music recedes to nothing, leaving the squeaking sound of a night bird outside my window. It really has been a long day. I turn over onto my stomach and within minutes I am asleep, dreaming of a time when there will be real peace because these children have thoroughly understood what has prevented it.

I will give you details as things progress,
Marvin

Lesson 16
Thinking in New Ways

"I tell the children today that all of us have creative opportunities, if we are able to see the world in a new light—one that allows insight and possibility. This is where our work remains. Our young people are so used to violence that it is difficult for them to see a world without it. But the young people at Common Ground Society are a new breed of Liberians. They are brave new children who are freeing themselves from prejudice, and from the kind of conditioned thinking that created the conflict here in Liberia."

— *Marvin Garbeh Davis*

Dear Dr. T and Jean…

Christmas will be here in two weeks. Already new stalls are being erected along Tubman Street. Old, abandoned booths are being refurbished in preparation for the season's sales. Stores and shops are stocking their shelves with new goods and provisions. Everywhere I turn, I hear someone say, "My Christmas is on you," meaning "I'm asking you for a Christmas gift." This is our tradition here; Christmas is the time for asking friends and relatives for gifts. It is the time for sharing. Everyone—even those who have nothing—go to great lengths to find something for relatives and friends. I am looking forward to seeing bowls of rice and fufu crisscrossing communities on Christmas and New Year's Day.

Already my children at the Peace School are on my back. Whenever they meet me in the street or come to the school, they remind me, "My Christmas is on you." Last year, I had a Christmas party on Christmas Eve for the Peace School. We had not been able to secure any funds for that activity. In post-war Liberia, Christmas is much more spartan than when I was a child.

The kids have nowhere to go, especially in a town like Buchanan. There are no ice-cream shops, no dance halls, not even any playgrounds for children here. On Christmas Day, the children just roam the streets from one end of Tubman to the other. Many parents just let their children wander.

There have been reports of young people buying alcohol, especially "drip," a locally popular drink that is sold in a long, thin plastic tube. Because it sells for five Liberian dollars, any child can get a bag on a big day like Christmas. Sadly, business people sell this drink to children as young as nine. Many of them get so drunk they cannot find their way home. The other day, I heard young people participating in the International Day of Children's Broadcasting, calling on adults in both government and shops to stop selling alcohol to children.

I'm interested that here, despite the strife, everyone still wants to make the best of Christmas. Many people go to any length to ensure that their families have enough food and their children have a small gift on that day. I have heard stories of people spending so much on Christmas that the day after Christmas, they go to bed hungry. By New Year's Day, they're looking for a place to secure credit just for food.

Today I am at school, talking with the children about how they can think in new ways. I read aloud a story on prejudice from your book, Dr. T. about a girl called Jean who had a dream about a completely different world from the one she lived in. In Jean's dream, all the children played with each other without fighting. Adults could not wait to get home to be with their families, and had time to play with their children after work. In her dream, Jean saw her father helping her mom with the dishes and also cleaning up on weekends. Her mother even helped with chores that were traditionally masculine. A trained carpenter, she built an extension to their house. In her dream world, Jean also saw that being a schoolteacher was the most respected and therefore most highly paid job. Jean watched TV programs that showed kind people who loved to learn and have fun. She watched exciting and adventuresome movies without any killing. Jean not only played basketball with her brother, but shared her likes and dislikes with him. She also talked about all the people they knew, and how they all cooperated with one another. How great it was to live free of conflict!

In Jean's dream world, there were neither people who were poor, nor people who had so much money that they didn't know what to do with it. Everyone knew how much was needed to go around and everyone got a fair and equal share of everything there was to be had—food, friends, toys and love. Nobody had to be taught to be good, and nobody was bad. To be happy meant living intelligently, honestly and peacefully. There were no soldiers and no wars, because people understood what created conflict, and knew how to prevent it. As a result, there was no need for lawyers, judges, and prisons. It was a lovely dream,

As I read the story aloud, the children looked transported to Jean's different world. But dawn came, and Jean woke up. As the story ended, the students jolted from the reverie.

I asked them what they thought about Jean's dream. "Is it perfect?" I asked them. "Does it set up an ideal that is impossible to achieve?"

"Jean's dream is a beautiful dream; I really wish to have been there with her in the dream. But then it is only a dream. We live in a different situation in our world today," Janet declares.

"That is true, Janet." We all live in a world different from Jean's dream world—a world in which prejudices run through our lives and affect us. It is these prejudices that we are trying to recognize here," I respond.

At this point, many of the students ask if it is possible for human beings to live in a world where children can play without fighting, or where movies can be made adventuresome without being murderous.

Instead of answering, I ask the children what *they* think. Joseph volunteers: "It is possible for children to live without fighting if they understand each other. It is also possible for people to watch movies that can be adventuresome without showing people killing each other. I have watched movies that show no killings."

"But how about living in a world without soldiers and police?" Trokon asks, pointing to Joseph. "It is still possible," Joseph answers. "Have you seen any soldiers on our streets since the elections?"

Marion intervenes. "I have not seen Liberian soldiers, but how about the Bangladesh soldiers around here? We have police on the streets, too."

"Didn't you hear that they are training our own soldiers?" Wodokueh interjects. "They will soon be on the streets again."

The class is in the mood for debate. As it is healthy, I flow with the children's arguments.

Thomas stands up. "The Bangladesh soldiers are peacemakers and will soon go home once we stop fighting. I don't think anything is wrong with the police, once they do the right thing, like take the bad guys off the streets."

A few years ago, before the recent elections, gunmen were seen everywhere on the streets here. They stood on street corners and prowled the communities as if looking for fights. They were a law unto themselves, randomly arresting and beating innocent citizens. Many of the children still vividly remember watching in trauma as Taylor's soldiers whipped, harassed and gun-butted their parents and other community members. Since I returned home, I have not seen any soldiers walking the streets. The children are dumbfounded by their absence. Except for the Bangladesh peacekeepers who provide security, we don't have soldiers along the streets anymore.

The debate continues with Cindy: "If there were no poor people and everyone was paid equally for the same job, no one would steal and kill. People steal and kill because they want something they can't get—things that others have and can't or won't share. Have you seen thieves breaking into the homes of poor people?"

I agreed with all the children. If all of us had all we needed, there would be no thieves, and police and soldiers would be out of work. I ask the children if they might like to live in Jean's kind of world.

"Who doesn't want to live in such a beautiful world?" Janet asks rhetorically.

"No one wants to suffer, fight and live in poverty," Benedicts adds.

At this juncture, I ask the children to tell me some of the differences between their world and Jean's.

"There is no poor person in Jean's dream world," Cindy states.

"There are no soldiers," Joseph adds.

"There are no prisons, and no courthouses or lawyers or judges," says Ben.

I ask the children if any part of Jean's dream world makes sense to them. Did they enjoy any particular part of her world? There is a flurry of answers.

"Jean's world does not make any sense to me, but I enjoyed the fact that there were no poor people," Ben explains.

"I like Jean's dream world, because qualified women can do a job that many consider men's work," Pius adds.

Now it's my turn to take some explanatory time. "Jean's dream world is possible in reality," I explain. "People can live in such a world. For example, Costa Rica, a country in Central America, has no army. All the money that could have been spent on the army goes to education. For many countries, this would be an unimaginable dream, but in that country, it is a fact. Some things we imagine to be impossible actually are possible with the right kind of attitude."

Then I share with them a wonderful experience. "Do you know that it is possible for us to live in our towns, villages and cities without having to go to courts when we have misunderstandings? That we can resolve our differences without police or soldiers?"

They look at me with shaking heads and wide eyes. "Well, it's not just a dream. This is one of the most touching, true stories I have seen happen in our community since I returned home.

"A young lady called Ruth rented a house with her little girl, about eight years old, and sublet one of her rooms to another young woman. On Christmas Day last year, Ruth left her daughter, alone and went out in the night. The little girl lit a candle which was sitting on a wooden table, and after some time fell asleep. The candle burned lower and lower until it caught the table on fire. Soon the mosquito net around the girl's bed burst into flames and roared up into the roof. The little girl awoke in the midst of the smoke, realized that the house was burning, and began crying loudly. The neighbors next door heard her, broke the door open and saved her, but could not save the house.

"As you know, we have no fire trucks or firemen in Buchanan, so the house burned to the ground. Also, because Buchanan has no bank here, most people have to keep their money in their house and wait until they have enough, before taking it to the bank in Monrovia. So Ruth lost her belongings as well as all the money she had saved in her home.

"The house did not belong to Ruth. Most people expected the owners to be so furious that they'd send Ruth to jail, or at least take her to court. Before it got to that point, however, the community held a meeting to try to resolve the matter. On my way to the gathering, I heard lots of people saying that there was no way the owners of the house would forgive Ruth. She would definitely have to pay for it.

"In front of everyone, Ruth stood with tears in her eyes, apologized to the owners and asked to be pardoned. Following this, community elders consulted several times with each of the family members who owned the house, and again with mediators. After all the meetings, they agreed to forgive Ruth. The owners of the house only asked her to rebuild it. They told her that they needed no money, only their house standing in its old place.

"Not only that, but one of them offered a place in their other house for Ruth until she could find a new place. Even the girl who had sublet a room from Ruth agreed to forgive her. People had pain in their hearts, but they shook hands, hugged and were then ready to move ahead.

"So you see, the entire conciliatory process was resolved with no police or soldier involvement. Courts and judges did not have any input in the case. Those who had doubted a resolution of the matter by the community went home stunned.

"Do you realize how many people expected the owners of the house to make Ruth's life even more miserable by sending her to court or jail? Do you see how this story has a bit of Jean's dream world?"

Gradually, the children are beginning to understand that Jean's fantasy world can be a reality today. They are beginning to see the world through Jean's dream—grasping new insights, beholding new possibilities.

I continually reiterate to my students that prejudice has negative effects on all human beings. I also emphasize that the heaviness with which prejudice is transmitted varies with each individual or culture's outlook on life. But I am quick to tell the children that some good decisions also go out into the world which affect the lives of people positively, reminding them of Costa Rica's lack of army and our local community's wise decision to resolve the fire incident peacefully. But this is possible only if human beings think and act intelligently.

The clouds of prejudice in the children's minds are steadily disappearing. One of my students gives me an example that I want to share with you both.

"I was attending a school where flogging was the main way to discipline," said Jimmy. "Then my parents moved us to Buchanan last year so I enrolled in a different school. Here I learned about cooperative discipline. Students, teachers, administrators and parents share in different ways to enforce rules. No teacher is allowed to beat any student in my new school.

"I was surprised. For a long time, I believed that flogging was the only way to discipline. I could not believe any school could work without a whip."

"Yes, Jimmy," I said. "When people get used to a particular way of life, no matter how abusive, it is difficult to imagine anything else. If people get used to fighting as a means of resolving problems, then settling differences peacefully seems strange.

"But today, all of us have creative opportunities. If we are able to see the world in a new light, we can also see a world of insight and possibility."

This is where our work remains. Our young people are so used to violence, that it is difficult for them to see a world without it. But the young people at Common Ground Society are a new breed of Liberians. They are brave new children who are freeing themselves from prejudice, and from the kind of conditioned thinking that created the conflict here in Liberia. They are beginning to understand that there can be a new way. They have started not only conceiving prejudice, but also perceiving it. So now, they can see prejudice in action—right as it is happening— which enables them to stop it instantly, right where they are standing.

Today in class, we also talk about brain science, as your lesson provides.

"This project is designed to weed out the roots of prejudice that lead to panic and conflict," I begin. "First, it will help you recognize misinformation in the brain. Then it will help you restructure the brain with correct and accurate responses that will undo conditioned programming and lead to understanding. In this way you'll see prejudice in action, right as it is happening. You'll be able to see prejudice quickly enough to stop it before it begins."

The brain science project uses a chart with two columns Let me show ours to you:

WHAT CREATES CONFLICT? Conditioned Responses	WHAT PERMITS PEACE? Intelligent Questions
A conditioned image appears in the brain. *Example: Krahn people are mean.*	I have heard something about this, but is it true? *Example: Is it true that Krahn people are really mean?*
The image provokes conditioned thoughts and feelings. *Example: That Krahn man is mean.*	Do I have to think this way about Krahn people? *Example: Aren't all human beings mean to a certain extent?*
Prejudgment (prejudice) takes place. *Example: I will have nothing to do with this man because he is Krahn.*	I will look at all the evidence myself *Example: I will try to know this Krahn man.*
Conclusion: This situation is dangerous. *Example: I have to look out for that Krahn man and all Krahn people.*	Conclusion. I see nothing dangerous or bad about this Krahn man. *Example: He is one of us. He is Liberian. He is a human being.*
Because of the conclusions drawn from these conditioned responses, the perceived threats lead to fear. Because of these fears, we fight or flee. Perceiving an arising need to defend ourselves, we prepare for conflict.	Because of the conclusions drawn from these intelligent questions, instead of threats, there is an inner calm. We relax and enjoy ourselves. There is a feeling of confidence. A desire to resolve, reconcile and reach for new insight occurs. In this state, peace reigns.

During this brain science project, the children and I establish the fact that when we experience a conditioned response, our brain is doing what it is supposed to do, which is preparing us to deal with a threat. In the case of the discussion illustrated in our chart, the threat is *imagined*. The reaction is based on *mistaken information*—thoughts and feelings of fear and danger due to *false programming*. This false information creates conflict and hence prevents peace.

"The key," I say to the children, "is to Stop! Think! Run a check on your thoughts. There is no need to be afraid of your thoughts, because they are only thoughts. Thoughts don't hurt people, so there is no need to run from them. Remember to ask yourselves in this 'Stop! Think!' moment:

+ Is the information I just received true or false?
+ Do I have all the information I need to make an intelligent decision?
+ Did I get all the facts or did I get someone else's mistaken opinion?

"By asking these questions, we are relaxing and understanding the situation. Rather than being frightened, we are more in control of our thinking, so we are feeling calmer. As a result, we feel more confident and ready to become part of the solution, rather than part of the problem. We are prepared to resolve our thoughts and feelings. We are understanding WHAT PERMITS PEACE!"

People create conflict by "false self-talk," which is mental programming, or prejudice. I teach the children to run a check when they experience false self-talk. I tell them what you have taught me:

+ The old part of our brain is what is reacting, because of fear. Remember that the old brain doesn't know the difference between an imagined threat and a real one. The old brain reacts as if the imagined threat is real.

+ The old part of our brain's "fight or flight" reaction triggers us to act on an imaginary threat, which confuses the new brain's understanding of conflict.

+ The new part of our brain just describes or thinks about the prejudice and the conflict it has created, but the old part perceives the description as "real," as a signal to act to protect itself by either fighting or running away.

+ Be aware that false thoughts create anxiety and fear, and can lead to conflict.

"Understand that those false thoughts are learned, and can be unlearned," I say to the children. "Know that every thought has its own chemistry. Whatever we think, we feel. Stop your old, conditioned way of thinking by seeing the falseness of it. Examine the facts and replace false information with truthful statements."

At the end of today's lesson I leave the children with this clue. "When you see that you are starting to create conflict, imagine a big, red, STOP sign in your minds. This will help you arrest your conditioned thoughts. Don't try to cover them up. Stay with them and notice the effects they are having on your behavior toward others. STOP and THINK before you react. Ask yourself questions. As soon as you notice false, fearful thinking, inhale for two seconds, exhale for four seconds. Let go, and slow your thoughts down. Look for the truth. Then remember to follow the Intelligent Questioning steps we just reviewed in class to check whether your first thoughts and feelings are true or false. After this, you can replace any false information with true information, as we did on the chart."

Today I decide to walk home. I do this often during the evening hours, since I barely have time to exercise. Besides, this is my way of seeing the community, getting to know the people and understanding their conditions. It is more interesting to walk down Tubman

Street. I can look into the faces of people and imagine what's going on in their heads. In a car, I don't see anybody. I just zing past them.

On Tubman Street, right after the Welcome Sign, a group of young men are patching the main road with dirt and rocks. Two young boys are standing right in the middle of the road where a temporary checkpoint has been erected. They stop drivers of all commercial vehicles and ask them to pay a small fee. The boys will share the money with the workers after the repair is completed. It is a way of giving something to their community, and provides a popular means of livelihood for many young people in our country.

Everyone is trying to find a way to make a living around here. I pass an old man looking in a rubbish bin along the road. At every street corner, people are working at some business or other. The variety of wares along the street show clearly how determined people are to make something of their lives. This is very difficult for Liberians; they have seen life in many shades of gray.

Three little girls walk hand in hand, singing lines from a Christmas carol in squeaky unison. Gradually I stroll closer to Jecko Town, the community, where I live. A few days ago, many wooden counters stood empty. But now, everyone wants to take advantage of the selling season. So the owners have returned, and are getting ready for business. A small group of women are supervising youths erecting their stalls. They pay adolescents to do the work, but if they don't watch them, many would take the money and procrastinate on the job.

Darkness is beginning to gather. To avoid a jagged hole in the middle of the road, I turn onto a narrow, dusty lane that leads to my house. Many residents are already in their homes, probably lying awake on their beds or conversing in groups in their parlors. As I see faint lights emanating from their lanterns and candles, I hope that they are happy. I reflect on how odd it seems for hundreds of people to be living in a dozen small houses while I pass them all by without seeing a single one.

A few meters from my house, I stumble on a rock in the road. If the major roads across the country remain derelict, I think it's a sign that these small roads to towns in and out of the capital will take another decade to be safely navigable.

At home, I hurriedly take my bath and climb into bed. Tonight our generator is down, so I have lit my lantern. I hate candles, because there is no way to control them once I am overtaken by sleep. By contrast, the lantern burns only until the kerosene runs out, so there is no fear of fire.

It has been a long day, but it has also been a wonderful one. I always look forward to The Peace School. The children give me so much pleasure.

I will keep in touch,
Marvin

Lesson 17

Perception Is Everything

"Children in Liberia find it difficult to imagine life without war. Many of the Peace School students were born during the war. All their lives, these children have seen only violence, hunger and death. Having suffered physical and psychological trauma, they have been denied many of the joys of childhood."

— *Marvin Garbeh Davis*

Dear Dr. T and Jean…

Today is the last class before we finally close for Christmas break. I want to make sure that the children are home in time for Christmas with their families. Some students have to sell wares during the season, to enable their parents to buy them gifts. Some children will need to see uncles and aunts who will give them money they can use to set up their own business during the last few days before the holiday. Some will buy cold water from cold-water depots, at five dollars for two bags which they then resell on the street at twice the price. The profit is used to buy clothes and other things they need for Christmas. Some sell auction goods, cool aid, doughnuts or soap for business people who pay them a small commission. Some of the children would like to travel to Monrovia to visit relatives who work there in civil service or business. As a visitor under a relative's roof, they may receive something for Christmas. In other words, everyone wants to have a merry Christmas and all are prepared to do anything to have it.

In our last few lessons, I have been challenging my students to believe in the possibility of their own right-side-up world, and to accept that the possibility exists. When I look at their faces, I can see that many of them doubt it. Those who do entertain the idea still hold vestiges of doubt, because all they know is war. Can you imagine, Dr. T and Jean, growing up in war, knowing nothing else?

Their doubt stems from fear of embracing a new way of seeing events around them. For those who have been traumatized, it can be frightening to try to shift and see the world in a different light. So I encourage them. "If you start to become aware of your fearful, false thinking, then a right-side- up world is possible."

I understand why many children doubt that a right-side-up world could come into existence in this part of the world. They have lived in terrible conflict for a very long time. We have been fighting ever since many of them inhaled their first breath of air. To change and see life in a new way is difficult, for some, impossible. Many of the Peace School students were born during the war. All their lives, these children have seen only violence, hunger and death. Having suffered physical and psychological trauma, they have been denied many of the joys of childhood.

The other day I heard a group of children arguing outside my office about how their lives would have been different if the war had never happened. "We would be enjoying electricity instead of reading by candlelight," one of them remarked.

Another said, "We would be watching TV at home, instead of paying money to go to a video club."

I not only agree with these children, I empathize with them. These are children as old as fourteen who have never tasted ice cream, seen a TV, or had sufficient food or clothing. In these modern times, it is a primitive and very sad life.

Our children are conditioned to violence and poverty, but our work is to help the children at least imagine something different, to show them that even if they were born and raised in the shadow of war, it is possible to imagine peace.

This brings me to the lesson I am teaching today, called "Perception Is Everything," and indeed this is true. We are what we think. Descartes put it squarely when he said, "I think, therefore I am."

But I would add what you have told me, Dr. T., and so I say, "I think, therefore I am *what I think I am.*"

This pertains to what we are teaching these young people about prejudice. It is only conditioned thought that triggers the emotions. The emotions in turn trigger the old part of the brain's "fight or flight" hardwired mechanism. This hardwiring creates conflict and, in the extreme, war. It is as simple as that.

Intellectuals, politicians and religious leaders who are determined to misuse power will say that this is much too simplistic. They don't want to change, because they have a vested interest in keeping the conflict going. They believe that the problem is "out there" somewhere. I have heard them saying, "I am just reporting on what is happening."

They falsely assume that the problem is an intellectual one. They are not aware that the very "I" that is doing the seeing and the problem solving is the entity that is creating the conflict. If they could face the facts fully, they would instead be saying, "I think that *I* am separate from the conflict but *I* am the source of the conflict in the self-protective ways *I* have built up to fortify myself against recognizing the truth of what is going on!"

Perception can pierce their illusion of being separate from the conflict by showing us that what is "out there" is actually "in here." To help us integrate this perception, we could say to ourselves, "Every time I project my conditioned views, I recreate and sustain the conflict by insisting that there is a division between *me* and everything that is *not me*."

This seems to be the source of conflict. We are always trying to act on what we create, but never get to the source of it by looking inwards at who we are, and at the conditioned ways we are programmed to think. So to help these young people understand the root of the conflict, we have to move from the outer situation of war at the political level, back to the fundamental root of it: the way we have been conditioned to think.

Thus, today's lesson is very important for I am teaching the children to question their false and fearful thinking, thereby eliminating their mental roadblocks to peaceable living.

First, we have to be aware of when we are creating conflict. Then, to be free of prejudicial conditioned thoughts by recognizing them for what they are and not identifying with them, we need to imagine a big red STOP sign in our minds. When we can do this, our conditioned thoughts and feelings can be recognized and allowed to move through our consciousness unimpeded.

"Be open to your fearful thoughts," I say to the children. "Don't cover them up. You need to see the effects your fears have on your thoughts. You also need to see how your fears affect your behavior toward other people. Remember to stop and think before you act, because this moment in time, this interval when a person stops and thinks, allows for new thinking.

"We are going to do a small exercise together, to help you become calmer and more powerful in handling fearful thinking. Think of the last time you noticed you felt fear because of some false thinking. Now, try this:

- "Inhale for two to four seconds.
- "Exhale for two to four seconds.
- "Repeat these slow breaths a few times.
- "Allow yourself to let go and slow down.
- "Take this moment to look for the truth by asking:
    1. What's the evidence?
    2. Is this true?
    3. Where did this come from?
    4. Do I have to think this way?

"Doing this exercise allows you to replace any false thinking with a true statement. Do you notice how, at the end of this exercise, we have come to the STOP! THINK! Moment?" They are all sitting there with calmly thoughtful expressions on their faces, nodding their heads.

For a long time, we have been talking about this ability to stop and think before react-ing. With each, frequent repetition, we reach a new perspective. Every beautiful insight carries the tremendous benefit of helping us understand what prevents peace. I use several images of comparison for my students, in order to help them really understand this im-portant insight:

"Imagine that you've stumbled on a new idea," I say. "It comes like a flash of lightning. You are suddenly forced into being absolutely still. You can't move, because you are over-whelmed. You suddenly realize that something you have seen or heard many times—and have believed—may be untrue, and your body suddenly recognizes it. You feel like you have even stopped breathing for a moment because you are so totally focused on that new idea. Nothing else in the world exists. It strikes you that no one has ever had such an idea before, that you are the first to make this new discovery. That's how it feels in the STOP! THINK! moment."

Sometimes, I give the students this portrayal of the insight: "In the STOP! THINK! moment, nothing exists but the 'here and now', exactly where you are. In these expanded seconds, there is no conflict. It is like locking the world up in your head and setting the key aside. When we stop, it is like being removed from a war zone and sent to a new location, where we *see* the conflict and *understand* that we do not have to join that old army of our past thoughts. Reaching this understanding of peace can be a rocky, arduous journey. The world we live in causes us to feel angry, sad and out of control, sometimes on a daily basis."

Understanding what prevents peace demands a lot of attention, time and patience. As human beings, we create conflict time and again, no matter how much we want peace. The main impasse is those old, inherited fears that we still allow to threaten us. We feel that ancestral need to defend ourselves in order to survive, and forget to question its veracity.

"Always remember that you don't have to think and act the way human beings have been behaving for thousands of years," I say to my children. "You don't have to live in the shadow of your forgotten ancestors. Instead, when you are faced with conflict, you can allow intel-ligence. This is why you are here in the Peace School.

"Many people cannot remain calm in stressful situations," I add, "which more than likely affects their relationships with others. It may even affect their health. Such people do not know how to relax or how to achieve a sense of calm in a tense situation.

"But you already know," I point out. "You are the new generation, educated with the un-derstanding and ability to respond intelligently to conflict, using insight that will enable you to act intelligently.

"All you need is to be *aware*, always alert enough to question intelligently when you sense false and fearful thinking. Just remember to ask those four, crucial questions from our ex-ercise today:

1. What is the evidence for what I am hearing?
2. Is what I am hearing true?
3. Where did this information come from?
4. Do I have to think this way, or is there a better way?

"What does asking ourselves these questions do for us?" I ask my students.
"Puts us in a STOP! THINK! moment," they say in unison.
"Yes," I answer, "and that puts us on the road to where?"
"To understanding!" they proudly answer. Just as this feeling of comprehension makes us feel open, confident, and filled with a desire to peacefully resolve conflict rather than

overflow with hate and start fighting, I see the same deep feeling of comprehension on my students' faces.

Together, we summarize the facts and then the steps: Understanding what prevents peace involves becoming aware of incoming information and questioning whether it is true or false. Conflict is caused by false self-talk that is mental programming, or prejudice. We can be free of this conditioning by learning and practicing a few steps:

- Understand that false thoughts create anxiety and fear which both lead to conflict.
- Be aware that the old brain's function is to fight or run away, and that it doesn't know whether a threat is real or imagined.
- Realize that blindly accepting mistaken information is a habit that can be unlearned.
- Know that every thought has its own chemistry. Thoughts produce feelings in the same way that feelings produce thoughts. Together our thoughts and feelings lead to understanding or to a primitive fight or flight reaction that underlies conflict and drives us to war.
- Listen to anxious thoughts. They contain lessons.
- Stop old, automatic misinformation by identifying with its falsehoods. Replace lies with truth.

The children and I perform an exercise to help them really see the differences. Here's the chart we created together:

REPLACING FALSE THINKING WITH TRUE INFORMATION

Examples of False Thinking	Examples of True Information
All Bassa people are lazy.	All such broad statements are stereotypes, based on conditioned thinking. Individuals are different.
Foreigners are strange and frightening.	A foreigner is just someone from another country. If I were in another country, I would be a foreigner too.
"We" need to defend ourselves against "them." Those people are a threat to our beliefs. My country is better than theirs.	Beliefs can separate people. Others probably feel as threatened by our beliefs as we feel about theirs. There is no "them." If I learn to understand other people, I will certainly feel more comfortable with everybody. We all share the same home—Earth.
These people have weird customs.	What a boring world it would be if we were all the same. Every culture has different customs, and the customs of other cultures are always interesting if we learn to understand them.
Their way of dressing is strange.	Clothes are only customs. They have nothing to do with the person inside.
Their dialect is too odd. They look and act different.	Our language probably sounds odd to them too. Wouldn't it be fun to learn a few words in their language?

Anger is a product of fear. Thus, when we are angry with someone whom we perceive as different and threatening, we are actually just hiding our fear. We feel what we think. Understanding this allows us to realize that we have a choice: to stay angry or to uncover the fear and deal with it.

Our conditioned brain usually shows these fears as thoughts that begin with "What if", and presents frightening images. Here are some "What if's" common to us in Liberia:

What if they came from a different county?
What if they were here to take over our country?
What if they were Kpelle people? We know Kpelle people don't like us.
What if they are part of a different belief system?
What if they want us to live like them?

The children admit that such questions run through their minds when they see someone who seems strange, whether they're from a different church, school, location, or team. I remind them that our thoughts affect our behavior. It is therefore important for us to try to replace our fearful thoughts with more realistic thoughts such as:

What if they are no different from us?
What if they had new and interesting ideas to build our country?
What if they want us to be their friends?
What if we see them as human beings?
What if they just want to live in peace?

"Thinking this way can open more doors and help make us more friendly," I say to the children. "It is therefore important for us to examine our thoughts, in order to understand whether they are false or true, and whether their effects on us and others are negative or positive.

"In concluding our lesson today, I want to remind you that all our troubles start with a single thought. The thought creates feelings. The feelings create actions. We can either react in a fight or flight way and continue the conflict, or we can stop prejudice in our brain, right at the start, when we are first aware of it. So I ask you, 'What is the intelligent thing to do?'"

Thanks for everything,
Marvin

Lesson 18

Rights and Responsibilities

"We, the children of Liberia, ask the adults—our parents, teachers, school administrators, and political leaders—to guarantee us the right to feel safe from being bullied at home, at school and in our communities. We feel afraid of what has happened in our country with people killing each other. We understand that this was caused in part by bullying, created by prejudice. We ask you, the people of our country and of the world, to consider seriously the dangers of bullying, and to provide us with programs that teach us how to understand and resolve this problem peacefully. If you can help us now, then we will be able to grow into adults without becoming bullies, and without hurting each other even more."

— Marvin Garbeh Davis

Dear Dr. T and Jean…

The issue of rights is raging like a blazing fire across the length and breadth of this country. It is a new phenomenon in post-war Liberia. Not a day goes by without news about our rights—children's rights, women's rights, medical rights, legal rights, cultural rights, environmental rights—the list goes on and on. Everyone we meet is quick to point out some aspect of our civil liberties and its associated entitlement. Even on the radio, we hear human rights organizations making a lot of noise on the subject. Some schools in Liberia are now teaching human rights as part of their school curriculum. Likely because the rights of people in this land have been abused so much and for so long, our new democratic administration is making everyone fight for what is theirs.

It is productive to talk about rights and to teach our young children about theirs. Sadly, however, too many overlook the responsibilities that go hand-in-hand with those rights.

I was talking with some parents recently who told me they were holding back on disciplining their children, because they were afraid they would be taken to court. One parent said to me, "This whole human rights business is driving us crazy. Our children are now our parents. If we want to punish them, we are afraid of being accused of child abuse. If we even want them to do some chores at home, we think about child labor laws."

Many people blame the Western world for all these problems. They say if Westerners did not make human rights a precondition to providing aids and grants, we would not be where we are today. Many people attribute social ills in our society to the Western world's demand for human rights and freedom. Some people even argue that the issue of human rights is not African, and if we want to talk about human rights, we should discuss it from the African perspective. This issue has become a touchy problem, most likely because there are so many positions.

I have heard Africans say that the human rights issue is the white man's idea. They work hard to have what they have in their countries, and their countries are developed. Africans work hard, too, and also want their countries to be developed. Now that we want to discipline our young people because we feel this contributes to the country's well-being, the Western world is accusing us of ignoring human rights. "Human rights are not for poor people," says one parent. "They are for the rich." Despite this outcry, human rights organizations are springing up in our country and our people are showing up in their offices every day.

Many people acknowledge that at the heart of the Liberian conflict, there has been a lack of respect for human rights. Now that there is a new administration that advocates rights for everyone, people should be very keen about them, and they are. However, I hear only a few voices talking about the responsibilities that balance our rights. In many cases, I hear people demanding rights without doing the accompanying work.

People are so embroiled in getting their rights that they forget that obtaining them is only the first part of the process. When a child demands her right to education, she must be made aware of her responsibility, which is to study well, and work toward success in life. When a child considers it his right to play music he wants to hear, he needs to understand that with this right comes a responsibility to play that music at a moderate level so that neighbors are not bothered.

Today in class, I inform the children that, as human beings, they are entitled to certain rights—in their families, schools, communities and in the world. For instance, at home, they have the right to be clothed, to be fed, to be cared for when they are sick, to be kept free of conflict and to be protected from harm. "Do you believe you are entitled to other rights at home? I ask.

"The right to be entertained—watching TV at home," says Marion.

"The right to eat three times daily," John adds.

"The right to play," Aminata stresses.

"The right to visit your friends," Cindy says.

We also discuss some of the rights they are entitled to at school: to be educated, to develop knowledge and skills in order to find a good job that will allow them to enjoy an intelligent, healthy life, to be trained to be physically and mentally fit, to be protected from bullies that could hurt them, to be able to freely and respectfully question the views of others, and to be able to think and talk about what they want without censorship.

Janet adds, "The right to have teachers who will always come to school—on time."

Martin stresses, "The right to pursue education in an environment where there will be no threat." Understandably, many children emphasize this point, remembering when their schools were invaded during the war.

John concludes with "The right to learn in a conducive atmosphere."

I steer the discussion into the next area of human rights. "In our communities, we should have the ability to speak and write freely about what we see as injustice. We should be able to speak against practices that are unfair to others, and we should feel secure where we live." The children dive in.

"Everyone should have a hand water pump close to their homes," says Martin. Apparently Martin lives far away from the hand pump that was installed by a non-profit organization. The distance varies. Many walk only several meters, while others have to hike many kilometers to get pipe-borne water.

Thomas says. "A community should have a place where children can read and find books to borrow and return."

"A community should have transportation to and from school," declares Emmanuel.

"A community should have a playground intended only for children to play games," says John.

Cindy finishes with "There must be a clinic in every community."

Next, we move to world rights. We all agree that we should feel safe, be free of the terrible effects of war, be able to enjoy the beauty of the earth and its many interesting people, and be free to choose capable people to represent us in government. The children are quick to point out more rights.

Wodokueh begins. "The freedom to travel to and in any part of the world."

Even though I know the answer before I ask, I can't resist. "Which part of the world would you love to see?"

Simultaneously, many of them shout, "America!" You see, Dr. T and Jean, all the young people here want to live there. For them, that is the real world, because everything seems possible in America.

Trying to help them understand, I say, "It is not all bread and butter in America. Prejudice lives there too, still visible in what people say, in what's printed in the press, and in what people see on television."

Trokon says, "You just let me get there, and I will give you my own viewpoint!"

"The freedom to work anywhere you like," says Jerrilyn.

All during this session, at my request, the children have been enumerating their rights. So far, not one has suggested a responsibility that goes with the right they feel they are entitled to. This is troubling. It seems the children are just imitating adults. I realize that I must help them connect rights with responsibilities.

At this point, I ask, "Do all the people in the world enjoy the same rights?"

"No!" they call in unison.

But Janet adds, "The children in America eat three times a day. I eat only once or sometimes twice, and that is mainly the first week after my dad gets his salary."

"That's true, Janet," I respond. There are certainly citizens of some countries in the world who have certain rights and freedoms that others don't enjoy. Does anyone know of any country whose citizens enjoy rights that we don't have here in Liberia?"

"America! America!" they scream in harmony.

The children are aware that even though other countries enjoy more rights than they, prejudice still exists everywhere. "Some people say unfair things about one group of people," I emphasize, "and that group may snap back with some prejudice in return. People abuse freedoms such as free speech to say scandalous and libelous things about others.

"Education," I explain, "is a right, but there is a responsibility that goes with this right. One must respond to this opportunity by being very serious about one's studies and working hard at school. So it is with freedom of speech. Just because a person has the right to speak his mind, doesn't mean that he has the right to say anything false or malicious about others. If he does, he is not accepting the responsibility that is attached to his right to free speech."

I then use the opportunity to explain the difference. "A privilege is a special opportunity, and a right is an entitlement we have because we are human beings. Our rights need to be looked upon as special opportunities that we earn by being responsible. We must use our privileges and our rights intelligently, not just for ourselves, but also for the betterment of the world."

The foundation of free countries of the world is democracy. A democracy is a form of government where the population of a society has power over the government. One such right is the freedom of speech. If we use our right to freedom of speech irresponsibly, we devalue that right. We have the right to liberty, but this does not mean we are free to do anything that pleases us, whether at home, at school, or in the world. It is abusive to pursue our rights in contradiction to the health or happiness of others. Our freedom cannot be exercised when it adversely affects others. In Liberia we say, where your rights end, someone else's rights begin.

The foundation of democracy is clear and intelligent thinking, and the opportunity to act in ways that bring equality and peace to all humanity. If we live in a country that wants us to think in a fixed, conditioned mode, then we are not free to learn. Sadly, this is the case in many countries around the world. Some leaders want to control their citizens' thoughts and actions. The reason is simple: they are afraid to let people make their own choices. They assume that if people speak freely, they are likely to criticize or override their government.

"Always remember," I say to my students, "if you are conditioned to think in only one way, you will not be able to make intelligent decisions. You will not be able to see the truth and act upon it, because all the details that could help you make a sound decision will not be at your disposal.

"Just as you have the right to freedom of speech, you are also entitled to the right to be educated intelligently. So remember to accept the responsibilities that go along with entitlements. You have a right to accurate information, to be able to gather all sides of a story. And you have the responsibility to use this information truthfully and honestly. Accurate information is the only route to intelligent decisions in our lives, and the only path to taking responsibility for our actions.

"Sometimes you may feel incapable of making intelligent and responsible decisions, but it will only be because you lack accurate information. The warning signs include such phrases as 'They say…' or 'Rumor has it…'

"Avoiding prejudice is your right *and* your responsibility. To do this, you need to remember the following:

- ✦ Question everything! Assume nothing!
- ✦ Gather accurate information.
- ✦ Don't judge anyone or anything. Observe. Think for yourself.
- ✦ Interrogate questionable authority.
- ✦ Examine your own thinking.
- ✦ Act rather than react.
- ✦ Look for root causes.

"We often have an urge to protect ourselves. But we really only have two choices. Should we hide behind lies or learn the truth?"

"Learn the truth," the children chorus, while nodding their heads.

Today the students construct another chart in class. This one has to do with rights and responsibilities. They take turns contributing one of our rights directly to the flip chart while the rest of the children suggest a corresponding responsibility. This is the chart.

MY RIGHTS AND MY RESPONSIBILITIES	
IF THIS IS MY RIGHT...	**THEN THIS IS MY RESPONSIBILITY:**
I can say what I think any time I choose.	I must use speech in an intelligent, constructive way.
I need to make intelligent decisions about my life.	I need to make sure I have accurate information.
I can take any action to protect myself against danger any time.	I need to act, based on clear thought— and not REact in a conditioned way.
I need to be free of disease.	I must take care of my health needs by making intelligent decisions about diet, exercise and rest.
I have a right to my opinion.	I need to be aware that my opinion may not be based on fact.
I have a right to travel.	I need to act courteously when visiting other areas of the world (by respecting different customs).

I congratulate the children on their good work. We discuss how these rights stem from the prejudices we have learned. For example, when we believe that we are entitled to the first right on our chart ("I can say what I think any time I choose") we must ask ourselves a list of questions to discover whether it is truly a right, or simply a bullying tactic based on old prejudices:

- Where does this belief come from?
- Where did you learn this?
- Do you think this belief is a fact or an opinion?
- If it is an opinion, do you think it may be the result of prejudice?
- How strongly do you feel about this right?
- What is the responsibility that goes hand-in-hand with this right?
- How strongly do you feel about this responsibility?
- Do you feel as strongly about this responsibility as you feel about the right?
- Do you think prejudice is a factor in this difference?
- Can you tell whether your "right" is a conditioned belief or an intelligent decision?
- Is it time to ask your fellow students, outside this classroom, if they believe your rights and responsibilities show any sign of prejudice?

I alert the children to the fact that proverbs, 'wise' sayings or aphorisms can be other sources of prejudice. "Here is a list of some of our common proverbs here in our Liberia," I say. "People base many of their decisions on them. I'd like you to notice how some of these sayings contradict each other."

- Look before you leap.
- He who hesitates is lost.

- You can't teach an old dog new tricks.
- It's never too late to learn.

- Out of sight, out of mind.
- Absence makes the heart grow fonder.

- Two heads are better than one.
- If you want something done, do it yourself.

- Where there's a will, there's a way.
- Time and tide wait for no man.

- Many hands make light work.
- Too many cooks spoil the broth.

We discuss the merit in these wise sayings. I point out that their chief use seems to be to support decisions already concluded. This is a source of prejudice among our people. It would be considered unwise or unintelligent to base your action on an old saying, whatever its content.

Just because some pairs of old sayings are mutually exclusive, it does not mean that we should reject them. While many sayings are of value in our lives, some are a hindrance. For instance, "All is fair in love and war." No civilized society would ever agree with this, if they reflected on the unspeakable atrocities committed in warfare. As for love, there is no moral code in the world that sanctions rape, adultery or incest, simply because the committer perceives himself to be seized by fervent love. Only those who intend to force themselves upon others would utter such a saying, as justification for having already made up their minds to cause harm.

"Once prejudice is in gear, it can create tremendous suffering," I remind the students.

"Just as our old, stale thinking has created prejudice, our new, fresh thinking can be the source of freedom from prejudice. All we have to do is develop our insight—our ability to be aware and to see. This will help us walk the path to peace. Acting from intelligence rather than prejudice is the highest form of action. Do you want to be part of this action so that our country can free itself of war?"

"Yes!" the children exclaim, nodding their heads vigorously.

Understanding prejudice as conditioned thinking is actually quite straightforward. Because we are the ones who have created it, we can come to an understanding of it and end it. But there are some people who don't want us, the "average" people, to understand and be free of prejudice. They want to keep us in a state of ignorance and exploit our lack of knowledge for their own personal gain.

I say to the children, "It is your responsibility to learn to recognize prejudice—in yourself as well as others—and to *see* the ways *you* have been programmed to think and obey without question. By putting aside all that is not responsible behavior, you will come upon your innate rights, those that are natural to you. Because they emanate from intelligence, they are universal and timeless.

"Before asserting any rights, it is important to differentiate between rights based on a rebound reaction, and rights based on careful, intelligent questioning. Reactive 'rights' are those claimed after a period of longing, or after having lost all rights during a war. Sometimes, just at such moments, we hear a strong speaker who knows how to play on our emotions and our fatigue, making claims about how our rights have been compromised. We have dreamt about these ideals and have imagined living in other countries that seem to have those rights, but we've never examined the actual facts. So just when we are most tired and most anxious, we must be even more cautious by questioning what such a speaker is really saying, and make sure we seek rights based on an intelligent understanding of what truly *prevents* human rights. This is how we naturally and responsibly come upon our true rights. In this, there is intelligence and love. And where there is intelligence and love, there is the greatest entitlement of all—to be free of conflict."

When I say things like this to them, I sometimes wonder if they are mature enough to grasp what it all means. But having grown up in war, they have matured far beyond their years. I can see the understanding in their eyes.

You created a Bill of Rights Dr. T, which I have adapted for the children and for the reader, as it has much to do with prejudice and the effects of bullying on us here in Liberia.

I wish the President of Liberia would adopt this for our children as well as for our adults, so everyone could become aware of what causes prejudice and bullying. In my heart, I feel that we could then avoid another terrible civil war like the one we just had and are still suffering from.

CHILDREN'S BILL OF RIGHTS AND RESPONSIBILITIES FOR A BULLY-FREE SOCIETY

BULLYING: THE REPEATED intimidation of others by the real or threatened infliction of physical, verbal, written, or emotional abuse, or through attacks on the person or property of another.

Proclamation

We, the children of Liberia, ask the adults—our parents, teachers, school administrators, and political leaders—to guarantee us the right to feel safe from being bullied at home, at school and in our communities. We feel afraid of what has happened in our country with people killing each other. We understand that this was caused mostly by bullying, created by prejudice. We ask you, the people of our country and of the world, to consider seriously the dangers of bullying, and to provide young people with programs that teach us how to understand and resolve this crisis peacefully. If you can help us now, then we can become adults without becoming bullies, and without hurting each other even more.

My Rights and Responsibilities

- I have the right to be free from bullying and physical harm and the responsibility to learn ways of resolving conflict peacefully.

- I have the right to be free from hurtful names and the responsibility to understand what would make me want to call others hurtful names.

- I have the right to be free from intimidation regardless of my membership in a group, and the responsibility to understand what it means to belong to a "group."

- I have the right to be free from taunting due to others' perceived differences of me, and the responsibility to be respectful of others regardless of how differently I have been taught to perceive them.

- I have the right to be free from bullying because of race, gender or culture and the responsibility to educate myself about why this happens.

- I have the right to be free from bullying regardless of my physical appearance and the responsibility not to pick on myself regardless of what others may think of me.

- I have the right to be free from teasing regardless of how much smarter other people think they are compared to me, and the responsibility to educate myself to be as intelligent as I can be.

- I have the right to be free from bullying regardless of how athletic I am compared to others, and the responsibility to find endeavors that both give me a sense of physical well being and provide me with the chance to personally excel.

- I have the right to be free from bullying regardless of my size or strength, and the responsibility to find ways that will strengthen me.

- I have the right to learn the skills to understand and handle bullies without hurting or being hurt, and the responsibility to teach others these skills so they will not get bullied.

- I have the right to protect myself from harm, and the responsibility to use these skills humanely.

Every child everywhere has a basic right to be treated with respect and the responsibility in turn to respect all others.

We call on you to support the Children's Bill of Rights for A Bully-Free Society and we encourage all of you who live or work with children to help them create a safe world that is free of bullying.

Sincerely yours,
Marvin

Lesson 19
Seeing the Big Picture

Our young people are our most endangered species. Today our world has achieved brilliance without wisdom and intelligence, power without control and conscience. Today we know more about war than we know about peace, more about killing than living. Now it is time for us to understand why, despite the tremendous technological advances we have made, members of the human race—the only true race—are still unable to live together in peace.

— *Marvin Garbeh Davis*

Dear Dr. T and Jean…

I am impressed, though not fully content, with the work we are doing with young people here. This impression comes from the fact that the children have begun freely discussing the issues of prejudice and how it can be prevented.

Considering the number of children in Buchanan who want to enroll in the Peace School program, we have taught only a small number. because of problems with space, resources and logistics. But as the saying goes, small drops of water make a mighty ocean. I am sure some of these young people will help to reshape this country. Hence, I am happy about the children whose lives have been touched by our program. We can refer to these children as the Brave New Generation of Liberians. With their new understanding of conflict—specifically prejudice, which is at the heart of human conflict—they will start a new Liberia with the requisite tools for relating in ways that enhance peace. Although it is a small group, I am sure they will stand like bright lanterns on top of a hill and illuminate the darkness of prejudice that binds humanity in lives of chaos.

Here's an example of the kind of discussion and debate that has been going on in the class lately among the children: Stephen, from the Monrovia Junction Community, came to class late. As he entered, Christopher said: "Why is it that you people from the Monrovia Junction area are always late for Peace School?"

Marion responded: "That is prejudice, Christopher. Stephen is the only person from Monrovia Junction who is late right now, and you don't know why he is late. To include all the children from Monrovia Junction is not fair."

"I am sorry," Christopher apologized, giving Stephen an opportunity to explain that his taxi had broken down near the Tarr Bar community, so he'd had to walk to Peace School.

I am impressed by how the children handled this conflict—resolving it intelligently without my intervention. The children are learning to understand what prevents peace. I find happiness in such exchanges among them.

This brings me to the big picture I have been conjuring up these last few weeks, Dr. T. Maybe it is only a dream, but that's the way Common Ground started. What would life be without dreams anyway?

You see, I have been thinking lately about establishing a special kind of school in Liberia, beyond the after-school program I teach now. I see this is as the way to the future, the way of rebuilding and reshaping our country and the world. I am talking about a school where many young people will go to understand themselves and in so doing, understand not only the place of thought in such areas as science and technology, but also how thought can become conditioned, creating conflict in human relationships. I want it to be a school where young people will learn the totality of their own lives.

For a long time in our country, schools have been a place for learning about how to be successful, which most define as getting a degree, getting a career and starting out in life. Our school system is concerned only with making people successful teachers, doctors, and lawyers and forgets to teach people about life and relationships. It has focused only on training for academic skills, omitting relationship skills.

We have seen the results in our own country today. After all this education, we have lost everything we have taken so many years to build. Had we taught our children to learn how to live with each other, respect diversity and see differences as a source of interacting rather than fighting, we would have had peace instead of war.

Even after the war, nobody is talking about teaching young people the art of human relationships. I don't know whether there is a sense of stubbornness or a lack of realization that keeps us engaging our children in getting an education that will provide them big salaries and a "good" life, while ignoring the teaching of values that will enhance and broaden the way they relate with other people. The foundation of all education is self-understanding. Once we can understand ourselves as people, then a career and security can be built. If self-understanding is the primary intent of education, then the divisive conflict that comes from ignorance and self-centered thinking will be over-ridden and all the rest can flow.

To teach our children about the art of living, we need to think holistically. It is important for them to learn skills that enable them to understand how to survive and cope with the stress of life itself. Starting with a curriculum that is grounded in understanding themselves, we can gradually expand the lessons in compassionate living arts to help them understand their families, their schoolmates, the broader community and finally their fellow human beings in the world at large.

When I tell people that we are teaching our young children to understand the root causes of conflict in human relationships, many of them find it difficult to understand why we would bother. They think we are wasting the children's time.

Our people are consumed with preparing young people academically. Everyone wants his child to be successful. All adults push their children very hard to succeed. It is admirable to educate our young people to strive for excellence technologically and academically, but at the same time we must educate them to fundamentally understand themselves.

Life may be difficult, but this is not. We know we can do it, as we have already begun it here at the Common Ground Peace School. It is time we started creating similar educational environments to produce sane and intelligent human beings in schools, homes and communities.

In this new kind of school, I am thinking that the graduates will not only get a job that pays well, but will seek what they love in life. In this kind of school, children will understand that it is good to pursue their own desires and interests. They will understand that competition is destructive, and that young people need to accept each other as human beings—not as representations of tribes, churches, nationalities or races.

I think this is possible. We are at a critical juncture in life here. We have the power to turn toward total destruction or toward total creativity. With the proper tools and resources, we can truly help our young people understand and live in peace. Why wouldn't we do this? I have come to the realization that if we don't understand and teach the process of thought, the complexities of self, and the structures that our thinking creates, our children will get caught up in "life as usual" and we will miss this golden opportunity.

Our young people are our most endangered species. Today our world has achieved brilliance without wisdom and intelligence, power without control and conscience. Today we know more about war than we know about peace, more about killing than living. Now it is time for us to understand why, despite the tremendous technological advances we have made, members of the human race—the only true race—are still unable to live together in peace.

This is the big picture for me and for the children at Common Ground. It's a picture we are beginning to fully embrace. We have started on our way to doing this by helping our children recognize their own fears.

I have taught the children to understand that prejudice is conditioned thinking, which in turn is fed by fear. A Bassa person says unfair things about the Kpelle man because of fear. People hate foreigners because of fear-mongering misconceptions. Sometimes difficult to recognize, fear hides beneath our anger, within our sorrow, inside the bully, intertwining the unhappy person.

But fear can exist in a happy person, too. Little Janet told me in class that she happily joined a group of girls who were bullying another girl from a different school because she was afraid that otherwise, her friends would see her as a coward. As U.S. President

Franklin Delano Roosevelt said in his 1933 inauguration speech, "The only thing we have to fear is fear itself." He was referring to the economic conditions resulting from the Great Depression of 1929. He was saying that if we could not shake our pessimistic outlook, it would be tough to turn things around.

As part of the big picture we are embracing, I often remind the children in the Peace School that prejudice begins with one thought. That thought affects how we feel. Those thoughts and feelings affect our behavior. We then act the way we feel by translating our thoughts into what we say and do. Thus all our conditioned behavior and any of our prejudices begin with our thoughts. The difference between being an angry, unhappy bully and being a friendly, open person is how we think. If we think honest, true thoughts, that is how we will act.

Because it is the most important lesson, I have been emphasizing the STOP and THINK concept in a variety of ways.

"Whenever you feel a thought creeping into your mind," I remind the children, "just stop and look at the thought, no matter what it is. You don't need to judge it as good or bad, because this doesn't help. Just look at your thought, see it, and do not resist it. You are simply an observer, looking at your thought as if it were a newspaper you were reading."

This is a simple but important concept, and as we are practicing it every day, it is helping us all. The children and I have realized that it is up to everyone. We can each stop prejudice in our brains, right at the start, when it first comes up—and end it in a moment!

I have come to realize that the whole problem of understanding prejudice and preventing it is an ongoing process, not a single event. We need to work at it every day. By being constantly vigilant, questioning, observing, and recognizing prejudice as it happens, we can stop it in its tracks.

To be free of prejudice, we need to acknowledge that horrible events such as wars and genocide are really happening. With such acknowledgement, we can question how they happen. In this process, we must remain aware of conditioned reactions of any kind. We must ask ourselves, "Why do I believe that?"

I have noticed, from my interactions with the children and from some of their responses, that the problem of prejudice stems from scary thoughts. I tell my children that it is natural for them to feel scared sometimes, but that it is also important to understand that scary thoughts are at the root of prejudice, too.

Fearing each other can stop us from creating a world where people can live together in peace. Fear can hinder us from creating a right-side-up world, because when we live in fear of each other, we can't respect our differences; nor can we learn from each other. Scary thoughts about others affect our behavior. But we have the power to change our thoughts from scary to realistic. Unlike scary thoughts that come from fear, realistic thoughts come from intelligent, clear thinking. While scary thoughts can easily lead us to prejudice, realistic thoughts lead us to peace.

Some of the students mistake scary thoughts for imagination, so I explain to them that there is nothing wrong with having a strong imagination, which can certainly lead to creative thoughts. We just need to know when we are using our imagination and when we are being realistic—and to be able to see the difference. It is good for us to know that we are what we think. That is, our thoughts produce all that we are. Thinking for ourselves can help free us from prejudice. If we are free of prejudice, we can make a world free of prejudice. If we have this extraordinary power, why wouldn't we use it?

Democracy is a new word used by many young people here, so I decided to tell them the real essence of democracy. "I know all of you know something about democracy," I said, "but the true essence of democracy is the freedom to find out for yourself what is true. This means the ability to get the clearest understanding of a subject or a problem, free of any prejudice and conditioned thinking."

This is the challenge for all of us. To get rid of prejudice, one has to learn to find information independently. We need to go after the truth without conditioned thoughts or prejudice. When we hear gossip, we should find out the truth before reacting to it—even if the subject of conversation is not a friend, does not go to our school, does not live in the same community or does not belong to our preferred political party. It is important to undertake such investigations with a clean mind.

This is the challenge for our young people. They live in a society where people can easily tell lies. It is difficult to discern the truth. The newspapers carry a lot of stories filled with prejudice. Those who have money can easily assassinate another person's character by simply paying an editor or buying space in the paper. Our young people are accustomed to hearing lies every day, so it is difficult to embrace the truth. People in authority make promises they can't keep. Parents take sides based on their own prejudices, and make their children think like them. In our society, people are too weak to investigate. They swallow all the information they hear, especially when it agrees with their own prejudices. It is difficult to make intelligent decisions here.

But it is my hope that the young people in our Peace School will be different. I anticipate that they will use the knowledge they are acquiring to make intelligent decisions. I trust they will use the insight and tools from their new education to understand each other better. But my most fervent desire is that they will learn to think and act for themselves on the basis of independent evidence.

It is going to be a challenging adventure. They will have to learn to live with others well, allow truth to prevail in all their dealings, and understand and really see that the truth is in their hands. With the education they are acquiring, they hold the key. All they have to do is open the door and walk through.

Every day I hear my fellow countrymen read the depressingly long list of serious problems that continue to assail us. Many have propounded theories that can help solve our numerous tribulations, but many others still ask, "What is it that we can do to bring us out of our present predicament?"

There are those who say perhaps technology will save us and want to count our nation among the great nations of the world. I agree with those who raise their hands for technology, but I believe that advancement in technology will not solve our problems. It might instead compound them. Some think that leaders of government will save us, but despite the good intentions of many leaders of the world—as well as the UN, world movements and other groups—we seem to agree on little and accomplish less.

It is disturbing to hear from people who think that an established belief system is our salvation. Perhaps if there were only one such system in the world, a sensible and compassionate one at that, such a dream could be within reach. But this thought is just one of many fantasies. Far from one, we have hundreds of traditional belief systems about spirituality and its practice, almost all of which consider themselves vastly superior to the others, each one claiming to be the chosen one.

We have serious problems in our society, all part of a large interconnected web. I believe that the solution to our numerous social dilemmas lies in the right kind of education. Education has the power to uplift the human mind and spirit, and has a profound place in social considerations. I am speaking of an education that goes beyond formal instruction, one that promotes self-inquiry. I am also referring to an intelligence that goes beyond the academic, one that investigates conditioned thinking. We are what we think, and what we think creates the world we live in.

If we learn how to think clearly, we might understand our self-destructive tendencies and start to do something about them. I am talking about reasonable thinking, since our thoughts are often based on blind, instinctual or impulsive responses, especially when emotions, pleasant or unpleasant, intrude. Despite the fact that our reasoning power distinguishes us from other creatures on earth, many of us reason poorly. Yet we have no special training in expanding this capacity.

In Liberia, some people see themselves more clearly than others. However, many see themselves as "us" and others as "them"—the enemy. Many people have no interest in the truth for truth's sake. What they are interested in is being right—and winning.

It is my hope that our young people will continually pursue the truth as they travel this world. Discovering the truth has a lot to do with intelligent thinking. It is also my hope that our children will not walk in our footsteps; otherwise they will continue to make little social progress. When I see the progress our students have made at the Peace School, I am very encouraged that they will not recreate our errors, and that they will influence other people to want to understand themselves. In so doing, they will widen the scope of our learning together.

Best regards,
Marvin

Lesson 20

The Discoveries We've Made

"At our Peace School, the children know they are valued. Their worth is confirmed as others express that they care about them and about their feelings. When a student greets a friend here, it is a gentle touch that comforts, that reaches inside and soothes, bringing peace and a sense of belonging. These children have learned that despite the alarming speed of the world outside, the tempo inside the Peace School is different. There is stillness, and there is power in stillness. We learn to gather facts and develop a new and intelligent way of solving problems. Instead of feeling obliged to mutely accept what others say, everyone is encouraged to question and think for themselves."

— *Marvin Garbeh Davis*

Dear Dr. T. and Jean:

And so I have come to the end of another Atrium Society curriculum with a different group of children. Working with different students from a variety of backgrounds, communities and families is exhilarating. It has been a wonderful experience, a journey full of signposts. But importantly, it has been a journey full of discovery, not only for the children but also for me. Together, as we have asked questions and researched the roots of human conflict, we have been able to see the prejudice that created our war.

During the past few months, we have laughed and dreamt and watched the sunset together. When the September rains would not stop, together we waited in the parlors of the office or huddled impatiently on the front porch. Together in the dry season, we held our noses to stop the dust from invading our nostrils. I shared in the life of these children—the quiet and the shy, as well as the outspoken, courageous and fickle. I shared in their disappointment and joy, each of them adding a portion of their lives to mine. Today is my last lesson with this special group of children; I have already started missing them. But I know as they go that I will be able to look back and say we all did this together.

Peace education is a special kind of learning, and it is profound in our Peace School. Every day we learn to honor individual differences. There are no demands on the children: the children are in no competition, there is no good or bad student, bright or dull child, and therefore there is no threat to them. This is probably why they talk to me so freely. The education here is vibrant, creative and enriching. The children have let go of their conditioned attitudes. In the Peace School, change means growth. Here in the school we hold together: each person looks out for the other.

At our Peace School, the children know they are valued. Their worth is confirmed as others express that they care about them and about their feelings. When a student greets a friend here, it is a gentle touch that comforts, that reaches inside and soothes, bringing peace and a sense of belonging. These children have learned that despite the alarming speed of the world outside, the tempo inside our school is different. There is stillness, and there is power in stillness. We learn to gather facts and develop a new and intelligent way of solving problems. Instead of feeling obliged to mutely accept what others say, everyone is encouraged to question and think for themselves.

Here we know that simple treasures such as winks, hugs, handshakes and holding hands are meant to be enjoyed. A soft voice is filled with patience, and reaches out to help, never to provoke, judge, compare, degrade or lower self worth. Together the children and I have made amazing discoveries. One is finding out the truth for ourselves.

Over the past months, I have taught my children to avoid uttering the phrase, "they say…" In Liberia, when we hear "they say…," it means someone is passing on information that he or she does not have any evidence for. Many people listen to the radio and accept every crumb of information "they say." This way of spreading misinformation from one place to another has cost many people their reputations, jobs, families and social contacts.

In Liberia, people believe that there is a little truth in every "they say…" Liberians believe that where there is smoke, there is fire—meaning every bit of misinformation has a certain amount of truth in it.

So on this journey, I have made special efforts to encourage my students to live like detectives in their schools, communities and in the world. "Whenever you hear any bit of gossip," I say, "take it as a signal to rev up the analytical gears in your brain and don your investigative hat. Using your power to think independently, you will establish the truth."

The children have discovered that prejudice is like a house of mirrors. All our mental images of others are created by us alone. In the Peace School, the children have firsthand experience with prejudice. Most importantly, we have discovered that without prejudiced people, there can be no prejudice in the world.

"Experiencing it personally made me understand the real meaning of prejudice," Johnny says.

Marion says, "Prejudice is like death. Unless you have lost a loved one, you will never understand how someone feels when he or she loses a relative or other loved one."

"Prejudice separates people," adds Samuel. "It creates walls between people and nations."

Samuel uses a personal example. "When I moved back home with my parents from the refugee camp in Ghana, the children in my new school never wanted to play with me. They laughed at me and mimicked my accent that had changed slightly because of my long stay in Ghanaian schools. They laughed at my intonation every day. I was like a punching bag during recess and on the way home. During those days, I just wanted to return to Ghana where I felt at home and could relax in school. Every day here, I felt lonely and separated from everyone at school. This experience has taught me a lesson whenever I think about how I felt. The pain was too much, and I don't want to be part of any group that dislikes someone only because of his accent."

Experience is the best teacher indeed. Samuel's experience had taught him the value of never treating anyone unkindly for being different.

Living in tribe-like groups is a threat to the security and survival of the human race. In Samuel's case, the children in his school saw him as an outsider, someone who did not belong to their group because of his Ghanaian accent. So they unleashed mean jokes on him. Why do we humans do this? Is it fear? Is the fear based on prejudice? What kind?

Any prejudice that happened in the past can continue to make us unhappy in the present. To understand prejudice, we first need to be aware of it; otherwise we will remain numb to life around us. We will endlessly accept the opinions of others, without finding out the facts for ourselves. Worse, we will act on this false information.

"The only enemy you have," I say to my students, "is the one you create in your brains. And the only way to end prejudice is to observe it in the making. We must try to avoid perfection. No one is perfect, and trying to be perfect creates conflict inside us. Instead of fighting, we can reason. Our brains are far stronger than our fists."

Today is a review session. It is a time for the children to make their own assessments of all the lessons they have learned. It is their day to talk to me. It is the day that we patch up any old wounds and look forward to renewed relationships in our country. We want to remain friends after the Peace School closes. So we reflect on the discoveries we've made, the nuggets of truth and wisdom we have accumulated. We refresh these discoveries not by memorizing them, but by putting them in proper perspective. It is like pointing a flashlight into a corner of a house where we keep a special treasure. We know it is there and can pick it out with eyes closed. But the light of intelligence will keep shining for you to see clearly. In our review, we remind ourselves:

- When we observe clearly for ourselves, we can stop prejudice. If we take time to observe prejudice as it is happening, rather than relying on someone else's judgment, we can stop prejudice in its tracks. The best way to understand the meaning of prejudice is first-hand experience. We never know if the shoe pinches until we wear it. If we have experienced the effects of prejudice, we will be motivated to avoid inflicting the same pain on others.

- We may be living in modern times, but we continue to live and behave in tribe-like groups. This is a threat to the welfare of the human race. It separates us by creating fear of each other's "tribe." Fear creates conflict. It is fear that makes us hate and speak evilly about others. When we don't want to make friends with a stranger, it's because we are afraid.

- The attitude of our ancestors continues to be ingrained in our brain cells. It is as if we are prisoners of our forgotten ancestors, forever living out their old, habitual, destructive patterns of behavior. These old tribal ways continue to make us prisoners of the past. There is only one race, the Human Race, and its survival depends upon our understanding that we are all members of one tribe. We can only change the world when we think for ourselves. It is difficult, but as the Chinese say, a journey of a thousand miles begins with the first step.

On my way home, I start to think about the young people who have completed the curriculum today. What does the future hold for these young boys and girls who have been journeying with me on the path of discovery, uncovering the roots of prejudice? What will become of them? Will they be true peace ambassadors?

How can I find out? I just hope that they will continue to travel up the Path to Peace, using their minds intelligently to live in the world free of the pain of prejudice. This is going to happen; I believe in infinite possibilities. To have peace in the world, we must first understand what prevents peace within ourselves. We cannot have peace with hate and prejudice in our hearts.

I can only hope that as ambassadors of peace, they will find the nourishment to sustain their journeys, take the time to feast on refreshing knowledge, and imbibe in a rich diet of intelligence in order to maintain the strength to continue their challenging pilgrimage.

So I bid them good-bye. I tell them, my little brothers and sisters, one thing: "If you want peace, don't find fault with others and don't find fault with yourselves. We all have faults. Learn to see faults without judgment. Learn to make the whole world your own. No one is a stranger. Speak with one voice—the voice of truth, of intelligence. Then we are one people—people of the world. Then there is no separation, because there is no conflict. We now understand what keeps us apart, what prevents peace, by putting aside all that which has divided us.

Therefore, by this intelligent process, we come upon it, not by trying to get peace, but by understanding that this only creates conflict—for whose peace shall we follow? Whose peace is the right one? Ironically, our passionate thinking about peace has divided us into opposing ideologies that have for millennia kept us apart and created tremendous suffering.

Trying to bring about peace is what creates conflict. Seeing the truth of this, conflict ends. With its end, all the established belief systems that all our conscientious thinking has devised to try to create peace also end. In so doing, we have eliminated the very dilemma that has separated us.

Most people don't understand this straightforward and profound insight. They want to "do" something to bring about peace according to the established system of belief into which they were indoctrinated. But what they don't realize is that the very identification with a fragmentary belief system is what divides us and hence creates conflict. This is a logical fact. We can see this now here in Liberia, with the warring factions that created conflict under the guise of creating peace. This is a great error in thinking.

People think that being peaceful is thinking, and hence acting, peacefully. That's what thinking does. It compares, judges and then tries to come up with a solution to the "problem." This has a place in science and technology, but in changing human behavior, it creates a judgment of what should and should not be. More commonly, people label it "good" or "bad." In this way, the "problem" of conflict versus peace becomes a moral issue, whereas in reality, it is a mechanical one in the way the brain has been conditioned to bring about peace through the imposition of ideals. But whose ideals shall prevail?

The thinking mechanism itself thinks that it can do something about creating peaceful behavior, overlooking the fact that its own thinking is the cause of the predicament. It says that the crisis is out there in the world. But those thoughts are projecting that blame outwardly, claiming it as a "problem" that needs to be solved.

What is needed is to have an immediate insight into this falsehood, to actually see that the thinking mechanism is constantly recreating this divisive behavior by its very nature. Under this false notion, it proposes "peaceful solutions" that will end the conflict. Ironically, it is blind to its own mechanistic, primeval thinking, so it is unable to see how its own process creates discord. Thought, in other words, is hiding from itself under the false assumption that it is bringing about peace, whereas it is actually doing the opposite. But thought is only doing what it does—comparing, judging, trying to eliminate the "negative" and affirming the "positive." It is a mechanical process that labels, and then juggles the labels to suit its initial conditioning, like a computer with preset programs.

So we have questioned this process with our students and have seen that the faculty of thinking cannot bring about peace at the core of conflict. The faculty of intelligence called insight is the ability to see the truth or falsehood of things, and using thought, it describes what is occurring. That thought is based on the observation of what is occurring in the moment; it is an accurate reflection of the fact, but it would be a misuse of thought to use that reflection as the judgment of what should or should not be.

Through your peace education books and curricula, we have demonstrated this faculty of insight to the young people here. Perhaps because they are young, they are not yet conditioned enough to reject insight in favor of some established ideology. Most adults do not understand this simple truth, and therefore go on creating conflict in the name of peace. This is what the phrase "preventing peace" means, and it is the most important point to understand. When are we going to realize this? What will it take to see the simple truth of this? Will we need to have another war to show us that the way we are trying to bring about peace is actually preventing it?

Or by learning what prevents peace, are we now acting with intelligence and is it this intelligence that can put aside all that which prevents peace and in so doing allow peace to happen? We have told the young people that they are brave new children who can go out into the world with their education here at Common Ground Society and avoid taking on the conditioning that creates conflict between peoples. They can now see the futility of trying to bring about peace by idealistic means, by adhering to some tribal, ethnocentric belief system that got us into conflict in the first place. They now understand how easily people are conditioned and how this mostly unexamined conditioning pervades society. They understand that prejudicial bullying at school and at home is in essence the same prejudicial bullying that created the war they just went through, that the structure and nature of playground bullying is the same as battlefield bullying.

In the process of inquiring into all this, their intelligence has been awakened. This intelligence sees beyond the isolating confines society imposed on them to conform to outdated and divisive traditions. They now understand how physical survival at one time depended on the adherence to a system of belief that created the need for psychological identification to the group. They realize that this identification to a particular ideology, which once guaranteed physical survival, now prevents it. They now see that they have to think and act as individuals who can, by putting aside the conditioned thinking that prevents peace, embrace the whole human race beyond a narrow, exclusive, cultural or nationalistic view.

In understanding all this, they will not enter into the old ways, but move forward to create a new world, one free of conflict created by conditioned thinking. We wish them well and tell them that it is now up to them to carry forth these insights, so they have the opportunity to act with dignity and intelligence in all they do. This is all we can do. It is a tremendous task.

These are only twenty young people, but they are the seeds of humanity. They can grow into adulthood demonstrating that no matter how one has been conditioned to violence— and these young people have had more than most in this world—that there is the possibility that the human race can be free and live in peace. As the anthropologist Margaret Meade once said, "Never doubt that a small group of thoughtful, committed citizens can change the world; indeed, it's the only thing that ever has."

Your friend,
Marvin

P.S.

Thank you, Dr. T, for creating the books and the curricula you have donated to us here in Liberia. They enabled me to teach our young people about the prejudice that created war. Since they now understand that tribalism has created this vicious cycle of human destruction, I think that they will be able to change it.

And many thanks to you, Jean, for your programs and for the years you spent training me in peace education. Without your training and materials, I would not have been able to help these young people develop into the intelligent human beings I now see. They are being freed from the conditions that have created conflict here. As a result, I feel they will now be able to move forward and change Liberia—and the world. What has happened here is the world's problem. As you have said, "We are the world, and the world is us."

Thanks for everything,
Marvin

Dear Jean and Dr. T:

Greetings! I have not been able to speak to you both directly since you started knowing our family, especially my husband. I am aware of everything you and Marvin have discussed over the year, especially since I joined him with the children in Gambia in 2003.

I decided to speak to you now, since we have the Internet with us here at the office. I want to use this time to thank you for everything you have done for our family, especially my husband. I want to thank you for the numerous gifts you sent me. Particularly, when you paid the taxi fare and sent me the money for the cost of the surgery when our son was born in the hospital. I am very grateful. I have kept silent for too long and now it is time I sent you my own words of gratitude.

I have been married to Marvin for 9 years now, which excludes the many years we dated and lived together. When we married, his father had already died, so only his mother came for the wedding. We could not say anything of importance to each other, because I cannot speak Marvin's local language. I have not seen any of his real uncles and aunts since we got married. I am saying this to show how Marvin is a kind of self-made person. He is strong and hardworking, but most importantly, he is intelligent.

But you have added a lot more to his life in recent years. Sometimes now, he considers you as his parents. You mean a lot to him. Every day I hear him say "Dr. T or Jean says…" Your name is our household word. All my children know your names. I hope someday all of us will meet. He has lately developed a big passion for peace education work, especially when it comes to working with young people. There is not a day here when young people fail to come to see him.

I am happy for him too. The changes in his life have come to affect our family in a very positive way. His way of thinking and doing things is quite different now. Of course I don't enjoy it some of the time, when he wants me to show evidence for everything I say or hear. "If you don't show evidence for things you say about others, then it is prejudice," Marvin says.

Since our return home, he has been doing fine. I want to thank you for the support you continue to give his work here. This year, I decided to give my time to the office too, even though we have a baby to take care of. As I am sure he told you, he never asked me for help this year. However, if strangers were supporting my husband, then what about me? I wanted to show him I am with him, so I just decided to give him my hand.

Marvin and the Common Ground are popular names in Buchanan. He is invited to all the programs here in Buchanan, to speak or make remarks. This week alone he was guest speaker at two youth programs. I am proud of him. I am only afraid that he might change his mind and go into politics. But I will not sit here and allow him anyway. Liberian politics is death. He can serve his country the way he is doing now. It is my prayer that he keeps doing what he is doing and improves on his education so that he can be of more service to the young people in this country.

The children and I send our best wishes and want to say thank you for everything. I told him I was writing you today, and he said it was good that I thought of doing so.

Please continue to help Marvin. Sometimes when I watch him, I know that there is a lot he wants to do. I don't have much, but I have decided to be with him all the way. I want to learn the ropes at Common Ground, so that when he travels to Monrovia, I can do the work sufficiently without him. I am still going through the curriculum with him. Presently, we are going through your curriculum, "War—What Is It Good For?" This is the next one we will be teaching the children at the peace school.

I will try and write once in a while when I have the time.

Affectionately yours,
Emily

Afterword: The Outcome of the Peace School

WE ASKED MARVIN *to let us know what some of the children had learned as a result of attending the peace school. The following comments are a very promising sign, considering that these children grew up in war, and thus knew only hostile ways to relate to each other. The subsequent dialog between Marvin and his students is also a very positive indication that even these young people raised in war can, with the right education, go beyond a conditioned mindset. Whereas before all they knew was one way of relating to each other now they have learned that there is another way, one that does not lead to conflict, but to peace.*

— *Terrence and Jean Webster-Doyle*

I held an interview with four of our students, Cindy Reeves, John Pius Onumah, Shad Whypaly and Julia Gbearr, who recently finished the Peace School. The interview was about their hopes for Liberia. How do they envisage the country in the coming years? Do they see lasting peace or another war in the making? The basis for the interview was to see how the curriculum on prejudice affected their outlook now.

Marvin: "What do you think Liberia is going to be like in the future?"

Cindy: "The country is going to be good. I am very sure things are going to be all right for us."

John Pius: "I think things will be okay. The other day, my father told me that they have electricity in some parts of Monrovia now. In other parts, people are drinking pipe-borne water. And many children don't have to walk miles to get water, because they are building hand pumps in the communities."

Shad: "The country will be fine. Did you hear that they are going to start to fix the road from Buchanan to Monrovia? I am sure you saw the young people marching on Tubman Street for a college to be built in Buchanan. Maybe by the time I am finished with high school, I will continue my college education right here in Buchanan."

Julia: "For many years my father could not get a job. He recently got employed with Mittal Steel. For me, things are going to be good again. When many parents get a job, they will be able to look after their children well."

Marvin: "Do you think people are going to fight again? I mean do you think we will have another war again?"

Cindy: "It is hard to tell, but for me, I am not going to fight a war. Nobody will make me fight a war, because I know war is evil. Right now, I am helping young people like myself to understand that confusion is not good. The way I see it, many children will not want to fight a war again, especially when they come to think of what happened here."

John Pius: "For me, I can say no. No one will fight a war again. War is bad. You can see everybody is talking about peace, because peace is better than any war. If we have peace, we can do those things we want: go to school, look for a job, travel and have our own families. I will not fight. I know why people fight; I know what stops people from having peace. So others will fight. Well, that is it, but for me John Pius, I will never fight and I will help to stop people from fighting."

Shad: "Others may want to fight, but for me, I will never fight. What is the use of fighting? I am a different person now and I hope many children will understand that fighting a war is wrong. We should settle our problems without fighting. The way things are now, it is going to be hard to fight again. Everybody is doing something now, because peace is here."

Julia: "People will have small misunderstandings here and there. But I don't think people will fight a war again. What we must learn now is to help people settle differences without fighting again. If we can settle our small differences, then we will not have big palavers that can bring wars."

Marvin: "You spent a year in the Peace School learning about prejudice and other causes of human conflict. How has your time in the peace school helped you in your life?"

Cindy: "The peace school has helped me in many ways. For example, I used to act according to how people wanted me to be. If people wanted me to fight back, I just did it to please them. Now I have a very strong mind. I think clearly before I act. Nobody makes me do what they want. The other day, some girls were mocking me. You know I am tall and lean. So they were saying that I am thin because I don't eat good food. They wanted me to stand up and make palaver and finally fight. I just walked away. I knew what they were saying was false. I eat good food and my mother says she used to be thin like me, but as she grew, she added more weight. So whenever I have to make a choice, I use my mind. The peace school helped to make my mind strong."

John Pius: "The peace school is a very good place. It is different from a real school where you learn English and Mathematics. The peace school has helped me to make decisions based on facts and not hearsay. Before I agree with someone about something, I find out the truth for myself. In the peace school, we learn that not knowing the facts and making a decision can lead to conflict. It is true. I am the prefect of my class, and one day our teacher left the cupboard key with me. My friends had their test papers in the cupboard. All of them knew I had the key. A boy in the class came running to tell me that the teacher wanted me to divide the test papers, and I said no. I asked him many questions and when he could not answer, I knew he was lying. For example, I said, 'Where did you see the teacher? When did you see him? Why did he want me to divide the papers when he was coming right back to class?' When he failed to give me answers, I just told him 'No.' I never had all the facts; I wanted to hear my teacher's side of the story."

Shad: "The peace school has helped me to learn not to have bad feelings about others without knowing them. For instance, when someone says, 'John is a bad boy,' I will not agree with the person. I will want to know if John really is bad. I will try to know John myself. I learned in the peace school that people sometimes say bad things about others only because they are different. Maybe the person says John is bad because he comes from a different tribe, school, or church. We sometimes hate because we feel others are different from us. To me, we are all human beings, and there is no need to treat other people badly because they are different from us. This can create confusion, hate and war."

Julia: "One big lesson I have learned from the peace school is learning to put up with people. I used to get vexed and hate someone if they did not act the way I wanted them to behave. I stopped my friendships with many girls because they did not want to behave my way. The peace school has taught me to understand that we should not hate others because they want to be themselves. No one has all the right ideas about how to live. We all have different ideas about life, so we must learn to live with others even if they have different ideas. Sometimes I used to have ideas about certain girls because of where they came from, or the school they attended. For example, my friend Marie is a Bassa girl, but she loves red so I used to say to her, 'If you don't change your red dress, I am not walking with you.' Why? I used to believe that only Kpelle girls should wear red dresses. From my peace school, I know this was a conditioned attitude. Color has nothing to do with a person. We are all human beings, no matter what color we like."

Marvin: "Can you tell me how you used to respond to conflict before you came to the peace school?"

Cindy: "Before I started the peace school, I used to always wish to be a very huge person. I wanted to be strong so that I could just pay back others when they did something bad to me. But most importantly, I wanted to use my body to bully people. I am surprised I don't think like that anymore. Even though I am not big now, I can use my head to solve many problems which would require a big body."

Pius: "Like Cindy, I hated being a small boy. Other children used to call me names and all I wanted was to beat them up. I learned new things in the peace school. Even though I am small, I have learned that you don't have to fight physically to beat someone; you can also win by using your mind. Now I don't worry about my body size too much."

Shad: "Many of the things people fight for are not the truth. I used to fight when anyone said something against me. Now I understand that most of the time, what people say is how they feel and think. And their thinking has to do with how they learn things in life. So when someone says something against my tribe, for instance, calling me stupid because I am a Kpelle boy, I just walk away. I don't blame the person, because maybe this is all the person has been taught about Kpelle people. I know that I am not stupid, so why fight someone for something that is not true?"

Julia: "For me, I believe that one thing that can cause war is carrying false information from one person to another. And many people don't try to find out the truth. They accept anything people tell them. I don't want to be someone like that again, and I am happy that I went to the peace school. If you bring me gossip, I'll ask you, 'Where did you hear that? Who told you? Did you find out the truth yourself?' These questions make people stop gossiping. I want to be like Sherlock Homes, our detective in peace school."

About The Atrium Society

THE ATRIUM SOCIETY, a non-political, non-sectarian, non-profit organization, concerns itself with the fundamental issues which prevent understanding and cooperation in human affairs.

Starting with the fact that our minds are conditioned by our origin of birth, education, and experiences, the Atrium Society's intent is to bring this issue of conditioning to the forefront of our awareness. Observing the fact of conditioning and becoming directly aware of the movement of thought and action bring us face-to-face with the actuality of ourselves. Seeing who we actually are, not merely who we think we are, reveals the potential for a transformation of our ways of being and relating.

The Atrium Society's fundamental objective is to create and develop a new field of study called BioCognetic Peace Education™ (Cognitive, Emotive, Bio-Reactive Conditioning)— The Scientific Study of Human Conflict—Created by Conditioned Thinking.

Atrium Society
atriumsociety@gmail.com
www.youthpeaceliteracy.org
Tel: 800-848-6021

About The Common Ground Society

THE COMMON GROUND Society is a legally registered, non-political, non-partisan, non-sectarian, non-profit organization dedicated to working with young people through after school peace education programs. Its goals are to build an understanding of what prevents peace, to help young people recognize the root causes of violence within themselves and society, and thus to develop the skills to resolve conflicts peacefully.

Common Ground Society Liberia
P. O. Box 5217, Monrovia, Liberia West Africa
Email: cgsliberia@gmail.com
Phone: +231-6-432655

About BioCognetic Peace Education™

The Scientific Study of Human Conflict Created by Conditioned Thinking

Background

BioCognetic Peace Education™ is the basis for everything in this book. It is the foundation for the curriculum of peace education as taught by Marvin Davis. To clarify how conditioned, prejudicial thinking creates conflict, Dr. Terrence and Jean Webster-Doyle created the BioCognetic Peace Education™ context for understanding the whole of psychological conditioning—how it impacts the human brain mentally, emotionally and physically, and how it extends from the playground to the battlefield. This pioneering field is based on the initial insights of modern notable thinkers, including quantum physicist Dr. David Bohm, educational philosopher Jiddu Krishnamurti, and authors Aldous Huxley and George Orwell.

Creating the Intent and Process

The first step in this process was to create a rationale for a consistent, scientific, empirical framework to comprehend conditioned, prejudicial thinking as a whole. The second step was to expand awareness of the nature, structure and implications of conditioned, prejudicial thinking that leads to human conflict at all levels. The third step was to expand awareness of conditioned thinking beyond its psychological make-up to include a holistic insight into the involuntary, automatic, three-stage, reactive configuration of conditioning in the mechanical disorganization of the human brain that produces an internal environment of discord. The next logical step was to create a significant justification to bring this urgent issue to the forefront of education as an essential subject matter in teaching young people to understand and peacefully resolve hurtful conflict created by conditioned, prejudicial thinking. The final step was to create appropriate educational resources and training for teachers to teach about the cause and effect of conditioned thinking. (http://www.atriumsoc.org/resources-overview.php)

BioCognetic Peace Education™ and Youth-At-Risk

As stated above, the main intent of BioCognetic Peace Education™ is to design a comprehensive insight for teaching young people about the basic factors of conflict-creating conditioning and escalation-prevention. BioCognetic Peace Education™ is also designed to provide therapists with a thorough understanding of the multiple causes of prejudicial conditioning, so they may assist At-Risk youth to cope with the effects of bullying. Thus, BioCognetic Peace Education™ can be effectively applied as a multi-purpose program.

Cognitive-Emotive-Bio-reactive Conditioning

From the individual to the group, conflict begins identically with conditioned pre-judgments. An unexamined thought initiates a domino effect of fearful emotions which in turn trigger the biological fight-or-flight system. Although this may be necessary when there is real danger, it is inappropriate when prompted by an unverified, imagined threat. This cognitive, emotive, bio-reactive coupling produces a powerful psychosomatic reaction of conflict internally and externally. In BioCognetic Peace Education™ this situation is called a "CEB" or a "Cognitive-Emotive-Bio-reactive." The term CEB encompasses the whole of prejudicial conditioning, not just the cognitive or mental process initiating this domino effect of the three-stage process. As soon as one becomes conscious of this process, one can avoid conflict at the primary prevention level. In other words, by recognizing the underlying structure at this fundamental level, one can prevent detrimental conflict from happening as it occurs, and therefore be free from having to react out of it. But this awareness is based on the assumption that the fundamental, bio-reactive, holding pattern of this part of the brain can be properly attended to.

BioCognetic Peace Education™ and Bullying

BioCognetic Peace Education™ has been expressly designed to reflect the nature and structure of bullying that creates any conflict in the way we have been conditioned to think and act. BioCognetic Peace Education™ uses the relevant context of bullying to demonstrate the cause and effect of prejudicial conditioning because all ages can relate to it. Young people can most easily understand prejudicial conditioning if it is grounded in their real, daily experiences. From the concrete rather than the abstract, they can come to understand what prejudicial conditioning is, how if affects them, and how it impacts the world. (http://www.atriumsoc.org/framework.php)

MAP S.T.A.R.S. ™ —Self-Defence for Self-Understanding

At the same time young people are taught about the fundamental structure and nature of bullying, they are introduced to a specially-designed system of mental and physical self-defence skills called MAP S.T.A.R.S. (Mental and Physical Safe Tactical Alert Response System). In this way, the young person not only gains insight into the initial impulse of conditioned, prejudicial thinking at the primary or prevention level, but also learns to work out conflict at the secondary or resolution level by the use of verbal, de-escalation techniques. In addition, the young person at the tertiary or management level builds confidence through avoiding a freeze, fight or flight reaction to an immediate potential threat and future supposed threats that are caused by the bio-reactive fight or flight system which gives the prejudicial conditioning its biological authority. By inhibiting the reinforcement of old, psychological and emotional impulses, this unique process creates a space in the biologically reactive system for creative, new actions.

Dispelling Cognitive Distortions

When an event occurs that disturbs us, automatic thoughts enter our brain so fast and so mechanically that we don't notice them. And if we don't notice them, we certainly won't question them. Still, they affect our attitude, our mood, our body and our ability to function clearly. These thoughts, based on either false information or a misperception of reality, are often referred to as "cognitive distortions."

When a conditioned thought/emotion triggers one of these distortions, it typically stimulates the bio-reactive survival system in the old brain. This situation occurs when we can't see through the falsehood, and the old brain is reacting to the image as if it were true. But if we can counteract this with an observational viewpoint, we can see how a conditioned, prejudicial image (say, of a bully) can jump in and lie to us about a need to protect ourselves.

Looping or Biocognosis™

However, the problem occurs when we can't see through the falsehood and the old brain is reacting to it as if it were true. Whether in bullying situations or in regular daily life, recurring cognitive distortions cause us unnecessary conflict. Even when the outer stimulus of a bully, for example, is removed, this triggering process can get internalized. In BioCognetics™ this is called "looping" or "biocognosis™", as the stimulus spins around and around, with the old bio-reactive brain constantly sending messages of a "threat" to the cognitive and emotive parts of the system, when, in fact, there is none at all.

Fight or Flight System Triggered by an Imaginary Threat

It is most significant that this biological flight or flight system can be triggered inappropriately by an image of a threat when the actual threat is not there. This part of the brain cannot differentiate between an actual threat and a supposed one. Behind the psycho-emotive conditioning, this deeper biological ("bio-reactive") conditioning holds or locks the initial psychological image of a threat in place. No amount of rationalization can reach that deeper place. We have to get to it by the back door: that is, by going through the body to give the deeper, biological/bio-reactive conditioning what it wants—to feel confident that it can fight, that this more primitive part of the brain can deal with the threat by preparing the body to defend itself. This part of the brain only "knows" that there is a "threat" created by an image and to it, it is "real." This is very evident in young people we call Youth-At-Risk who have been continuously abused and therefore perceive the world as a threat, even though they may be in a non-threatening situation. In other words, the biological fight or flight system—the bio-reactive part of the old brain survival system— is stuck in the "on" position.

Disrupting the Biocognosis™ Looping Pattern

To disrupt this biocognosis™ looping pattern, young people are taken into a safe, controlled environment where they are taught the MAP S.T.A.R.S. ™ set of self- defence techniques. This purposely triggers the flight or fight mechanism while simultaneously instilling the confidence to be able to "fight". All the old brain really desires is to feel able to protect itself from harm, whether real or imaginary. Remarkably, even a little physical training goes a long way. This process has worked especially well with youth-at-risk as a therapeutic process, although it is applicable to everyone, whether they have been a victim of serious bullying or not. As the participants integrate their newfound insights with the newly acquired physical ability to handle hostile situations, prejudicial, conditioned ideas of imagined enemies fade and automatic triggers are extinguished.

Psychosomatic Homeopathy

In the same way that homeopathy works through a system of "like curing like," developing this specialized set of self-defence skills cures the need to use those skills. The primitive brain acknowledges them with confidence, and relaxes. As one becomes conscious of this newfound insight into prejudicial, conditioned patterns of thinking, feeling and acting, one becomes aware of the potential to be creative in each fresh, new moment. Thus, Biocognetics™ brings an enhanced proprioception both physically and mentally to the very foundation of conflict. Through role-playing, developing cognitive awareness and expanding their insight into conditioned, prejudicial thinking, young people thrive in this environment of non-violent alternatives for resolving conflict.

Atrium Society's Peace Education Resources

BOOKS FOR YOUNG PEOPLE

- *Why Is Everybody Always Picking on Me? A Guide to Handling Bullies (English)**
- *Why Is Everybody Always Picking on Me? A Guide to Handling Bullies (Russian)*
- *Why Is Everybody Picking on Us? Understanding the Roots of Prejudice*
- *Facing the Double-Edged Sword: The Art of Karate for Young People**
- *Tug of War: Peace through Understanding Conflict**
- *Fighting the Invisible Enemy: Understanding the Effects of Conditioning**
- *Eye of the Hurricane**
- *Maze of the Fire Dragon**
- *Flight of the Golden Eagle**
- *Breaking the Chains of the Ancient Warrior*
- *Operation Warhawks: How Young People Become Warriors*
- *Martial Arts Masters: Black Belt Warriors for Peace*
- *Respect: The Martial Arts Code of Conduct*
- *My First Martial Arts Book*

BOOKS FOR ADULTS

- *Growing Up Sane: Understanding the Conditioned Mind*
- *Brave New Child: Education for the 21st Century*
- *The Religious Impulse: The Quest for Freedom*
- *Peace–The Enemy of Freedom: The Myth of Nonviolence*
- *Karate: The Art of Empty Self**
- *One Encounter—One Chance**
- *Dr. Webster-Doyle's Martial Arts Guide for Parents***
- *The Complete Guide to the Bully-Victim Cycle: From the Playground to the Battlefield*
- *Shadows of Forgotten Ancestors*
- *BioCognetic Peace Education™: The Scientific Study of Human Conflict Created by Conditioned Thinking*

CURRICULA

- *Why Is Everybody Always Picking on Me? A Guide to Handling Bullies*
- *Why Is Everybody Picking on Us? Understanding the Roots of Prejudice*
- *Why Are We Always Picking on Each Other? War – What Is It Good For?*
- *Why Are We Always Letting the Bullies Pick on Them?*
- *The Bystander: Villain or Victim?*
- *Why Are They Always Getting Picked On? Youth-at-Risk*
- *Why Am I Always Picking on Myself? Making Friends with Your Inner Bully*
- *Why Do We Bully? Understanding the Causes of Bullying*
- *Derrotar al Matón Sin Luchar (Spanish Bully curriculum)*

+ *Defeat the Bully without Fighting*
+ *Defeat the Bully the Smart Way*
+ *Character for Kids Life Skills*
+ *Who Put This War in My Brain?*
+ *Awareness: Exploring the Roots of Conflict*
+ *Mastering Martial Arts Manners*
+ *Respect: The Act That Conquers Fear*
+ *Respect: The Martial Arts Code of Conduct*
+ *Understanding: Creating Peace*
+ *As Easy As A.B.C. Part One – Twelve Ways to Act with Respect*
+ *As Easy As A.B.C. Part Two – Twelve Ways to Walk Away with Confidence*
+ *Stranger Heightened Awareness Response Program*
+ *P.A.L.S. Positive Action Life Skills: 12 Personal, Social, Coping Skills*
+ *R & R: Rights and Responsibilities*
+ *Understanding: Creating Peace – Two Levels*

WORKBOOKS

+ *Why Is Everybody Always Picking on Me? A Guide to Handling Bullies*
+ *Why Is Everybody Picking on Us? Understanding the Roots of Prejudice*
+ *Awareness: Exploring the Roots of Conflict*
+ *Martial Arts for Peace: MAP S.T.A.R.S.™* (Mental and Physical Safe Tactical Awareness System)

PROGRAMS

+ *The Bully Buster System*
+ *The Character for Kids Kit*
+ *The Character Development—Life Skills (Comprehensive) Program*

VIDEOS

+ *Solving Conflict Peacefully: Martial Arts for Peace*
+ *Education for Peace in the 21st Century: The Atrium School*
+ *How to Defeat the Bully the Smart Way: Part One and Part Two*

TRAININGS/SEMINARS/CONFERENCES

+ "Brave New Child: Education for a New Generation"
+ "The Bully/Victim Cycle: From the Playground to the Battlefield"
+ "Youth-At-Risk: MAP S.T.A.R.S™."
+ "Martial Arts for Peace: Character Development and Conflict Education"
+ "Metamorphosis Responsive Seminars"
+ "BioCognetic Peace Education™: The Scientific Study of Human Conflict"
+ "Isn't It about Time? Teaching Peace Education"

*Winner of the Benjamin Franklin Award (2 Golds and 7 Silvers)
**Winner of the National Parenting Gold Award

International Commendations and Awards
For Atrium Society's Books and Programs

THE BOOKS AND *programs of the Atrium Society have won widespread praise as resources for helping young people understand how to resolve conflict peacefully. Here are a few of the accolades:*

+ Awarded the Robert Burns Medal for literature by Austria's Albert Schweitzer Society, for "outstanding merits in the field of peace-promotion"

+ Acclaimed at the Soviet Peace Fund Conference in Moscow and published in Russia by Moscow's Library for Foreign Literature and Magistr Publications

+ Selected by the International Association of Educators for World Peace for their Central American peace education project in Panama and El Salvador

+ On permanent display at the International Museum of Peace and Solidarity in Samarkind, Uzbekistan, the Commonwealth of Independent States

+ Selected by the National PTA as a recommended resource for parents

+ Endorsed by *Scouting* magazine and *Sports Illustrated for Kids*

+ Nine-time winner of the Benjamin Franklin Awards for Excellence in Independent Publishing—for six consecutive years, sometimes more than once each year.

+ *Why Is Everybody Always Picking on Me*: cited by the *Omega New Age Directory* as one of the Ten Best Books, for its "atmosphere of universal benevolence and practical application"

+ Approved by the New York City Board of Education

+ Selected by the American Booksellers Association for its resource listing of "Children's Books About Peace"

+ "These topics are excellent and highly relevant. If each of the major countries of the world were to have ten Drs. Webster-Doyle, world peace is guaranteed to be achieved over a period of just one generation."

—Dr. Charles Mercieca, Executive Vice President
International Association of Educators for World Peace
NGO, United Nations (ECOSOC), UNICEF & UNESCO

- "Every publication from the pen of this author should make a significant contribution to peace within and without. Highly recommended!"
  —*New Age Publishers and Retailers Alliance Trade Journal*

- Dr. Terrence Webster-Doyle is an "eloquent leader of the movement to combine principles of education, psychology and the martial arts to teach young people to resolve conflict peacefully."
  —*The Center for Applied Psychology, Inc.*

- "Webster-Doyle's insight is that by recognizing, understanding, and accepting our violent tendencies, we can avoid acting them out. These new books … are good for teachers and parents of elementary school children who need appropriate language and activities to help children deal with their feelings and the violence-provoking parts of the environment. To this reviewer, they are realistic and practical."
  —*Young Children*
  (Magazine of the National Association for the Education of Young Children)

- "We use his books and thoroughly endorse the usefulness of his methods which have high potential in schools."
  —*Stuart W. Twemlow, M.D.*
  Psychiatry and Psychoanalysis, Menninger Clinic, Topeka,
  KS Instructor, Martial Arts School

- "The books of Dr. Webster-Doyle are the first attempt I have seen to explain to young people and adults the concept of martial arts as a peaceful, nonviolent 'way of life' and to give students the tools to accomplish this goal."
  —*Linda Lee Cadwell*
  Widow of the late Bruce Lee

- "Helps young people deal with conflict and violence by describing practical skills for peace"
  —*Holistic Education Review*

- "I realize *Why Is Everybody Always Picking On Me? is* urgent for every child and adult …My daughter couldn't stop reading it!"
  —*Marina Dubrovskaya,*
  Assistant Director Dept. of Sociology, Lenin Library, Moscow, Russia

- "Your book (*Why Is Everybody Always Picking on Me?*) has really helped me ignore the bullies, and in a way, stop bullying others."
  —*4th grader*

- "The materials were very helpful to the facilitators who conducted the workshop on bullying strategies."
  —*New Jersey State Bar Foundation*

- The book, *Why Is Everybody Always Picking on Me?* was presented at the National Conference on Peacemaking & Conflict Resolution.

…To name only a few

Eight Stages of Bullying
From the Playground to the Battlefield

By Dr. Terrence And Jean Webster-Doyle

1. **Why do we bully?** When we can understand the causes of bullying—which are rooted in the way we have been conditioned to think—we can prevent it.

2. **Why is everybody always picking on me?** When a bully finds a victim to torment, there are always reasons. A victim benefits from understanding these reasons and recognizing how a bully thinks. The victim also needs to learn how to avoid, resolve and manage bullying.

3. **Why am I always picking on myself?** Each of us has an "inner bully"—an internal voice that nags and intimidates us. This originates from being bullied, and then gets internalized so that it becomes a continuous, inward, self-defeating process.

4. **Why can't I do what I want?** Young people need to learn that for every right there is a corresponding responsibility. Leaning this makes for a balanced frame of mind in one's relationships with others and the world.

5. **Why is everybody always picking on us?** When we learn to hate and fear because someone else is different, then we are caught in prejudice. Whether it is prejudice against skin color, nationality, gender, sexual preference or religion, it only creates pain and suffering.

6. **Why are we always letting the bullies pick on them?** Most bystanders don't want to get involved in a bullying situation. Some bystanders release their hostility by encouraging a bullying situation. But knowledgeable bystanders can be powerful and resourceful, if they can understand how to intervene and stop bullying.

7. **Why are they always getting picked on?** Youth-at-risk are bullied both by fellow youth and by adults. To help prevent it, youth, parents and teachers must all understand how and why they are targeted.

8. **Why are we always picking on each other?** Wars break out because one group of people bullies another. In order to understand what creates this, we need to understand that the basic structures that created bullying on the playground are the very same ones that created all such behavior—including the worst bullying of them all: war.

Biographical Information

Founder and President of the Atrium Society

Jean Webster-Doyle, AEPT, MTT, is an educator, yoga teacher and the creator of Metamorphosis Training Seminars and Harmonious Mind Yoga. Ms. Webster-Doyle was educated at Sarah Lawrence College, New York University and the University of Madrid.

She has traveled worldwide educating people about the causes of conflict due to conditioned thinking, and has co-created numerous books and programs on the subject. She has taught prenatal therapy for mentally handicapped children and is the creator and editor of *Taking Time*, a newsletter about understanding the conditioned mind. Ms. Webster-Doyle is the co-founder of the Atrium School and the Rainy Mountain Outdoor Education School. She is also a master teacher and trainer in Education for Peace.

Director of the Atrium Society

Terrence Webster-Doyle, Ph.D., AEPT, founded and directed three independent schools and has taught at the secondary, community college, and university levels in Education, India Studies, Psychology, and Philosophy. He has worked in juvenile delinquency prevention and has developed counseling programs for youth-at-risk. Dr. Webster-Doyle earned a Master of Psychology and a Doctor of Health and Human Services. He has a lifetime secondary and community college teaching credential. He has been awarded a 6th degree black belt in the art of karate, and has studied and taught the martial arts for over 45 years. Dr. Webster-Doyle has also produced numerous conferences and workshops on New Directions in Education. He is the founder and director of the Martial Arts for Peace Association, director of the Atrium Society, and co-director of the Atrium School, which explores psychological conditioning. A prolific writer, Dr. Webster-Doyle has written 54 internationally acclaimed, award winning, peace education books and curricula.

Founder and Director of the **Common Ground Society Peace School**

Marvin Garbeh Davis, ACPE, was born on March 10, 1973, in the Liberian Agricultural Company (LAC) Plantations Hospital, Grand Bassa County, Liberia. He has an AA degree in Accounting and a BA in History/English. He was employed by the Center for Law and Human Rights in Liberia, where he worked as an editor for the *Human Rights Review*, a weekly paper that reported human rights abuses in the country. When he had to flee under threat of death during Liberia's 14-year civil war, Mr. Davis worked as the Secretary General of the Association of Liberians in Gambia. Among many occupations, Mr. Davis has been an elementary school teacher, coordinator of the Peace Pal Club at the SOS Children's Youth Village, and Secretary General of the Association of Liberian Refugees. He has taught "Education for Peace" to more than 40 young children in The Gambia, using peace books and curricula donated by the Atrium Society. Mr. Davis is certified as an Education for Peace teacher by the Atrium Society USA. He is currently founder and director of the Common Ground Society Peace School, a non-profit peace organization in Buchanan, Liberia.

Atrium Society's
Youth Peace Literacy Book Donation Project

**In a world where children are surrounded by violence and war,
we can help build a more peaceful future,
one book at a time.**

Children are being conditioned to fear and hate.

The fundamental intent of YPL—Youth Peace Literacy—Book Donation Project is to address what prevents peace—that is, what creates conflict, individually and globally.

The most important element of a free society is democratic thinking. Conflict in human relationships is created by thinking that is conditioned to a particular, fragmentary point of view due to the particular environment one has grown up in. Our minds are conditioned by origin of birth, education and experiences. The intent of YPL and the Atrium Society is to bring this issue of conditioning, and the tremendous conflict it creates, to the forefront of our awareness through donations of books that address this vital concern.

Conditioned thinking prevents democratic thinking and action because it fixes antiquated, ethnocentric beliefs into dogmatic, rigid patterns of behavior that divide people into opposing tribal ideologies. The foundation of a humane and intelligent society is open-minded, enlightened, free inquiry—that is, the freedom to think without any restrictions or pressures due to fear or coercion of any kind. In this way, people can intelligently question the underlying conditioning that creates this fragmentation.

The intent of democratic thinking needs to be promoted worldwide if we are to end these destructive divisions and therefore work together peacefully. The books of the Atrium Society do just that—they teach young people to freely inquire, to creatively question the conditioned assumptions of society that have for millennia caused such terrible pain and suffering. These books do not promote any system of belief, nor do they attempt to persuade readers to any particular point of view, no matter how noble it may seem to be. Instead, they create the basis for a truly democratic, civilized society by allowing for intelligent dialogue and enlightened inquiry.

We ask you to help us enlighten the minds of children around the world who are oppressed by autocratic, political, religious and/or traditional nationalistic systems of belief that hinder democratic thinking and living. Please contact us for more information about how to contribute to Youth Peace Literacy, urgently needed in the world today. Your donation, of even one book, can help free a child from the bondage of conditioned thinking.

Call us at 800–848–6021 or
look up YPL at
http://www.atriumsociety.org or http://www.youthpeaceliteracy.org

ISBN 142511947-6

Edwards Brothers Malloy
Ann Arbor MI. USA
October 30, 2012